Divorce in Medieval England

Divorce in Medieval England is intended to reorient scholarly perceptions concerning divorce in the medieval period. Divorce, as we think of it today, is usually considered to be a modern invention. This book challenges that viewpoint, documenting the many and varied uses of divorce in the medieval period and highlighting the fact that couples regularly divorced on the grounds of spousal incompatibility. Because the medieval church was determined to uphold the sacrament of marriage whenever possible, divorce in the medieval period was a much more complicated process than it is today. Thus, this book steps readers through the process of divorce, including: official and unofficial grounds for divorce, the fundamentals of the process, the risks involved, financial implications for wives who were legally disabled thanks to the rules of coverture, the custody and support of children, and finally, what happens after a divorce. Readers will gain a much greater appreciation of marriage and women's position in later medieval England.

Sara M. Butler is Associate Professor of Medieval History at Loyola University New Orleans. Her first book was *The Language of Abuse: Marital Violence in Later Medieval England* (2007). She has published also on suicide, violence against children, abortion, and medical practitioners at law.

Routledge Research in Medieval Studies

1 **Agrarian Change and Crisis in Europe, 1200–1500**
Edited by Harry Kitsikopoulos

2 **Pluralism in the Middle Ages**
Ragnhild Johnsrud Zorgati

3 **Theorizing Medieval Geopolitics**
War and World Order in the Age of the Crusades
Andrew A. Latham

4 **Divorce in Medieval England**
From One to Two Persons in Law
Sara M. Butler

Divorce in Medieval England

From One to Two Persons in Law

Sara M. Butler

Routledge
Taylor & Francis Group
NEW YORK LONDON

First published 2013
by Routledge
711 Third Avenue, New York, NY 10017

Simultaneously published in the UK
by Routledge
2 Park Square, Milton Park, Abingdon, Oxon OX14 4RN

Routledge is an imprint of the Taylor & Francis Group, an informa business

Library of Congress Cataloging-in-Publication Data

Butler, Sara M. (Sara Margaret)
Divorce in medieval England : from one to two persons in law / by Sara M. Butler.
pages cm.— (Routledge research in medieval studies ; 3)
Includes bibliographical references and index.
1 Divorce—England—History—To 1500. 2. Marriage—England—History—To 1500. 3. England—Social conditions—1066–1687. 4. Great Britain—History—1066–1687. I. Title.
HQ876.B88 2013
306.890942—dc23
2012042910

ISBN13: 978-0-415-82516-0 (hbk)
ISBN13: 978-0-203-47006-0 (ebk)

Typeset in Sabon
by IBT Global.

Contents

Abbreviations

C	Chancery
Canterbury	Canterbury Cathedral Archives
CCR	*Calendar of Close Rolls*
CP	Court of Common Pleas
CPMRCL	*Calendar of the Plea and Memoranda Rolls of the City of London*
CPR	*Calendar of Patent Rolls*
CPRRGBI	*Calendar of Papal Registers Relating to Great Britain and Ireland*
GL	London, Guildhall Library
KB	King's Bench
LAO	Lincolnshire Archives Office
PP	*Petitions to the Pope*
REQ	Court of Requests
SC	Special Collections
TNA PRO	The National Archives, Public Record Office
Y.B.	Year Book
YBI CP	York Borthwick Institute, Cause Papers

Acknowledgments

This book is evidence that research and teaching are meant to go hand in hand. In large part, the impetus for this book comes from the confusion and indignation voiced by students in various incarnations of the course entitled "Between Eve and Mary: Women in Medieval Europe," a class I have been teaching regularly for the past ten years. Students in this class have persistently returned to questions that I had a great deal of difficulty answering. Many of those queries focused on the lot of medieval wives. This book is my attempt, finally, to provide definitive answers to those outstanding questions.

I am indebted to a number of institutions for the funding that produced this research. Although I did not realize it at the time, the project was begun on a Social Sciences and Research Council of Canada post-doctoral fellowship. Since that time, I have had a variety of internal research grants from Loyola University New Orleans to continue my archival research. The staff at the National Archives and the J. Edgar and Louise S. Monroe Library's Interlibrary Loan Department both deserve heartfelt thanks for facilitating the research for this study. I would also like to single out a number of new electronic initiatives that I found helpful for locating relevant material. David J. Seipp is responsible for the creation of an online index of the English Year Books that was enormously valuable: David J. Seipp, "Seipp's Abridgement," School of Law, Boston University, http://www.bu.edu/law/seipp/. G.R. Boynton's "Calendar of Patent Rolls Search," hosted by the University of Iowa at http://www.uiowa.edu/~acadtech/patentrolls/, is very user friendly and was also of great assistance. And, finally, the digital library "British History Online," created by the Institute of Historical Research and the History of Parliament Trust, http://www.british-history.ac.uk/, was absolutely vital to my research.

For feedback, encouragement and inspiration, I would like to thank Krista Kesselring, Margaret McGlynn, Shannon McSheffrey, Anthony Musson, Cynthia Neville, Tim Stretton, the various audiences at Kalamazoo and the University of Exeter who have cheerfully suffered through earlier renditions of my work and the anonymous readers for this press, who offered very productive and encouraging reviews. Krista Kesselring and Tim Stretton also hosted a conference on the subject of "Married Women and the Law" in June 2011 that was very inspirational and helped me round out my perceptions on the limitations of marriage. Members of the History Department at Loyola University of New Orleans have offered their staunch support and confidence in me, patiently listening to me rave about dead people and helping me balance teaching, service and research. Mark Fernandez and David Moore need to be singled out for their heroic efforts to keep me sane. Family and friends who deserve to be recognized for their continued support are: Carol and Brian Butler, Alice Clark, Karen Reichard, and John Sebastian. For support on the home front, my husband, Mark LaBine, deserves much credit for his parenting without complaint during my research trips abroad. My children, Cade, Genevieve and Miranda, must also be included for their unwavering confidence that Mommy can do anything.

Portions of this book have been published in other venues. "Runaway Wives: Husband Desertion in Medieval England," *Journal of Social History* 40.2 (December 2006): 337–59, appears in parts of chapters one and three. It appears here with kind permission from the *Journal of Social History* and Oxford University Press. An article I wrote some time ago on medieval alimony forms the base of chapter four: "Maintenance Agreements and Male Responsibility in Later Medieval England," in A.J. Musson, ed., *Boundaries of the Law* (Farnham: Ashgate, 2005), pp. 68–83. This material is reprinted with permission from the publishers. Finally, some of the material from "The Law as a Weapon in Marital Disputes: Evidence from the Late Medieval Court of Chancery, 1424–1529," *Journal of British Studies* 43.3 (July 2004): 291–316, appears also in chapter one. It is reprinted with permission from *Journal of British Studies*.

Please note: all quotations have been translated into modern English for accessibility. Unless otherwise indicated, the translations are my own.

Introduction

The thirteenth-century dispute over the validity of the marriage of William and Alice de Cardunville is a potent reminder of the ways in which views of marriage have evolved since the Middle Ages. Alice probably believed she had done quite well for herself when she married William, one of the king's tenants-in-chief and thus a man of some authority, owning substantial landed estates in Southampton. The two were married solemnly at church door, as both law and custom dictated. They lived together for the next sixteen years, during which time they had several children, although only one four-year-old son, Richard, was still living when the marriage came under fire. Despite the lengthy period that William and Alice cohabited as husband and wife, William's former lover, Joan, abruptly reappeared in his life. Joan purported to have borne William a son, sharing the same name as his young son with Alice, twenty-four years previously. She also alleged to be his wife and was determined to prove that claim in the court Christian. Although the two had never had a proper wedding, Joan asserted that he had at one time pledged his faith to her, and thus the court ruled that intent made a marriage: it declared Alice and William's subsequent union invalid, and the church mandated William to return to Joan. With such a disturbing upheaval in his life, it is no wonder that William passed away the following year. William's death breathed new life into the question of just who actually was his valid wife and thus the mother of his heir. Although the ecclesiastical court had confidently upheld the first relationship, the royal inquisition held at Salisbury in the year 1254 doubted that Joan was his valid wife, because she and William had not been "solemnly espoused at the church door." Nor were the king's officials willing to endorse the marriage to Alice over that of Joan. Ultimately, officials settled on making Robert de Cardunville, William's brother, his heir, thus denying the legality of both marriages and both sons as heirs.[1]

The plight of Alice, Joan and William reveals that, even at a time when marriage was thought to be indissoluble, marital bonds were easily broken. Misconception largely perpetuates the myth of the modernity of divorce. Although the medieval world also employed the word divorce (*divorcium*), because it was not regularly granted at the will of the couple simply because they no longer wished to be married, it is assumed to be another beast altogether.[2] In reality, no matter how loudly the medieval church proclaimed the indissolubility of marriage, the real issue at stake was "the prerogative of the church to decide"; divorce was indeed attainable, providing the church approved it and the couple paid for it.[3] The medieval church's loyalty to the permanence of the marital union (however inconsistent) meant that "divorce" as a formal category in the era encompassed a greater subset of variables than it does today. Specifically, medieval divorce entailed two distinct scenarios when sanctioned by the church. First, divorce implied a judicial separation (*divorcium a mensa et thoro*) in which the couple remained married but was no longer required to live together or to render the conjugal debt (that is, to have intercourse). The English church rarely condoned separations but theoretically might grant them on the grounds of heresy, adultery and cruelty. Second, divorce also signified an annulment (*divorcium a vinculo*)—that is, a formal statement issued by the church that the marriage had never been valid. Impediments that laid the groundwork for an annulment were numerous: among others, non-age, force and fear, impotence, bigamy (known in the Middle Ages as pre-contract) and various forms of incest (consanguinity, affinity, sponsorship).[4] Given the greater strictures involved, undoubtedly a formalized divorce was rarer in the medieval era and required much more perseverance and ingenuity to present a lawsuit that conformed to the church's rhetoric of divorce. William's relationship with Joan above, however, confirms that not all couples carried out their divorces through official channels; self-divorce, as Richard Helmholz has dubbed it, was the inexpensive and less-public alternative.[5] In the case of William and Joan, the informality of their divorce mirrored that of their marriage; cohabitation without a formal declaration of marriage may have even been the norm for those lacking significant property. As James Brundage has suggested, "[f]ormal proceedings were far more common when the parties were socially prominent and when large amounts of property were at issue"; clandestine marriage was thus quite appropriate for those lower down on the social scale.[6] In general, the medieval church wanted no superfluous ceremony or criteria to stand in the way of marriage; as St. Paul pronounced, "it is better to marry than burn."[7] A valid marriage might be contracted anywhere, without witnesses, and using any language as long as the couple expressed their intent in the present tense (*verba de presenti*); the future tense (*verba de futuro*), of course, was reserved for betrothals. If a couple followed an exchange of vows in the future tense with sexual intercourse, however, the union was equally binding (the act confirmed the intention).[8] With such minimalist guidelines, some couples differed significantly in perceptions of their relationship status; while a man might believe he was only betrothed because he had said he "wants to marry her," the woman might interpret those same words as a valid marriage. Misunderstandings of this nature were the reason why the church strenuously advocated (and even punished those who did not participate in) the publication of the banns three Sundays in a row, followed by an exchange of vows in the presence of a priest and witnesses at the church door (a process the church referred to as "solemnization").[9] England also stands out from its continental counterparts because of the lack of written record in terms of marriage agreements. Elsewhere in Europe, families hired a notary public to record the exchange of property that took place upon marriage; in contrast, English contracts were oral.[10] Often the only hard evidence of a marriage was the exchange of a gift, such as a ring, to affirm and publicize one's commitment.[11] Given the highly casual nature of medieval English marriages, that their marriages sometimes ended in an equally relaxed manner should come as no surprise.

The perquisite to clandestine marriage, as the church referred to such informal unions, was that "[a] marriage contract which was unknown to the church authorities could also be dissolved without their knowledge."[12] Self-divorce comes closest to our modern usage of divorce to dissolve the marriages of incompatible individuals. Granted, self-divorce was not easily accomplished: Philippa Maddern's most recent study on serial monogamy not only confirms the regularity of informal divorces but contends that geographic mobility was central to assisting couples in remarrying without worrying about the legal implications of bigamy.[13] Not all couples were capable of moving households, though, so formal divorce was a vital option despite the burden of paperwork and lawyers' fees.

Because marriage significantly altered the status of a woman in law and society, the process of divorce was more challenging to bring about. Drawing inspiration from scripture, medieval English law adopted the fiction of coverture, treating the husband and wife as one person in law, represented in the person of the husband. Hence, the husband became the couple's financial manager, responsible for the governance of all property (both landed and movable). As a *feme covert*, the wife became a dependant of the husband at law and might not appear in court singly unless it was to sue for the death of her husband or personal injury. An ecclesiastical decree of divorce, of either kind, obviously entailed changes to a couple's status with respect to coverture. In a judicial separation, the legal fiction of unity of person still existed, but a woman had to discover the means to support herself and exist in society apart from her husband. In an annulment, the couple did indeed transition from being one person in law to two. Although coverture was a legal fiction, it had a very real impact on the ability of a wife to act independently within medieval society. The goal of this book is to answer many of those questions outstanding about the experience of divorce, such as, how did a couple transition from being one person to two in the process of divorce? What difficulties did individuals encounter during and after the process of divorce? Given the limitations of coverture, how did a wife regain her personhood? Finally, what challenges did she face when she asserted her newfound independence?

It is imperative to clarify from the beginning that this study examines the practice, not the theory, of divorce. Brundage, Connor McCarthy and Charles Reid, Jr., among others, have studied in profound depth the canonical views concerning the dissolubility of marriage.[14] Although their findings act as a guide in the absence of more definitive evidence of the practice of English law, there is no need to rehearse those arguments here once more. Rather, this study sides with Helmholz's view that "[t]he English Church courts did not put into practice every part of the medieval canon law."[15] Divorce was a very normative, human experience that cannot be conveyed adequately by the legislation of celibate clergy, many of whom lived in a "world without women."[16] Admittedly, the records of divorce proceedings offer evidence of marital breakdown at its worst. Those couples appearing in court, generally, were at the end of their ropes, determined to separate whatever the cost. Thus, the more typical divorce—that is, self-divorce—is not as visible. However, the legal record more generally captures snapshots of marital life when couples appeared before the courts in cases tangential to, or arising from, divorce. Property disputes, disciplinary actions for adultery, fornication, non-cohabitation and litigation concerning restitution of conjugal rights all contribute in different ways to gaining a more profound understanding of the medieval process of divorce.

A word of caution: historians are necessarily constrained by the curial process. Most royal records, and many ecclesiastical, are short and formulaic and lack the intimate detail that might allow us great insight into the process of marital breakdown. Even in chancery or in instance litigation in the consistory courts where litigants had much more leeway in the writing of bills and depositions, a paid clerk drafted all the documentation, just as a paid lawyer advised the litigants.[17] Mediation by a scribe or lawyer was only one obstacle. Litigants who appeared in court were there with a mission: lawyers coached their stories precisely to achieve their objective of obtaining (or thwarting) a divorce. This is not to blacken the character of all litigants by implying that they were invariably dishonest. Although some prevarication should be expected, we need to take into account that filtering took place: litigants presented their stories from their own unique perspectives. Faulty or favorable memories, as well as a degree of desperation, may lead to a very one-sided explanation of marital breakdown. What is more, as with divorces today, when the accusations start to fly, angry and resentful spouses defend themselves with their own mud-slinging. All allegations made in a divorce suit, thus, must be taken with a grain of salt.

LOOKING FOR EVIDENCE OF DIVORCE

In Helmholz's seminal study on marriage litigation in 1974, he notes that "[t]he most striking fact about divorce litigation in medieval England is how little of it there was."[18] In the strictest sense, this is true. However, as

Alice, Joan and William above demonstrate, not all couples sued for divorce as such. Their circumstances involved not one, but two divorces. Joan and William participated in a self-divorce decades before Joan resurfaced. The second divorce most likely was sued as multi-party litigation over the validity of a marriage. The decision had the incidental effect of divorcing Alice and William. If we were to look at rates of divorce, those rates would probably only include one of the two divorces, and yet, it is impossible to deny the experiences of both divorces in their lives. The frequency of self-divorce undercuts our efforts to count cases; so many of the suits for restitution of conjugal rights (that is, a request to resume cohabitation and payment of the conjugal debt), disciplinary actions for non-cohabitation and adultery and pre-contract suits mask the fact that couples long ago divorced themselves. The rates can only be so helpful in this respect. It is clear that only those couples whose separations had become notorious appear in the records of the church courts. Separated spouses who went on to engage in adulterous relationships or even other marriages were the chief offenders. It is not hard to imagine that husbands and wives who led chaste lives or moved to new communities may have easily escaped notice. When a wife took the initiative to self-divorce, the records are particularly obscure. Spurned husbands were probably unwilling to confess publicly that their wives had left them. Abandonment by a wife was explicit evidence of a husband's inability to govern his household properly. Accordingly, many husbands were most likely too embarrassed to inform the courts upon their wives' departures (or, they may also have been too busy celebrating over their absence).

Helmholz's observation also reflects the nature of the ecclesiastical records. To date, those who have studied marriage and divorce have set their sights primarily on the courts Christian. This study does not intend to replicate the fine work of Helmholz, Frederik Pedersen or Charles Donahue, Jr.[19] Although the church courts were capable of addressing the spiritual side of the equation, many of the grievances couples had about their divorces (either formal or informal) were matters for the king's courts. Any issues relating to the conveyance of property (through dowry, dower, curtesy or inheritance) fell squarely into the jurisdiction of the common law courts. Because the church was so vehemently pro-marriage, some couples preferred to avoid them altogether and go to the English chancellor in the hopes of convincing him to address their grievances equitably. The court of Chancery existed for those cases that did not fit neatly into the rubric of the common law courts (as was the case with many of the unusual grievances arising from marital dissolution). This court was also ideal to bring truces to matrimonial wars in which individuals manipulated the courts to harass unwitting spouses. Petitions to the court of Chancery have much to offer in terms of highlighting especially the role of women in medieval England. Recent studies have demonstrated that medieval women felt most comfortable in this legal setting. In an examination of bills of complaint sent to chancery between 1461 and 1515 by petitioners living in

Yorkshire, Emma Hawkes notes that fully 15 percent of the litigants were female. These figures have led her to argue "that women were significantly more likely to participate in legal activities in equity than in common law courts." Moreover, chancery bills appealed to notions of chivalry, "calling on the idea that the king should be the friend to the friendless, caring for widows and children. The use of this ideology may have made chancery a more attractive jurisdiction for women."[20] The versatility and effectiveness of chancery made it the ideal venue for resolution of marital disputes. For example, although late medieval common law justices were able to award damages for the non-performance of an oral or written agreement, this was the limit of their abilities. Chancery, on the other hand, was capable of both awarding damages and ordering the performance of the agreement.[21] In spousal disputes, this provision meant that the courts might effectively enforce maintenance contracts for separated wives. Although the church courts were capable of addressing this issue (and often did), chancery was more expedient. Chancery could have the delinquent husband arrested and cast in prison (without waiting the forty days required by the law of caption) and compel performance of the agreement. To a woman without any immediate support, chancery undoubtedly offered the most expeditious solution. The records of the court of Chancery, however, demonstrate that English medieval society was still not comfortable with wives suing their husbands (or vice versa) and chose instead to keep within the rules of coverture in which husband and wife were considered one person in law.[22] Hence, for example, there are no identifiable cases of medieval wives using the court of Chancery to plead suits against their husbands for violent trespass.[23] What the records do demonstrate is a shrewd use of the courts by both husbands and wives to maneuver around the rules of coverture and dictate the terms of marital separation. No study of marital disharmony in the medieval period, then, would be complete without an investigation of the records of the court of Chancery.

Because divorce and issues relating to divorce might appear in such a wide variety of courts, this study casts a broad net in the hopes of reconstructing an overall perspective of the dissolution of marriage in medieval England. Ecclesiastical materials, such as papal petitions, Episcopal registers, cause papers and some *ex officio* (that is, disciplinary actions), are combined with those of the royal courts (coroners' and eyre rolls), but also chancery bills. In order to flesh out the perspective also for the highest and lowest ranks of society, both of whom frequently bypassed the courts because of publicity or expense, royal communications (both close and patent) as well as manorial and mayor's courts' papers also contribute to this analysis. Finally, in order to get a better sense of the role played by the courts in their approach to cases of divorce, the Year Books are also included. The Year Books provide valuable insight into the process of law, an aspect that is hidden in the formulaic accounts of the eyre rolls. The Year Books record series of dialogues between king's justices and pleaders (an early form of barristers) relating to lawsuits that came before the king's courts. Thus, their discussions, although not binding, offer some perspective of how jurists sometimes approached specific situations. Moreover, because the Year Books played an important role in the education of lawyers and justices, the deliberations they record probably had a greater impact on the courtroom process than can be measured. The result of this investigation is, in essence, a hotchpotch of records that is not, in any way, intended to produce a thorough study of rates of divorce; rather, it hopes to offer an overall perspective on the ways in which medieval couples, at all levels of society, might approach the cumbersome problem of dissolving supposedly indissoluble unions.

WHY IS THIS STUDY IMPORTANT?

Scholars of the medieval family would generally agree that the lot of the medieval wife was not an easy one. Medieval husbands held the upper hand in the power relationship, both legally and socially. Although Lawrence Stone's view of married life in the Middle Ages as "brutal and often hostile, with little communication, [and] much wife-beating" has since been called into question, historians who have written more recently have still painted a somewhat unflattering picture.[24] Judith Bennett writes, "[m]edieval people thought of conjugality as a hierarchy headed by a husband who not only controlled his wife's financial assets and public behavior, but also freely enforced his will through physical violence."[25] Indeed, she argues that wife-beating was "a normal part of marriage."[26] Even Barbara Hanawalt, who has optimistically described peasant marriage in medieval England as a partnership (although not of equals), still concedes that occasional violence was accepted and expected in marriage.[27] The rules of coverture also left a wife economically vulnerable. Because all real and movable property legally belonged to the husband as head of the household, a wife who fell out of favor with her husband might well find herself expelled from the family home, without any resources to fall back on.[28] From a modern perspective, marital practices hardly provided any sense of reassurance. At a time when families more often than individuals took the lead in spousal selection and the chief criteria were inheritance and status, strong bonds of affection were not guaranteed to develop. Up against all these factors, some medieval wives might have found their fates difficult to accept. That is not to say that all medieval marriages were prisons instead of playgrounds; certainly, some medieval marriages have provided great evidence of marital affection. However, to quote Robert Palmer, "[m]arriage was a time for bargaining."[29] It was all too easy for a daughter's feelings to be "sacrifice[d] on the altar of the family's ambitions."[30] Thus, the potential for prolonged marital discontent was notably higher then than it is now.

Despite this dreary image of medieval marriage, wives generally accepted their positions—and not just passively. Some women actually fought to hold on to their wretched marriages, even when it was clear that their husbands were desperate for annulments. In examining the records of marriage litigation at the consistory court of York in the fourteenth and fifteenth centuries, Donahue makes a number of striking observations. He notes that not only were women more persistent in suing their cases, but they were far more likely to sue to enforce marriages than were men (even when the financial benefits "were not obvious") and far less likely to dissolve marriages than were men.[31] Andrew Finch, in his comparison of the dioceses of Hereford and Cerisy, makes a similar observation.[32] Findings of this nature would seem to suggest that women would do almost anything for the security of marriage, even if it meant staying in an unhealthy marriage or with a man who would really rather be married to someone else, as was often the case in multi-party litigation where pre-contract was the issue at contest. At any rate, Donahue's portrayal of the church courts as overwhelmingly pro-plaintiff reveals that many women got what they wanted.[33] Because the medieval church was even more determined to uphold the sacrament of marriage, female plaintiffs found a powerful ally in the courts and were often successful in their suits.

The reluctance of wives to divorce stemmed from legitimate concerns. Countless different factors explain their aversion. As a rule, most wives were too financially vulnerable to see divorce as a viable option; with children, in particular, the possibility of supporting a family as a single mother must have been daunting. Although alimony and child support both existed in the Middle Ages, the church lacked the manpower to enforce their payment effectively.[34] Economics were not the only concern: social stigma also played an immeasurable role. For much of the modern era, the stigma associated with divorce was sufficient to persuade many wives to remain in discontented and even abusive marriages for fear that family and society alike might ostracize them. In the Middle Ages, when marriage was a much more public institution, initiated and overseen by families, friends and neighbors, the disgrace of divorce was significantly more meaningful.[35] Petitions to the pope requesting dispensations for marriages where couples belatedly discovered they were related within prohibited degrees (and therefore risked being divorced by court order against their wills) furnish insight into the anxiety divorce produced. Both Robert Urswick and his wife, Margaret, in 1366 and Helen de Witmay and Roger de Donyngton in 1450 alluded to the "scandal" of divorce.[36] Some couples, admittedly being overly dramatic in the hopes of gaining sympathetic approval of their requests, went to much greater extremes. In 1460, the petition of Henry Drew and Joan Hamely depicted a crisis of near-fatal proportions, warning "dissension and scandals might probably arise between their kindred and affinity. . . . Henry would run danger of death, and Joan would be defamed and perhaps remain forever unwed."[37] Although it was certainly overstated, Joan and Henry addressed a very realistic concern: in an era in which the marriage of moneyed individuals was less about the bride and groom than it was about family alliances, an unexpected divorce, for whatever reason, might have disastrous consequences. The histrionic tenor of their petition was not atypical. A 1452 petition by Ralph Sympyl and his wife, Elizabeth Boid, contended that "if a divorce were to take place between them, who are by both parents of a race of great nobles, grave events might probably happen between their parents, kinsman and friends."[38] The Scottish couple Alexander de Suthirland and Margaret Maclayde in 1448 contended that a divorce would provoke "very great dissensions, brawls, and scandals . . . and the slaughter of more than five hundred men, and that Margaret would remain forever defamed."[39] This negative attitude towards the dissolution of marriage reflects broader apprehensions in late medieval England. The rise of Lollardy, in particular, brought these concerns to the fore, highlighting popular anxieties about the church's willingness to facilitate divorce, thus undermining the stability of the family. John Wycliffe's challenge to divorce targeted canon lawyers, arguing that they acted as "men of anti-Christ" when annulling unions.[40] The Lollard tract entitled *The Lanterne of Light* reiterated Wycliffe's stance, boldly describing divorce as "authorize[d] lechery."[41]

Such disparaging attitudes towards divorce make it clear how difficult it must have been to make the decision to end a marriage. In this environment, suing for divorce required great stamina and a strong sense that one was making the right decision. The court process presented additional obstacles to shake the confidence of even the most assured litigants. Much like today, medieval divorce was an expensive, often lengthy process, replete with name-calling, finger-pointing, and plenty of metaphorical bloodshed. Few emerged unscathed in terms of reputation or finances. Considering these factors gives us a much better sense of the kind of person who sued a case of divorce. This study is particularly important in light of the role played by women in marriage. The image of "desperate housewives" projected by women who fought to save their miserable marriages needs to be complemented with that of women who were equally resolute to escape marital misery, even if it meant defying society, the church and the law.

This study also tries to shed new light on medieval husbands in an attempt to understand why they chose to pursue the difficult path of divorce. Traditional notions that women wanted to get married and men wanted to get out of marriage are problematic. As the requests for dispensations above suggest, some husbands were similarly averse to divorce. In large part, a husband's economic success relied extensively on not only the property a wife brought into a marriage but also his wife's labor. Wives played an active role as business partners to men; thus, divorce affected not only a husband's marital state but possibly even his career. Marriage for a man brought with it many perquisites. English society recognized a man's social adulthood only once he became the head of a household. Moreover, good governance of one's household was an essential building block for a man's reputation within his community. A wife's desertion undermined a husband's masculinity in an exceedingly public way. With such weighty consequences, divorce was not a desirable option for men either.

THE ROLE OF COVERTURE IN THE DIVORCE PROCESS

The thirteenth-century legal treatise popularly ascribed to jurist Henry de Bracton best describes the rules of coverture. As *Bracton* noted, marriage merges the legal personalities of husband and wife. They are "so to speak, a single person, because they are one flesh and one blood." This symbolic vision of marriage had very tangible results, particularly in terms of property. *Bracton* explained, "the thing is the property of the wife, and the husband its custodian, since he rules his wife, in which case no answer will be made the husband without his wife nor conversely." [42] In theory, coverture was in the best interests of the marriage, "intended to remove from the marital union any potential for acrimony or disagreements over property interests, obligations, privileges, and other entitlements."[43] The implication in reality, however, was total erasure of a woman's legal personality, so much so that when she appeared in court to pursue a cause in which she had a vested interest, the court viewed her as her husband's attorney. Granted, for many women, the impact of the legal disability of wives in English common law on their actual lives was negligible. Women without landed property and those in amiable marriages most likely felt few repercussions from this oppressive ideology and may even have lived out their lives oblivious to it. Coverture reared its ugly head primarily in times of crisis—that is, when a husband failed to respect his wife's wishes with her property, or when a marriage ended through either death or divorce. It is important to recognize, though, that coverture in medieval England was not the authoritative institution it became by the eighteenth century. As Tim Stretton argues, "[w]hat had begun as a limited fiction applied in specific circumstances had grown to become a metaphor that helped to describe the marital state, then a doctrine that at first explained coverture and finally justified coverture."[44] The flexibility of the medieval approach in applying coverture is evident in the fact that when coverture was inconvenient for men, the courts ignored it. Criminal jurisdiction offers the best example: although coverture was not entirely absent from criminal law, the courts did not hold the husband responsible for his wife's felonies. The courts might also ignore coverture when it prevented them from upholding the law: although a wife on her own technically was permitted to bring an appeal only for the death of her husband or for personal injury, justices regularly overlooked the limiting rule when a wife's appeal was the sole means of prosecuting a known criminal.[45]

The process of divorce intensified the reality of this legal fiction by attempting to destabilize it. Divorce, in all its forms, had a very real impact on unity of person. As a result, coverture vividly shaped the experience of divorce. For a separated wife attempting to eke out a solitary existence, an unsupportive husband's continuing governance over lands and goods was crippling. Annulments were not necessarily much better; although a wife's goods and property theoretically returned to her upon divorce, laying claim to them sometimes seemed near impossible. The husband's reluctance to return a wife's belongings coupled with the challenge of achieving public recognition of a divorce drew many women into lengthy and unpleasant court proceedings in the hopes of recovering what was lawfully theirs.

Property was not the only realm in which coverture played a role. Because coverture obliterated a woman's legal identity, in a husband's absence, she was incapable of defending herself appropriately at law. In a 1478 case of trespass, the defendant, a married woman, appeared without her husband in tow, declaring that he had been gone overseas so long that she had no idea whether he was even still alive. Incapable of defending herself without him, the court convicted her. Her husband conveniently returned in time to sue a writ of error, and the court reversed the declaration of outlawry against her. Common law justices commented that, because of coverture, an outlawed wife could do nothing to resolve the situation without her husband; she might not even purchase a pardon in his absence. Thus, as one justice observed (humorously), a husband "could be well discharged of her, if she be a shrew, because if he did not want to sue to reverse the outlawry, she would never be received sole." These justices, then, saw outlawry as a potent form of divorce.[46] Although justices may have found this situation amusing, assuredly those wives who experienced such legal disability did not.

Coverture also asserted the power of a husband to govern his wife. In practice, this ideology merely encouraged marital violence. Medieval marriage accorded a man "hitting rights" over his wife. Husbands were expected to govern their wives with a firm hand. As Maddern has argued, "late medieval English people perceived violence as an instrument and a sign of good social order. From the highest hierarchy of heaven to the smallest independent sociopolitical unit (the household), violence was normatively thought to be rightly exercised in the maintenance of divinely instituted order."[47] Most medieval Englishmen would have interpreted a husband's violence as laudable, as it was "both the guarantee and the marker of political and social order."[48] Even in medieval England, however, violence had its limits. As a royal writ intended to protect wives from their husbands' abuse phrased it, the law expected a husband to "treat and govern her well and honestly, and to do no injury or ill to her body other than that permitted lawfully and reasonably to a husband for the purpose of control and punishment of his wife."[49] As one might expect, the ambiguity of these parameters awarded a husband great discretion in the doling out of punishment. A husband might legitimately employ violence to coerce a wife into remaining in a marriage despite her desire to divorce. In terms of judicial separations and informal divorces, a husband's continuing role as disciplinarian was defensible at law. In an annulment, the length of the duration until the church finalized a divorce meant a husband's right to punish remained during a time when, admittedly, a husband might find great fault with his wife's actions.

Coverture also frequently dictated the nature of the court from which a wife sought redress. Only the common law courts recognized coverture: thus, many wives preferred instead to take their property concerns relating to divorce proceedings to either chancery or ecclesiastical courts, where unity of person did not take center stage. Nonetheless, it is striking how deeply entrenched was the ideology of coverture in medieval society, such that courts freed from the constraints of this legal fiction still sometimes imposed it. For example, manorial and borough courts, although in principle not common law courts, sometimes held husbands responsible for their wives' misdemeanors, even when they were not present to witness the act. The borough court of Colchester (*Essex*) in 1311 included the complaint of Joan, wife of William Sprot, against Benedicta and Richard le Blunt. Joan and the court held Richard accountable when Benedicta assaulted Joan, chiefly because he failed to chastise his wife for her actions.[50] This is just one example among many. The proclivity of the courts to uphold coverture, even when not required to do so, meant that coverture played a much greater role in a wife's life than one might think.

Of course, coverture was not always a disability for wives. Certainly, the dominance a husband asserted in marriage sheltered some wives from legal accountability for their actions. As *Bracton* argued, the court might not hold a wife who participated in a crime with her husband liable, "because whether or not she was privy to the crime, she was under her husband's rod."[51] This ideology existed both in theory and in practice. The Wiltshire eyre of 1249 acquitted Christiana Sprot of a merchant's death. The murder was carried out by her husband, and the jury determined "that Christiana did not take part unless by the compulsion of her husband and her fear of him."[52] Coverture also provided a mask for women's accountability for debts incurred in her business dealings; rather than apply for *feme sole* status, a license that permitted a married woman to buy and sell as if she were single in order to continue her pre-marital business, many wives preferred to assert coverture to avoid paying their debts.[53] In terms of divorce, coverture promoted the expectation that a man support his wife during the proceedings for an annulment and perpetually if a judicial separation was the goal. A separated wife might even exploit this expectation through buying on credit, especially if her husband was reluctant to continue her support.

Coverture's role in shaping women's legal personalities was paramount; it also molded their lived experiences substantially, regardless of whether they realized it. Married women were at the mercy of their husbands' good will. The existence of this legal straightjacket helps us reassess the nature of a wife's decision to divorce and better understand the obstacles she might encounter on that path.

THIS STUDY IN BRIEF

Chapter 1 addresses the reasons why medieval men and women divorced. Canonists permitted both judicial separations and annulments for only a limited pool of reasons. This book, though, recognizes that the medieval church was highly regional and that not all regions implemented canon law in the same fashion. Thus, chapter 1 focuses only on those grounds for divorce that Englishmen and -women pleaded in divorce litigation. Medieval lawsuits guide us to a number of observations. First, men and women sought divorce for different reasons. Because family prosperity and advancement were tied so closely to marriage, marital high politics were often shockingly brutal. Some women accepted that violence; others fought against it with the church's support. Second, the divorce process displays a gap between canonical and lay perceptions. Although the church insisted that divorce "should be allowed only for serious causes—mere dislike or disgust with the appearance, habits, or character of the marital partner did not furnish adequate grounds for separation," the laity themselves did not always agree.[54] Some couples who wished to divorce for incompatibility did so; however, the church's rigid positioning required them to work around the process, either by self-divorcing or suing falsely for divorce on other grounds.

Chapter 2 walks through the fundamentals of the divorce process: what kind of person chose to pursue a divorce either inside or outside the courts? What were some of the causes of divorce? How did a person proceed through the legal system? Dissolving a marriage was an extensive procedure in the medieval period, with many far-reaching considerations ranging from expense to the length of the proceedings, as well as more basic questions of how a person was going to support him- or herself both financially and emotionally throughout the process and after. This chapter attempts to address the universality of divorce. No socio-economic class was more inclined to divorce than was any other, but a person's economic standing very much dictated his or her approach to, and the nature of, divorce. Rank also predicted a family's reaction to an individual's decision to dissolve a marriage. As this chapter suggests, marriage fulfilled exceptionally different goals, depending on one's position in the economic spectrum; thus, familial support often relied on the wider implications of a marriage's failure. Finally, status also dictated the nature of the resources available to a divorcing wife. Through an appeal to the king, a woman of high rank could mobilize the local sheriff and other royal officials to safeguard both herself and her property; women of lower rank generally had only their families and neighbors.

Divorcing one's spouse involved many risks. Chapter 3 underscores the nature of those risks, focusing primarily on the wife, for whom the stakes were highest. Many studies of marital disharmony center on women's role as victims. This study reveals instead women reared to be passive and to accept calmly their husbands' authority who chose instead to defy social norms and carve out their own futures, despite the attendant dangers. The economic dependence of married women as well as their legal disability meant that making the decision to divorce was far more perilous for women than it was for men. Although both jeopardized their reputations and souls, for women particularly divorce had a much greater sphere of influence, endangering also their children, their families and anyone else who chose to assist them in dissolving their marriages.

Some women decided against divorce because they had no independent means of support. Chapter 4 addresses how a wife supported herself both during and after the proceedings. In terms of a judicial separation, alimony, although not the guaranteed right some scholars have interpreted it to be, was a distinct possibility. The basics of alimony payments as well as the courts' ability to enforce their disbursement are both central to understanding the reality of separate living for medieval wives. Annulments, though, presented a very different scenario. Theoretically, an annulment meant the division of property to a premarital state, a feat that was not easily accomplished. Some husbands (and some wives) were hesitant to relinquish the property that they had previously enjoyed.

Chapter 5, undoubtedly the most challenging of the entire study, tackles one distinct form of property: children. Both the custody and support of the children of divorced parents are issues that scholarly circles do not usually address. Working from an assorted miscellany of sources, this chapter tries to fill in the gaps in our knowledge to understand medieval expectations of a child's rights as well as his or her parents' obligations in terms of custody and support. Although divorce records omit dialogues over such issues that we today would see as fundamental, they do include extensive discussions on the impact of divorce on their children's legitimacy. In theory, whether the children of divorced parents were bastardized by their divorce relates entirely to the nature of the divorce; in practice, there seems to have been much more leeway.

Continuing this theme, chapter 6 asks what happened after a divorce. With the rules of coverture, the law considered husband and wife as one person. How was it possible to transition from being one to two persons in law, and in reality? This chapter examines couple's efforts to prove their divorces, both in court and within society, seeking to understand how a couple performed the social rituals of divorce as well as its popular reception. Many of the records above imply that divorce was a scandalous, unthinkable affair. Did family and neighbors actually respond to couples who divorced in this manner? Did society respect a woman's newfound personhood? What continuing relationship did a couple have after the church dissolved their marriage, and were any problems uniquely associated with the process of medieval divorce?

1 Why Did They Leave?

If the medieval church did not consider incompatibility sufficient reason to leave one's spouse, then what did it believe was a good cause for divorce? This is not necessarily an easy question to answer. Time and place, in large part, are key factors. Canon law in the Middle Ages was an evolving body of legislation that developed over hundreds of years out of the highly specialized intellectual debates of academics. Their reasoning derived only partly from biblical precedent: Christian tradition, Roman law, natural law and even common sense all contributed to contemporary perceptions of acceptable grounds for divorce. The history of adultery as a justification for marital dissolution provides an excellent window into the process of developing canon law. Following biblical directive, early Christian legislation put forward by Constantine permitted divorce for adultery but restricted it to the wife as perpetrator. Although a wife could sue for divorce if her husband was engaged in murder, poisoning or grave robbery, the early Roman church did not see a man's adultery as a failing sufficient to grant divorce.[1] Under emperors Theodosius and Valentinian, this position changed: adultery by the husband also became a legitimate basis for divorce. This egalitarian perspective did not extend much beyond the fall of Rome, however. The Council of Friuli in 796 once again limited divorce only to a wife's adultery.[2] With Gratian's new textbook of canon law in the twelfth century, the tides turned against adultery. Although Gratian was willing to permit adultery as a legitimate rationale for a couple to separate, divorce was out of the question. Nonetheless, the evidentiary process was still highly gendered. As Rufinus later observed, the wife "was at a legal disadvantage, since a man was entitled to charge his wife with adultery on suspicion alone, while a woman could bring such a charge against her husband only with hard proof."[3] Even still, Peter Abelard, who taught canon law at the University of Paris in the twelfth century, instructed his students that men could divorce their wives for adultery but that canon law did not permit wives to do so.[4] In the thirteenth and fourteenth centuries, canonists shifted the focus of their query significantly. Although they consistently accepted the adultery of either partner as good grounds for separation, canonists were more interested in the implications of a separation on property, focusing especially on an adulterous wife's right to claim dower.[5]

As this case history suggests, canonical interpretations of the acceptability of adultery as justification for divorce have evolved greatly over time. Regional diversity is also a key factor. Although we glibly refer to the "medieval church," no such monumental, unified institution ever existed in the Middle Ages. Churches were decidedly regional; thus, English canon lawyers sometimes applied the law in different ways than their continental counterparts. To offer a pertinent example, although the English church courts rarely entertained the notion of permitting couples to separate, the Franco-Belgian courts of the same period had an "extensive separation jurisdiction," awarding an astonishingly high number of separations and boasting an exceptionally formalized process that even included hired arbiters to oversee the separation of marital goods.[6]

Given these limitations, this chapter does not aspire to universality; rather, it addresses only the practices of the English church concerning divorce litigation during the later medieval period. The only exceptions to this exclusively English focus are the communications resulting from English appeals to Rome. The nature of the sources inevitably guides this discussion. The medieval church permitted annulments only when valid impediments existed, implying that the marriage had never truly been valid. Thus, divorce litigation centered on those claims deemed acceptable by the church, such as incest, pre-contract (bigamy), under-age marriage, coerced marriage and impotence. Because of the visibility of those claims in the medieval records, this chapter addresses them first. The church awarded judicial separations only to couples whose marriages had evolved to a point where one or both spouses were endangered, either physically or spiritually. Although heresy was an acceptable justification for judicial separation, adultery and cruelty dominated the English suits for separation. Moreover, litigants tended to connect these allegations in their requests for separation; therefore, this chapter addresses adultery and cruelty jointly. Finally, self-divorce presents the most difficult obstacles in terms of discerning the context for marital dissolution. The sources that offer the most information are those of the ecclesiastical courts, in which the courts cited a wife for not adhering to her husband (or vice versa). In these circumstances, the responses of the individual give us some indication as to why he or she chose to self-divorce.

INCEST

Incest was one of the foremost causes for divorce. The reasoning behind the concern for incestuous marriage had nothing to do with modern fears of genetic disorders; rather, as Thomas Aquinas argued, the ban on couples marrying when too closely related had more to do with the need to create boundaries so that lust did not reign supreme in the close quarters of a household.[7] In the medieval context, couples divorced on these grounds frequently were divorced against their wills and sought to remarry. The church expected a couple to probe into their family backgrounds before entering into marriage. The publication of the banns three Sundays in advance of the wedding was an additional safeguard to detect any underlying issues that might be mortifying if discovered down the road.[8] However, the rules of incest in the medieval church were so convoluted that tracing impediments required a vast amount of research and good memory.[9] Canonists defined incest not only through blood relationships; sexual encounters and religious sponsorship also created lasting family relations that acted as impediments to marriage. How earnestly did couples apply themselves to uncovering incestuous relationships? The survival of genealogical trees among the church's records expresses a positive dedication by some couples to ensure the validity of their union. Affluent couples actually hired people to investigate their pedigrees: the dispensation awarded to John Moubray and Elisabeth de Vrer, daughter of the earl of Oxford, states specifically that "persons more skilled in the law than those consulted by [the couple] before marriage" had discovered the incestuous relationship, prompting their request for dispensation.[10] Because the church did not always practice what it preached, permitting couples to apply for a papal dispensation when too closely related (even when related within the second degree), some couples believed the church might not strenuously object when an impediment was discovered. [11] Regrettably, this erroneous perception provoked a good deal of suffering among couples divorced against their wills. The papal petitions record plenteous examples of couples divorced on the grounds of incest and then granted a dispensation with permission to remarry; but the Vatican priced dispensations well beyond the reach of the ordinary individual. The costs of saving a marriage were predicated also on a couple's ignorance: the church required couples who married knowing an impediment existed to make a financial settlement to a curial official. Consciously violating church law also led to a sentence of excommunication, which might only be alleviated by further fines from the affluent or physical penance from the poor. Altogether, this meant that some couples paid dearly for the privilege of remaining married, and there was no guarantee that the papal court would side with the spouses' wishes.

Of all the impediments, incest was the most open to manipulation, simply because it was so easy to create an impediment. Surely, for an individual wishing to get out of a marriage, a recently discovered (or manufactured) incestuous relationship was a good excuse.[12] Indeed, historians have argued repeatedly that "kings and nobles might have resisted church jurisdiction over marriage if they had not had the 'forbidden degrees' escape route to fall back on."[13] Even those lower down on the social scale took advantage of this loophole. Many divorces on these grounds have all the earmarks of invention. For example, in 1356, Christine Spicer petitioned the bishop of

Carlisle for a divorce from her husband, John de Distyngton. Grounds for divorce centered on a previous "carnal knowledge" of her daughter, Agnes. After interviewing all the concerned parties, the bishop sided with Christine and awarded a divorce.[14] How could the couple have married without knowing about this previous impediment? Even if John had kept it to himself, surely Christine's daughter would have spoken up. The most likely explanation for this divorce is that Christine wanted out of her marriage, and she knew her daughter would support her through perjury.[15] Divorces awarded on these grounds were common enough; each time the records describe the couple's "shocking" discovery that they are related within prohibited degrees, even though in many situations, it is hard to imagine how they could possibly have been that ignorant. For example, a 1414 mandate to the bishop of Lincoln relates how Richard Boteler and Joan Lymebrenner had learned only after they entered into a valid marriage that Richard had previously been married to Joan's aunt (her mother's sister).[16] How could the couple have not known this before they were married?

David D'Avray sees marriage within incestuous lines as a deliberate strategy among the wealthy. He notes, "[t]he more church justice blocked the path to divorce, the more the magnates tended to choose marriages which they knew could be annulled at need."[17] The impact on the church's reputation, however, was damning. Such "frequent annulments" inevitably "made the system look two-faced: unbreakable monogamy in principle, but a popular loophole to facilitate changing wives."[18] D'Avray's perspective on aristocratic resistance to the ecclesiastical model of marriage not only is critical for a clearer understanding of why medieval individuals resorted to divorce but reaffirms that England is not an anomaly. Georges Duby's 1978 study of marriage among the French aristocracy draws essentially the same conclusion.[19] The chief distinction between the two settings lay in the degree of animosity: where the French upper crust struggled with competing models of marriage (one ecclesiastical, the other secular and aristocratic), in England, as Frederik Pedersen has argued, the "struggle" was largely absent.[20] Although the English certainly had their own "coherent lay aristocratic agenda," they preferred passive resistance, exploiting the impediments to achieve their own ends.[21] Moreover, the manipulation of provisions for divorce in England was never restricted only to the moneyed ranks. Although the poor most likely engaged in self-divorce, wealthier peasants (the group Barbara Hanawalt has labeled "primary villagers") were accustomed also to employing the courts to address their marital problems.[22]

Although the laity sometimes saw incest as a strategy to undermine the permanence of the marital union, the church saw it as a means of protecting the sanctity of marriage. The church assiduously devoted itself to divorcing incestuous couples who befouled the institution. Its dedication is evident in the myriad cases of marital dissolution on the grounds of sponsorship. Although today the church sees religious sponsorship as creating more of an allegorical relationship between sponsor and child, the medieval church adopted a very different perspective: "Because the sponsors had become parents-in-God, or godparents, to the child, they were incorporated into his or her family. They became spiritual relatives of the child and of the child's parents, all of whom were bound to one another by mutual obligations of trust and help."[23] Once again, however, a gap existed between secular and ecclesiastical perceptions. Although the church considered godparentage to create a lasting family relationship, communities themselves plainly did not share this belief. Parents regularly appointed godparents for their children from among their neighbors and friends, generally that same pool of people with whom they exchanged their children in marriage. Godparentage tended to occur within social strata rather than across, such that "[m]erchants godparented the children of other merchants, artisans godparented those of artisans, the nobility other nobles."[24] Furthermore, the lines of sponsorship in a village multiplied not only through the greater number of births in the Middle Ages but also because the church assigned each child three godparents (two of his or her own sex, one of the opposite) at baptism and then again at confirmation.[25] The bonds of family established at baptism and confirmation were not limited only to the child and his sponsors: "sponsorship established a tie of coparenthood between the godparent and all of the adult members of the godchild's family."[26] With all of these obstacles working against them, a couple from the same village, for example, might easily find themselves related through sponsorship. Once again, although the church was often willing to provide a dispensation for couples who wished to remain married despite the impediment, the couple had to pay dearly for that dispensation. Sometimes the pope took pity on a couple: Isabel Martiner and John Cheyne of the diocese of Lincoln pleaded poverty when asking to remain in their marriage: John's first wife had been godmother at the baptism of one of Isabel's children from a former marriage, thus they required a papal dispensation to stay married but could not afford to pay for one. The pope granted the dispensation regardless.[27] Many couples clearly believed purchasing a dispensation was worthwhile, even when uncertainty existed. For example, the dispensation awarded to Thomas Gray and Alice de Elwyk of Durham diocese reveals that they were not entirely certain of the nature of the impediment that existed between them. Alice's mother had been godmother to one of the twins of Thomas's mother, but they were not sure whether she was godmother to Thomas or his twin brother.[28] Many couples married despite the impediment, simply because they had no other choice: the dispensation awarded to Thomas de Leuth and Alice, daughter of John Beteler of Wych, states that their impediment derived from the fact that Thomas was godfather at confirmation to Alice's son by a former husband. The couple knew of this impediment when they married, but, as Thomas declared, they married at a rather unfortunate time: "[he] knew no one else whom he could marry at the time of the pestilence."[29]

PRE-CONTRACT (BIGAMY)

Many scholars have highlighted the centrality of pre-contracts as a pretext for divorce.[30] The ease of marriage making in medieval England sometimes led to confusion over a couple's status. Lacking set vows, and with the popularity of conditional vows (that is, "I will marry you if . . ."), an individual hoping to self-divorce might creatively recast the exchange in an amply ambiguous manner. Canon law took a strong stand on the ineligibility of notoriously subjective conditional vows, such as, "I take you if I decide not to marry someone else," or "if you continue to please me." But it allowed many other equally problematic vows, such as, "I take you if you are skilled in baking, brewing, and weaving," or "I take you if my parents approve."[31] Self-divorce, then, might easily be justified because the condition was not met, and thus the individual assumed the vows were not binding. The room for vagueness caused by the church's modest guidelines for a valid marriage created a breeding ground for pre-contract suits.

Pre-contract was a relatively common situation and needs to be understood, to quote Philippa Maddern, as "serial monogamy," rather than actual bigamy.[32] Nonetheless, we should not assume that serial monogamy necessarily denotes free choice in marital union; in fact, sometimes, it was quite the opposite. Despite the church's bold and controversial declaration that a binding union required only the consent of the bride and the groom, both families and lords generally believed otherwise. Although some historians have described medieval English marriages as "astonishingly individualistic," in general, the medieval English thought marrying without consulting one's broader community was vulgar and inconsiderate.[33] As Diana O'Hara has argued, "[t]he final choice of partner, while it may indeed often have incorporated personal liking or love, was linked indissolubly to questions of family credit, economic worth and the successful handling of both courtship ritual and the sensitive negotiations that accompanied them."[34] Hence, "[s]ometimes free choice in marriage was to prefer to abide by the wishes of others."[35] This interpretation of "consent" was passive rather than active. Consent to marriage was best described as having "the power of refusal."[36]

When individuals neglected the normal rules of the courtship process, litigation was often the result. The marriage of Agnes Huntington to John of Bristol in February 1339 is an example of a couple exerting their own choice in marriage, despite the vehement disapproval of Agnes's mother and stepfather: her mother had even threatened that "she would draw a maternal curse upon herself" before consenting to any such contract.[37] The determination of Agnes's parents resulted in litigation before the dean of Christianity in the hopes of refuting the reality of their daughter's marriage. Through intimidation, Agnes's mother persuaded her to commit perjury, claiming that her vows had been conditional on parental consent, which was not to be forthcoming. The court pronounced John and Agnes free of marriage. Six years later, embroiled in a love match with a possibly abusive man, Agnes began to rethink her initial decision. The downfall of pre-contract litigation is that it nullified one marriage by upholding a previous one. However, in Agnes's mind, marriage to an old boyfriend (even if he did not agree) was preferable to continuing in a violent and unhappy union. Agnes initiated court proceedings before the archbishop of York on the grounds of pre-contract, hoping the church might release her from her bond to Simon Munkton.[38] Given the extent of family pressure exerted upon individuals, many families may have bulldozed young men and women into renouncing their rash, individualist decisions to marry, actions that they may have come to regret some time later upon mature reflection.

Some marriages fell apart because a husband, long-thought dead, suddenly reappeared to claim his wife who had remarried in his absence. War, trade and pilgrimages often kept men away from home for extended periods, and without any reliable means of long-distance communication, a wife might mistakenly believe he had not returned because he was no longer alive. Because marriage was central to a woman's identity in the Middle Ages, the church believed it was immoral to prohibit her from remarrying when her husband was presumed dead, although she had to wait a reasonable period before leaping to any conclusions. For most of the Middle Ages, ten years was the norm, although Pope Celestine III (*r.* 1191–98) reduced the waiting period to seven years.[39] Husbands who returned home to discover their wives newly married, especially when they were anticipating a jubilant homecoming, were usually unimpressed, but not always unsympathetic. When Bernard Brocas arrived home after years of fighting abroad, his wife, Agnes Vavasour, motivated by false reports of his death, had remarried and borne a son, whom she had named Bernard in kind reminiscence after her first husband. Although the church immediately declared Agnes's second marriage void on the grounds of pre-contract, Bernard sued for (and won) a divorce, charitably permitting Alice to keep her most valuable dowry estates.[40] Gilbert de Paris's petition to the king in the year 1298 makes it clear that sometimes wives were purposely misled to believe their husbands were dead. Gilbert claimed that he had entrusted his wife and all his lands, goods and chattels to Nicholas Rollaund while he was away fighting in the king's service in Flanders. During his absence, Rollaund informed Gilbert's wife that her husband had been killed in action. By the time Gilbert returned home, Gilbert's wife, lands, goods and chattels had all come into Rollaund's hands.[41]

Litigation emanating from pre-contracts stands out from the rest as being among some of the most confusing documentation imaginable. The intricate marital history of Elizabeth Barantyne is an excellent illustration of just how elaborate these cases might become, exhibiting especially the impact of pre-contract on issues of marital property. As dowager to her late husband, Reynold Barantyne, who died in 1441, Elizabeth was a very desirable match for any Englishman hoping to advance in the kingdom.

Sometime between 1441 and 1443, she entered into a marriage with John Upham. According to his bill to the chancellor, soon after that, John Tychbourne appeared, pretending that he had a pre-existing contract with Elizabeth and thus was her valid husband. Upham's version of the story paints Tychbourne as an abductor, determined only to get his hands on her property. He recounts how Tychbourne "took her away and wedded her against law and conscience" and since then had held her "in his governance." Upham's concern was not only for Elizabeth; during this time, "his" property (that is, presumably Elizabeth's dower lands) had come into Tychbourne's hands, and Upham wanted it back.[42] Tychbourne's formal response adopted an entirely different tone. He highlighted the validity of his marriage to Elizabeth. Their union was not coerced; the two had been married at church door, lawfully, with the assent of friends. Rather, in this scenario, Upham was the wicked abductor. He appeared in their lives while Elizabeth was visiting Brightwell. With the help of another woman, he carried her away and then initiated a false suit of divorce between Tychbourne and Elizabeth on the grounds of pre-contract, motivated by "covetousness to have his lands and tenements and goods." Since that time, Elizabeth had hired two bachelors of canon law to determine the matter. They had decided in favor of Elizabeth's union with Tychbourne, declaring Upham's union with Elizabeth void. Elizabeth was not entirely blameworthy, though, adding some credence to Upham's testimony; apparently, because of the "great hurt, cost, and shame" that Tychbourne had endured because of her, she granted all her lands, tenements, goods, chattels and bonds to her husband. Tychbourne then "sent her into Sussex unto a manor" to live on her own, with lands worth £20 to support herself.[43] Although Elizabeth's own voice is absent from the official record, by March 1445, the king took charge and was communicating with lawyers in order to end this matter. Apparently, Elizabeth had died, and Upham and Tychbourne were still in chancery fighting over her properties. The king's commission does at least offer some insight into whose story was most credible. He requested the lawyers to inquire into that strife, "wishing to know all herein from the day of the marriage of Elizabeth and John Upton [Upham] to the day of the divorce between her and John Tychbourne by reason of a pre-contract, and from the day of the divorce to the day when John Tychbourne delivered her from his possession, and the value of the goods and the extent of the lands."[44]

Because coverture awarded a husband governance of his wife's goods and lands, to some men, pre-contract may have seemed like an ideal way of augmenting one's holdings through marriage to a woman who would not otherwise be willing to consent. We have no way of knowing exactly what happened to Elizabeth Barantyne, but it is clear that both John Upham and John Tychbourne were concerned primarily for title to her lands. The fact that their dissension continued after her death reveals that she was probably also an heiress (dower lands had a lifetime limit, but a husband could legitimately lay claim to lands she had come into as an heiress). Elizabeth's position as a woman of wealth certainly complicated her situation, but many other lawsuits evolving out of pre-contracts suggest that the strategies employed by Upham and/or Tychbourne were typical. A chancery bill from an anxious father lower down on the social scale in the years 1467–72 discloses how married men manipulated church law in order to gain control of women's property. Edward Candell of Frome complained of the deviousness of William Godyhold, recently of Warminster in the diocese of Salisbury, a newcomer to Frome (*Som.*) and Edward's new son-in-law. After a chance meeting with a dyer of Warminster (*Wilts.*), Edward became aware that William was already married. His petition accuses William of marrying women in diverse dioceses across England for the sole purpose of gaining possession of their goods and riches. Edward turned to the chancellor for help only after the church had failed to locate the swindler, who went missing soon after the wedding.[45] John Mynton of Barking (*Essex*) was an even more accomplished fraud. When Alianore Lunte of Great Waltham (*Essex*) complained to the chancellor in 1474, she admitted to having given him all her goods and properties—that is, 100*s.* in cash, chattels worth 20 marks and many evidences—on only the promise of marriage. Since receiving them (and holding on to them very tightly), not only did he deny his earlier commitment, but she also discovered that he was married.[46] These men had identified the perfect swindle. When they entered into a bigamous union, they knew well the church would not uphold it, and thus the long-term risk was minimal—penance at best. At the same time, as chapter 4 discusses, the legal system was especially inept at assisting jilted wives in tracking down their delinquent husbands to recover their goods. William Godyhold and John Mynton represent a whole host of men in medieval society who learned to play the marriage game expertly and profited significantly, to the detriment of deserted wives across the kingdom.

Most pre-contracts brought to court in the Middle Ages were not swindles of this nature. Nevertheless, these cases highlight how effortlessly this particular impediment might be implemented to the benefit (or undoing) of another. The ease with which marriages were dissolved due to pre-contract suits has prompted D'Avray to ask, "[d]id not pre-contract cases make a mockery of indissolubility?" Answering his own question, he asserts quite astutely that "[o]n the contrary: pre-contract cases were premissed on the conviction that a marriage was indissoluble. The first marriage contract may have been informal, may have taken place in sinful circumstances, but even so, it overrode any subsequent marriage, however religious the ceremony."[47]

UNDER-AGE

The legislation of the Fourth Lateran Council in 1215 set out in explicit detail the acceptable ages at marriage for both men and women: a woman must be twelve to marry, a man fourteen. The church intended the ages to reflect physical maturity. It also expected these to be minimum ages, not maximums, and most English couples were much older when they entered into marriage. Recent studies emphasize that the English marriage pattern of the medieval period was, in fact, quite unusual in having husband and wife of roughly the same age at their first marriage, with women normally marrying in their early twenties to men in their later twenties.[48] However, families with a good deal of property, out of eagerness to secure a good future for their offspring and an advantageous alliance for the families, often prompted their children to enter into spousals at a much younger age. Canon law sanctioned this practice, providing the children involved were at least seven years of age and the union went unconsummated. Granted, the church did not consider the union an actual marriage, but rather a "formal legal agreement intimating intention to be married."[49] The union was formalized when, upon reaching marriageable ages, the couple consented to live together. Once again, it is critical to note that consent was passive—that is, it did not have to be publicly articulated: continued cohabitation itself was sufficient to make a valid marriage.[50]

In his study of marriage litigation in 1974, Richard Helmholz remarks that it was "surprising how few cases" of this nature "appear in the Act books."[51] The reason for this is that most couples did consent well enough once they crossed into their teenage years. Many others were probably older by the time they realized they wanted to revoke their consent, and by then it was simply too late. Some few brave youths defied their parents and chose to dissolve their marriages. A mandate to hear the cause between John de Segrave and Margaret Marescal of Lopham (*Norf.*) notes that they contracted marriage before she was of marriageable age and that she had never agreed to cohabit with him.[52] In 1346, Hugh Giffard and Elizabeth More, married when Hugh was nine and Elizabeth eleven, renounced their marriage.[53] Some requests for divorce illustrate the coercive nature of the parents' role in keeping the marriage together. Richard, earl of Arundel, and Isabella, daughter of Hugh le Despenser, were seven and eight (respectively) when they married. Their petition to divorce upon coming of age declared that it was "not by mutual consent, but by fear of their relatives . . . forced by blows to cohabit, so that a son was born."[54]

The parental perception of marriage as an important means of solidifying family alliances is underscored by the frequency of desperate attempts to salvage those alliances after the death of a bride or a groom. For example, William de Ravengham exchanged vows with Cassandra when she was only seven years old, but William died before they were able to consummate the marriage. She was then married to his brother, Thomas. The church was eventually drawn into an inquiry to document that their son, Thomas, was indeed legitimate, despite the fact that she was once married to her husband's brother.[55] Thomas Darden and his wife, Matilda, daughter of Richard de Stafford, eventually had to apply for a dispensation for their marriage, anxious about aspersions of incest: Thomas, at the age of ten, had married Katherine, Matilda's nine-year old sister. When she died, Thomas then married Matilda, who by then was eleven.[56] Serial matrimony within families of this nature highlights the role played by marriage in the high politics of moneyed families. Under-age marriages rarely led to divorce; in good part, the upper ranks of English society raised their children with the expectation that personal happiness took a backseat to family ambition.

COERCION (FORCE AND FEAR)

The story of Alice, widow of the fifteenth-century Norwich merchant Nicholas Crome, offers a somewhat typical experience of late medieval coerced marriage. As a woman with substantial landed estates, she became a regular target for marriage proposals. One particular suitor, in his eagerness to add her dower lands to his estate, overstepped the bounds of the normal process of courtship. A papal letter to the bishops of Ely, Lincoln and Beirut[57] from May 1482 recounts Alice's petition complaining of John Williamson, described as both "esquire" and "gentleman," who "violently ravished her and compelled her by force and fear to contract marriage with him." She testified that the marriage transpired without her consent in "sign, word or deed."[58] At the first opportunity, she fled to the court of James Goldwell, the bishop of Norwich, planning to have the union annulled; but the bishop refused to comply, obliging Alice to turn instead to the papal see for her appeal and resulting in the mandate to the three bishops to investigate further into the matter. Although the papal register provides no further information on the case, a chancery bill dated to the years 1483–85 shows that John and Alice were still married at that time, and John was just as intent as ever to gain control of her lands as *baron* to this *feme covert*. The bill was purportedly drafted at the request of John Williamson and his wife, Alice, mistakenly here recorded as having been the wife of "William" (rather than Nicholas) Crome (such a fundamental error is the first indication that she had little to do with preparing the bill). John requested the chancellor's assistance in "recovering" land, tenements, and their appurtenances that had originally belonged to Nicholas Crome, but before his death, Nicholas had enfeoffed William Sweyn, Robert Camond and John Brewyn to their use. After Nicholas's passing, John claimed that land should have come properly to Alice, her heirs and her assigns. John related that Alice had demanded many times that the trio make estate of the land, but they had declined. As her new husband, John was taking up the cause for her.[59]

On its own, the chancery bill makes John sound like the typical medieval second husband, concerned to help his demoralized wife in what frequently became an endless pursuit to petition for her dower lands.[60] Nonetheless, John Brewyn's response to the bill exposed the dubious nature of Williamson's petition. Brewyn declared that this inquiry was against Alice's will: John intended to sell the land, thus alienating it from Alice and her heirs and assigns, and the entire process was "contrary to all good conscience." Brewyn asked that the court send for Alice and examine her privately in order to discover what her "free will and intent" actually were.[61] Brewyn's suspicions were well founded. In 1486, Alice appeared in person before the chancellor, this time a recently divorced woman, as she asserted that a "lawful divorce is ready to be showed," and intent on punishing Thomas Roo, Thomas Bettys and Thomas Mathewe, men who assisted John in what she saw as a blatant attempt to wrest her dower lands from her possession. Her petition narrates in detail the story of her abduction. Referring to her abductor here as Wylliams instead of Williamson, she testified how he "led and brought your poor suppliant into Rederede[62] and there he shut her into an house within four locks by the space of five weeks." During that time, she "never came to hear mass, nor to see sacring," and John applied steady pressure for her to marry. In one dramatic episode, John summoned a priest so that Alice might repent her sins and be shriven, announcing his intention to kill her. Alice credited her continued existence to the generosity of one of his retainers. John drew a naked sword "and said he should slay her," but fearing John was not bluffing, the man threw himself down on his knee and begged John to save her life. Alice bought more time by giving John a hefty bribe of £40 in cash. Soon after that, John brought her to St. Catherine's (in Ludham, Norfolk), where he apparently had connections with the parish priest, and imprisoned her there for eighteen weeks. He chained her to the wall for much of this time, beating her repeatedly, all in the hopes of inducing her to tell him where she had put the deeds to her husband's lands. When he got nowhere with Alice, John wrote to her mother, saying that Alice wanted to sell the lands to pay their debts. Knowing that Nicholas's testament plainly stated the land was not to be sold, Alice's mother realized something was amiss and approached the mayor of Norwich on Alice's behalf, giving him the deeds for safekeeping and requesting that Alice be delivered from her prison. Presumably having spoken with Brewyn since her imprisonment, Alice mentioned specifically that during that time, John petitioned the chancellor to sue against Nicholas's feoffees for the land but noted that "they were charged to keep full their estate till they had other commandment by the court." Out of fear for her life, Alice had consented to enfeoff some of her former husband's lands to the use of Thomas Roo, Thomas Bettys and Thomas Mathewe, and thus she appeared in chancery hoping to recover that land. Astutely, she argued that the sale was void precisely because of her marriage, as it was known that husband and wife "are all one person in law," and thus "a wife may not give her husband during the coverture neither land nor good." The enfeoffment of John's cronies, then, was obviously invalid.[63] Specifically, Alice was commenting on how, after a marriage, the common law deemed void any feoffment of a wife's lands made during a marriage, because a wife's consent may have been coerced (as was Alice's situation).[64] Although chancery's decision does not survive, Alice's last will and testament does; it indicates that this experience did not impoverish her. At her death in 1518, she devised the funds to establish seven almshouses for poor widows in the parish of St. George Colegate, attesting that she died a wealthy woman but conscious of the vulnerability of widows and the need to support them.[65]

Given the penchant to equate women with the land they brought to a marriage, forced nuptials, such as those experienced by Alice Crome, were a perpetual danger, especially for heiresses and widows of means.[66] Here, it is critical to note that the church essentially set the guidelines for coercion (or "force and fear," as the courts phrased it). The church required enough force to move a constant man or woman, although it offered no sense of how the courts should apply this definition in practice. From his study of marriage litigation in medieval England, Helmholz concludes that the courtroom evidence implies a multi-faceted use of the requirement, but with rigid standards: "[t]here had to be proof of the real possibility of the use of force or of the imminent loss of one's expected inheritance. . . . The force and fear which moved a constant man had to be more than the insubstantial threat, the minor inconvenience, or the parent's urgent entreaty."[67] Individuals looking to prove coercion, then, would have sculpted their testimonies to meet those expectations. This holds true even when the forum was not ecclesiastical: if the plaintiff hoped eventually to sue in the church court also, for the sake of consistency, she or he needed to keep the church's standards in mind. Accordingly, some plaintiffs, like Alice Crome, may have overstated the brutality in the hopes of shocking justices into awards in their favor. Nonetheless, stories of coerced marriage from the medieval courts often include instances of beatings and threats. For example, in 1411, John Dale abducted Agnes, widow of Hugh Grantham, forced her to exchange vows of marriage, and then raped her.[68] In 1477, Robert Talbot dragged Alice Townely, to whom he was related within prohibited degrees, from her bed in the middle of the night and repeatedly submerged her in the river until she agreed to marry him. Reportedly, the wedding was followed by regular beatings, incarceration and isolation from her family.[69]

Men who coerced women into marriage were unusually adept at evading legal responsibility. Moreover, those who targeted young heiresses were encouraged by the simple fact that the English common law saw ravishment of ward as only a misdemeanor, not a felony; a man who abducted an heiress, then, took on minimal risk for his actions. The failure of the common law to take ravishment of ward seriously derives from the simple fact that many nobles seemed to have engaged in abduction and may even have seen it as an acceptable means of initiating a marriage. Primogeniture excluded younger sons from the patrimony, leaving them to their own devices to make their way in the world. Marriage to an heiress or a widow was the most direct path to social and financial success. Duby has documented the roving bands of aristocratic youth, constantly "on the lookout for an heiress. If they came across one, they tried to reserve her before she was nubile. Sometimes they took the child with them on their journey, and were prepared to restore her to her father if they should find a more desirable match on the way or if another 'youth' should come to claim her too insistently."[70] Although Duby's study centers on the French experience, Gwen Seabourne has recently argued that the English were no more chivalrous in their treatment of women. She observes that the abduction of heiresses was widespread in fourteenth-century England, prompting a commons petition of 1378 to address the issue directly. Indicting "the men of Chester and Lancaster," the petition recounts how the kidnappers regularly informed the girl's parents "to send a third of her goods as a portion for the daughter, and if they did not pay, they (the parents) would be killed."[71] The English experience differed also from the French in that violence was a key component. As Caroline Dunn observes, the would-be husband regularly employed rape as a tool, "designed to cement the marriage by its consummation" and also "to shame the victim into submitting to her newly married state and prevent her from initiating annulment proceedings in a church court."[72]

English common law offered little in terms of a resolution. The church was prepared to declare null and void those marriages carried out without a bride's consent. A mandate to the bishop of Lichfield in 1364 establishes that the church was well aware of this problem. The directive centers on the case of Isabella de Scaresbrek of York, who claimed she married Henry Molineux when she was ten years old, but directly afterwards John of York abducted her. The papal official described John as being "more desirous of patrimony than of matrimony," a telling phrase that appears on more than one occasion in the ecclesiastical records. Before her family was able to rescue her from John's grasp, he compelled her into an exchange of vows. When she came of marriageable age, she carried through her family's wishes and participated in a public wedding to Henry Molineux. In response, John of York hastened to the archbishop of York and claimed her as his wife. At this point, Isabella appealed to the pope, resulting in the mandate to the bishop of Lichfield that began this investigation.[73] Simultaneously, John pleaded a suit of ravishment of wife in the king's courts against Henry, contending that Isabella had been divorced from him before the bishop of Chester because she was too young to consent at the time of the wedding. Hence, she was, in fact, John's wife. Henry produced evidence of her divorce from John, which the church had since awarded. In the end, the ecclesiastical documentation was sufficient to quash the case, but John's charisma and false sincerity won over at least one judge, who argued that Isabella may not have been his wife in right, but she was certainly his wife in possession (thus, in this one judge's mind, validating his plea).[74]

The abduction of young girls of Isabella's age was a common tactic by men hoping to cement a union before she might exchange vows with anyone else. The Anglo-Irish knight Adam, called "Lenfant," of the diocese of Kildare, also abducted a child in the hopes of securing an heiress. Synolda was only nine years old when Adam kidnapped her from her parents. Royal officials tracked her down and returned her to her parents, but Adam insisted that their union had been consummated, leading her (or more likely her parents on her behalf) to appeal to the pope. Adam died before the pope's ruling.[75] The snatchings of both Isabella and Synolda demonstrate precisely why heiresses were usually married at such a young age: their guardians knew that if they did not marry them at the first opportunity, someone else might force through a marriage.

Women were not the only victims of coerced marriages; men were also sometimes victims, the key difference being who was doing the coercing. Rather than an eager suitor, the wife's parents or family were most often responsible for applying the pressure to marry. William Beaumond won his divorce from Joan Stafford after he claimed that he entered into a marriage with her "out of fear," despite the fact that they were related within the forbidden degrees.[76] The Year Book for 1338 recounts the story of a man known as John of F. who claimed to have been beaten, abducted and imprisoned until he paid a fine of £100 and entered into a marriage with the daughter of his abductors. He argued that he "had been compelled by force to marry her, and never afterwards assented to it."[77] Given the serious implications a woman's loss of virginity might have on the marriage market, as well as fears she might become a single mother, her family had good reason to feel violated by any sexual experimentation outside of wedlock. It is not hard to imagine that a woman's "deflowering" prompted many families to strong-arm reluctant grooms into an *impromptu* wedding. In William Rote's denial of his marriage to Agnes Wellys in 1475, his response explicitly recognizes the father's concerns about his daughter's sexual status. He notes that when he arrived at the house to share a jug of wine with Agnes's father, he was instead met with angry recrimination. John Wellys declared, "[y]ou have violated Agnes, my daughter, and have known her carnally. You will contract marriage with her if I have to force you and you will be sorry." Despite denying that the two had ever been intimate, Agnes and William proceeded almost immediately to an exchange of vows, John's dagger pressing forcefully into William's back. William's flight put the nuptials temporarily on hold, while Agnes's mother chased him down the street. Agnes herself ran after him, shouting, "[h]old the thief." Neighbors returned to the house several moments later with a reluctant William in arms. William submitted to more threats of legal action and social embarrassment before completing the marriage ceremony.[78] John, son of Ralph of Painsthorpe, described a similar situation in his request for an annulment on the grounds of force and fear. In the year 1334, John was awaiting his lover in her father's bakehouse when she arrived with her brother and his servant, both armed and ready for a wedding. At sword point, the two exchanged vows in the present tense. The archbishop of York later awarded John and his wife an annulment.[79]

IMPOTENCE

Sexual dissatisfaction may have been a more common motivation for desertion than one would think for this period. Augustine argued that marriage was a necessary remedy against sin, making marriage an individual's only licit sexual outlet (that is, providing intercourse occurred in the right position, under the appropriate conditions, and at the correct times of the year).[80] In its regular prosecution of fornicators and adulterers, the church stringently applied that perspective on all Christians. If the impotence or frigidity of one of the spouses prevented consummation of the marriage and the canonically prescribed trial period of three years had passed, then the church would grant an annulment.[81] Obtaining a divorce on these grounds, however, was not easy. When Agnes, widow of William Webster of Bromfield, sued for divorce from her husband, John Bowman, in 1367, even after three years of marriage and her husband's oath sworn on the Gospels, the church was not prepared to separate the couple. Rather, the bishop of Carlisle demanded "penance, and prayers and good works so that God would allow the consummation." They returned the next term to report that all their hard work had come to naught: they were still incapable of consummating the marriage. The bishop then set a trial date in which the couple brought seven kinsmen and neighbors to swear that "John could not consummate with Agnes or any other woman," at which point the bishop declared them divorced.[82] Records of the divorce of William del Park and Ellen Bogher in February 1356 show a similar reluctance by the bishop to foray into the realm of marital dissolution. Originally summoned to court for not having solemnized their marriage, they explained that they had not because "William's frigidity was such that he could not have intercourse with any woman, even though he and Ellen had been left together in bed." They, too, appeared in court with many witnesses, "whose testimony convinced the bishop that the alleged impediment was true."[83]

The motivation of wives to report their husbands' impotence to the church courts has received some criticism. Rather cynically, Edward Behrend-Martinez has argued, "wives who accused their husbands of impotence worked to destroy them publicly and politically. Rather than pitiful victims, such wives were vigorous, often victorious, defenders of their own self-interests."[84] Some husbands certainly reacted as if a wife were intent only on attacking her husband's masculine reputation. After all, what man wanted his wife to broadcast widely his sexual dysfunction? When Henry, vicar of Swalcliffe (*Oxon.*), appeared before the court of King's Bench in 1388 to respond to allegations of abducting Alice, wife of John Wyatt, and goods belonging to her husband, the story he presented demonstrates that some husbands reacted violently to the mere suggestion of desertion on these grounds. When Alice decided to sue for an annulment before the archdeacon of Oxford because of her husband's impotence, the court counseled her to leave her husband during the course of the proceedings, "because the said John Wyatt threatened the same Alice in life and limb because of her aforesaid suit not only before the said official there but also elsewhere before various law-worthy persons." Fearing for her life, Alice sought permission from the archdeacon to live in the custody of her uncle during the proceedings, the very same Henry, vicar of Swalcliffe, who was accused of her abduction. Permission was granted. According to Alice, the only goods she took with her were her clothes and the ring on her finger, apparently enough to fuel a demand by her husband for compensation of lost goods.[85] Although this case does not tell us whether the church, in fact, granted an annulment, it makes clear why some women were hesitant to sue on these grounds. An informal separation that friends and neighbors might rationalize as incompatibility was probably a safer option for most women than a formal and public declaration of male sexual inadequacy.

Behrend-Martinez's study is tied to the Basque region; although it is feasible that the medieval Basque approached the matter of impotence from a different perspective than the English, this pessimism still seems unwarranted and narrow-minded. In a world that equated femininity with motherhood, many women must have experienced disappointment and a sense of inadequacy while waiting three years for their annulments. Elizabeth Lambert of London enunciates this sentiment quite clearly in her fifteenth-century petition concerning her husband, William Schore, whom she describes as being "frigid and impotent." Because she was "desirous of being a mother and having offspring," she approached the official of London for a divorce. When he refused to cooperate, she appealed to the pope.[86] The centrality of motherhood to the lives of medieval women is also echoed in an *ex officio* case from the act book of the diocese of Canterbury. When the court summoned Juliana Hewet to accuse her of pimping her daughter, Helen, she and her daughter both appeared to deny wholly the allegations. Instead, Juliana argued that she had abducted Helen from her marriage. When asked why she refused to adhere to her husband, Helen replied that her husband was impotent, but she was now in the custody of an "honest man," with whom she had since become pregnant and given birth.[87] The record makes no mention of a suit for annulment on the grounds of impotence, presumably a critical detail that would have been included had she been engaged in such a suit. The birth of a child so soon after her removal from the marriage, however, makes two points clear. First, Helen was not to blame for the barren marriage. Second, being a mother was an important role she was eager to play.

Although historians have often interpreted claims of impotence as either a slander of a man's reputation or a fabrication to exploit the rules of annulment, the evidence itself suggests that sometimes we need to take those claims at face value. When John Sanderson of Weel and his wife, Tedia Lambhird, in the year 1370 petitioned to have their marriage annulled on the grounds of impotence, the court ordered a physical examination by three wise matrons. Their findings were conclusive: one of the women described John's penis as an "empty intestine of dead skin, not having any flesh in it or veins in the skin and the middle of its front is totally black."[88] Such a concise (and gruesome) description is unlikely to have been fabricated. The church seems to have felt the same way: not surprisingly, the court awarded the couple an annulment.

ADULTERY AND CRUELTY

All of the explanations proffered for divorce so far have been for annulments. In terms of judicial separations, the justifications were much more limited. Suits were restricted to heresy, adultery and cruelty. The church's expectations, though, were extreme. The English church courts interpreted adultery as having a concubine of a long-standing nature and cruelty as an attempt on a person's life.[89] Moreover, because society expected husbands to chastise their wives, proving "cruelty" was no easy feat. To quote Sharon Wright, "what we would consider assault was understood as correction: it was both a man's duty and his right."[90] Divorces on any of these grounds were not common in medieval England; they did exist, though, and women hoping to sue for divorce doubled their chances by combining allegations of cruelty and adultery.[91] For example, the petition of Anne, wife of John Cope, to the pope for a judicial separation in 1476 notes that John "committed adultery with divers other women and behaved to her with such violence that it was not safe for her to live with him."[92] Mabel Smith of Ware, wife of Robert Smyth of Sible Hedingham (*Essex*), claims in her 1457 petition that her husband "had shamelessly committed adultery with divers other women, and was treating her so cruelly that she could no longer cohabit with him without danger of her person." She was hoping for a judicial separation and the restoration of her dowry.[93] The level of violence indicated in some petitions suggests that women endured a high degree of violence before turning to the courts. In the 1457 petition of Cristina Sewale, wife of John Archer of London, she says that "John has so inhumanly beaten and wounded her beyond her deserts, even when she was pregnant, that he caused her to bring forth two still-born children, and has treated her and still treats her so cruelly that she is in fear of her life and cannot any longer remain with him." She, too, was asking for a judicial separation and the restoration of her dowry.[94] Violence also explains many informal divorces that appear in the records in disciplinary actions relating to non-cohabitation. Only after seeing her excommunication in writing would Margaret, wife of John Cutte of Drayton (*Bucks.*), allow herself to be coerced into reuniting with her husband, but she did so on condition that "her husband treat her in future well, decently, and favorably," a guarantee often sought by victims of abuse when forced to return to their spouses.[95] At times, wives were quick to resort to cruelty as a defense for their desertion. The wife of Henry Cook of Trottiscliffe (*Kent*) told the court of Rochester in 1347 that her husband had been both unfaithful and cruel.[96] High rank was no immunity to violence in marriage: accused by her husband of trying to poison him in 1292, in 1293 Lady Christiana Meynell claimed she left him because of his cruelty.[97]

Witness testimony presented in favor of Eleanor Brownynge's suit for a judicial separation demonstrates the kind of evidence a court expected to hear. William Saunder testified that

> on a day in summer seven years ago, this deponent, coming with a repaired gown to the home of a man named Burgoyn situated in the hospital of St. Bartholomew, saw Alexander with a naked dagger in his hand chasing after Eleanor, who was running in her tunic with her head uncovered and her hair streaming behind her. Because of fear, Eleanor ran to the house of the man named Burgoyn, where Eleanor's sister was. Eleanor's sister took her into the house and closed the door. Alexander, seeing this, shouted in a loud voice, swearing that he wanted to kill Eleanor the next time he saw her unless those in the house gave her up to him. When they would not do this, Alexander left. This deponent says in his conscience that Eleanor would have been killed or at least mutilated if she had not escaped into the house. He says moreover that within the last five years on a certain day, exactly when he does not recall, Alexander entered the tavern at the sign of the Sun on Lombard Street, London, where, in the presence of this deponent, he held a naked dagger in his hand, and threatened Eleanor with it. On account of his threat, Eleanor jumped at least the distance of four men long, which this deponent saw with his own eyes.[98]

The church awarded two distinct kinds of separation. Most separations severed a couple's obligation to cohabit and to render the conjugal debt. Occasionally, however, the court might only require the couple to reside separately, allowing the right to request payment of the conjugal debt to continue. The obvious benefit to a separation of this nature is that it protected the wife but also prevented both halves from being led into the sin of adultery. When Joanna the wife of Richard Peyfrer de Boklande came before the archbishop of Canterbury in the year 1295 to complain of her husband's behavior, she avoided using the term "divorce" altogether. Rather, because of her husband's adulteries, incest and abuse, she asked permission to reside with her father or in some other suitable location, at Richard's expense. Specifically, she asked that he pay her alimony of goods worth £10 to be paid at four equal terms over the course of the year for her maintenance, but also for "bearing the burdens of marriage." Perhaps to heighten her chances of persuading the courts, though, she noted that wherever she stayed, she would be ready to receive her husband's embraces. The courts agreed.[99] Joanna's decision to frame her request in that particular manner may also reflect the early date of her petition. Canon law in general took time to adapt to the idea of permitting separation on grounds of cruelty. Thus, Joanna's thirteenth-century petition probably reflects her lawyer's perception of the best deal on offer.

What is most striking is the existence of cases in which husbands solicited the courts for a separation on the grounds of their wives' cruelty. These are very unusual suits. Because of contemporary expectations of masculinity, not many men were willing to admit publicly that they were victims of abuse at the hands of their wives. The medieval era considered a violent wife a joke: in fact, the wife who reigned supreme, much like the celebrated Wife of Bath wished for her marriages, was a popular trope in the world of bawdy songs and literature, certain to elicit great laughter.[100] In this atmosphere, a man risked becoming a laughing matter in initiating a lawsuit on those grounds. Certainly, the persistence of some men in defying the gendered climate implies that there may well have been some truth to the allegations. A brief notation in the records of the court of the Archdeaconry of Buckingham from 1493 reports that Henry Bereaker Junior sought a divorce from his wife because of her cruelty. The wife denied it, and the court sought reconciliation.[101] The same court two years later adjudicated in the case of Roger Calaber, who sought a divorce from his wife, Elizabeth, on the grounds of her adultery and intoxication. Finding sufficient proof, the court granted them a judicial separation.[102] The following year in the same diocese, Robert Auditour sued his wife, Alicia, for cruelty and intoxication with the same result.[103] Certainly, all of these cases being clustered in the very late medieval period is significant. Men on the cusp of the early modern era may have been more willing to admit their wives' violence. A 1523 case of restitution of conjugal rights in Whalley, Lancashire, also produced an allegation of a wife's cruelty. When Alice, wife of Robert Spenser, asked to be restored to her husband's home, Robert responded that "he was mortally afraid of her." When the judge required him to take her back, Robert then changed his tune, claiming they were not legally married, because their relationship was within prohibited degrees. Soon after, it came to light that Robert had a live-in mistress.[104] In Robert's situation, asserting cruelty was clearly just one among many of the explanations he was willing to aver in order to escape marriage. In general, though, the records imply that husbands were usually the abusers, not the victims of abuse.

THE EVIDENCE FROM SELF-DIVORCES

Lawsuits inevitably needed to live up to the expectations of the law; thus, divorce litigation is predictable in terms of the accusations brought forward by plaintiffs. For example, there was no point in suing for a divorce on the grounds of intoxication on its own when the canon law did not see that as a justifiable basis for divorce (even though a spouse's desire to not continue living with a drunk may well have been the explanation for why a divorce was being sought). More to the point, no lawyer would take on such a case knowing that it would inevitably fail. Evidence drawn from self-divorces, then, has the potential to offer a more realistic perspective of why couples divorced simply because there was no need to conform to legal principles. Regrettably, the documentation undermines this noble aspiration. A self-divorce only made it into the legal record when it came to the attention of a court official that a couple was no longer cohabiting; as a result, many self-divorces probably went unnoticed. Even for documented self-divorces, however, our records are very limited. The court records reflect their goals: the court's intention was to identify spouses who had abandoned their marriages, have them agree to begin the penitential process and then reconcile the two. The reason why they left in the first place was not necessarily pertinent and thus is usually absent from the record. Generally, a spouse's rationale is included only when it continued to interfere in his or her willingness to undertake the penitential process. The vast majority provide no explanation whatsoever. To offer an example of the paltry detail included in some of these records: the register of the bishop of Salisbury for the years 1388–95 notes the case of Katherine atte Borwe, "who will not consort with Philip, her husband, nor receive him in her house, nor share any of her goods with him." The record notes that Thomas Cuttyng abetted her; but otherwise, the reader is left to imagine exactly what transpired, and whether Cuttyng was a lover, a brother or a neighbor.[105] Another case from the diocese of Salisbury in 1409 reads, "Isabel Cras of Lechelade [*Glos.*] cited for not living with [her] husband; did not come; suspended."[106] An even less informative notation: "Agnes Bevre does not adhere or consort with John Brewer her husband."[107] Lamentably, for cases of this nature, the historian cannot discover much about the motivation for spousal abandonment.

Some records only hint about reasons why a spouse left. One wife was thought to have left her husband because of physical infirmity. The register of the bishop of Salisbury for the years 1388–95 notes the case of Agnes Wormes, who left her blind husband, Ralph Irwyn, and reportedly refused him conjugal rights.[108] A good number of individuals were in the process of formalizing their separations when their spouses initiated suits against them in other courts. When the church raised the secular arm of the law to capture Lady Margery of Longford (*Staffs.*), she had already initiated an application for a judicial separation.[109] She was not the only one. A case brought before the mayor's court of London in 1305 notes that, because of a delay in addressing the complaint brought by William de Lyndesseye for goods worth £20 that his wife had "eloigned into the houses of William de Wynchelsee," a judicial separation had been celebrated between them, and the goods had already been delivered to Alice by the undersheriff.[110] Some other women, usually those fending off husbands looking for lost goods, claimed that the church courts had already granted them annulments for a variety of reasons, from pre-contract to consanguinity.[111] In the case of Agnes Mortimer, the archdeacon of London had already annulled her marriage with Simon Barber when Simon decided that he wanted her back. By the time his case of ravishment came before the court in 1369, she was married to her "abductor."[112]All of the records above relate to women's explanations for why they abandoned their spouses. Husbands offered a much different perspective of why their wives left. In some cases, the record explains the wife's departure as having been unreasonable. For example, when Emma, wife of Nicholas Swayn, left her husband in the year 1360, she apparently did so "for trivial and fabricated reasons."[113] Similarly, when Agnes Cossall left her husband, Edward Plompton, the records note that "without cause reasonable [she] willfully departed."[114] Robert Barbour asserted that his wife left "without cause"; Leonard Wright of London explained that his wife left "without any license or cause given by [him]," and he was willing to prove this by "record of his neighbors"; John Tikyll's wife left "without reasonable cause."[115] These responses may have been typical defenses of men determined not to be accused of driving their wives away, but in an age where the legacy of Eve loomed large, this may also have been a deliberate attempt to draw on stereotypical images of the "unreasonableness of women."[116] If women lack reason and are known to act in ways contrary to their best interests, then do we even need to worry about finding a reason why they left their husbands? For a husband who may have provoked his wife's desertion, there could be no better cover.

In other records, the husband's desire to shift the blame entirely to the wife is more pointed. He could do this in various ways. Some records do not explain why the wife left but add tone. For example, a matrimonial suit initiated by Thomas Wycense of Laudwick against his wife, Matilda, at the court of Canterbury in 1313 argued that his wife "maliciously absents herself."[117] At times, jilted husbands made an ignoble attempt to explain their wives' defection. For example, when Henry Cook of Trottiscliffe (*Kent*) and his wife were brought before the court of the bishop of Rochester on December 24, 1347, the husband claimed that "it was not his fault that his wife had left him." Rather, it was apparently his wife's fault for being a scold, even though, admittedly, he had also engaged in adultery, and his wife accused him of cruelty. [118] Henry's wife was not the only scold in the lot. Isabella Case, wife of Jankyn Dey of Hereford Diocese, was "a common defamer and sustainer of quarrels."[119] Joan Grokles was accused of "customarily leav[ing] her husband for long periods"; she was also a scold, "causing quarrels amongst her neighbors," and an adulteress, accused of adultery with one named man and with "strangers."[120] Two husbands accused their wives of being prostitutes. The records describe Agnes, wife of John Attepole, and Katherine, wife of John atte Mulle, as common prostitutes.[121] Many other husbands blamed their wives for adultery.

All of these accusations need to be taken with a grain of salt. Cases of desertion appearing in the ecclesiastical courts are examples of marriages in crisis. Just as divorce cases today often break down into expensive bouts of name-calling in the presence of a judge, we see similar accusations flying between estranged husbands and wives in medieval England. Accusations usually divided along gendered lines. Wives blamed their husbands for cruelty and adultery; husbands impugned their wives for being scolds and loose women. A shadow of doubt must be cast even on those accusations of prostitution. In the courts, *meretrix* had much the same meaning as the modern term "whore": were these women actually paid prostitutes or simply women of loose morals?[122] Alternately, was this just a popular insult hurled at a wife in a moment of anger during a rather unpleasant legal process? The case of William Newport seeking a divorce from his wife, Isabel, before the consistory court of London in January 1492 demonstrates just how difficult it is to take these aspersions at face value.[123] John Smyth, a neighbor to the couple for five or six years and witness for the plaintiff, reported that the two quarreled frequently, "to the great weariness and nuisance of their neighbors." During one particularly ugly spat, Isabel attempted to stab her husband with a pin from a brooch; when the assault failed, she attacked him verbally, calling him a cuckold. She derided him by saying that "she had made him a cuckold and would do it again if any man, a friar or other man, wanted to know her." The neighbor concluded that Isabel was a "whore and a strumpet who used in public to declare dishonest words and invited diverse men to know her."[124] William brought forward at least four other witnesses who claimed that Isabel was so violent that it was not safe for William to live with her. Several others testified that she constantly provoked his wrath; three witnesses claimed she stole from him, being a "waster and ruiner of William's goods," intent only "to make merry" with his hard-earned possessions.[125] In this situation, it is critical to note that these witnesses were appearing on behalf of the husband, who desperately wanted a divorce. Moreover, their evidence for Isabel's licentiousness was slim. Many witnesses for the plaintiff eagerly testified that Isabel claimed she had cuckolded her husband, that she adhered to "suspect, adulterous and evil disposed persons," but none were able to provide eyewitness testimony to actual adulterous behavior.[126] The most damning evidence came from John Foster's report that he "heard William Newport often saying that many times when he happened to be out of town and came home again, he found Isabel in bed with a certain man, at that time and still, as he believes, living in the county of Kent, whom Isabel named as her blood relative." [127] Yet Isabel's husband was the source behind that hearsay. Public knowledge and fame of her adulterous behavior would have carried much more weight in the medieval courtroom than in today's; more important still, her behavior justified any violence by William, who was clearly attempting to reassert his governance over his wife.[128] Nonetheless, for our purposes, it is imperative to acknowledge that even if Isabel did defame her husband as a cuckold, she may have been doing so only because it was a useful means of unmanning her husband in a public setting. Thomas Goodeale's deposition implies that emasculation was indeed

Isabel's intent. After a public dispute, Isabel reportedly stated, "[c]all not me Isabel Newport, but call me Isabel Horseley, for I had rather the bald whoreson cuckold were hanged than he should be my husband, and I trust that I shall find some good fellow that for my sake either this evening or tomorrow shall make him to piss above his girdlestead [waist]."[129]

To return to the matter at hand, the hostile nature of disputes, such as that between William and Isabel Newport, prevents us from gaining a clearer understanding of women's motivations for leaving their husbands. At least in cases of judicial separation or annulment, there must have been some substance to the allegations; a court proctor knew better than to take on a case that was unprovable. Otherwise, some caution should be exercised. The records do reveal, however, that wives left marriages for a wide variety of reasons. If cruelty had been the dominant factor, distinguishing these obstinately runaway wives from other cases of marital separation, it might seem that wives only left marriages because their lives were in danger. These runaway wives demonstrate that that was not the case.

Why men left their wives is not always much clearer, although the courts themselves targeted primarily cases of a man's non-cohabitation when adultery was involved. In fact, the request to resume marital cohabitation often appears as an appendage to a charge of adultery. For example, in 1298–99, when the archbishop of York summoned Sampson de Strelley and Elizabeth of Clipston to answer for their adultery in a relationship that had gone on for many years, the record does not even state which of the two was married until after it records their penances for adultery. Only then does it note that Sampson and his "legitimate wife" also appeared before the court and that Sampson was ordered to treat his wife with marital affection.[130] Granted, disciplinary cases such as these were usually the result of information from a concerned resident of the diocese, who may well have been the frustrated wife herself. Many others suggest that not only was the man engaged in an adulterous relationship, but that he had, in fact, moved on and remarried. The consistory court of Canterbury in 1469 noted that William Pegeon of Rainham (*Kent*) did not live with his wife but instead lived with another wife in Borstal.[131] The following year, it reprimanded also Thomas Neme of Staple (*Kent*); Thomas also did not live with his legitimate wife but was reported as having another.[132] It is important to note that adultery was not just a man's sin: many runaway wives were also apparently adulteresses. Adultery was probably a symptom of a faltering marriage rather than the cause. An inevitable conclusion of this study is that spouses may have been more successful in their desertions if they had managed to stay chaste. Adultery may also have made a return to marriage more difficult. Even if she had wanted to, could a woman like Agnes Day have easily returned to her husband after she had borne a child to another man?[133]

The surviving records are very much weighted against the husbands. Because husbands were significantly more capable of independent living and did not need to resort to lawsuits in order to fund their future existence, they did not appear as plaintiffs in marital litigation anywhere nearly as often as did women.[134] This fact confirms that the litigation cannot tell us the full story of what was really going on in medieval marriages. Requests by husbands for divorce were almost always on the grounds of incest or pre-contract. In those few exceptions, we have an opportunity to view how the pressures of marriage burdened men as well as women.

The requests for divorce discussed here do not represent all of the potential grounds in which couples might sue. A spouse might legitimately request a judicial separation from a heretic (what the church refers to as "spiritual fornication"). The church might also grant annulments for an impediment of crime—that is, where a man lived in adultery with a woman and then married her after the death of his first wife (the genders might also be reversed in this scenario). Examples of both situations, however, are exceedingly rare. Nonetheless, the records substantiate that the medieval English left their spouses for a great diversity of reasons, although the nature of their rationalizations often divided on gendered terms. Incest and bigamy were common grounds for both sexes in their suits for divorce. Although some men sued also for cruelty and coercion, women stood out as being especially likely to describe themselves as victims of the violence and pressures springing from medieval practices of marriage and inheritance as well as the era's highly patriarchal values.

Once again, it is critical to remember that the evidence examined in this chapter derives from the medieval courtroom. Because the church only recognized a small pool of reasons for divorce, individuals anxious to escape a marriage had to mold their grievances to fit the needs of the lawsuit. Although consanguinity might have been the plea a woman put forward for leaving her husband, in reality she may have felt that their personalities were simply incompatible. Even more importantly, we need to realize that many lawsuits may reflect collusion between spouses who mutually agreed that a divorce was in their best interests. Marriages involve reciprocal relationships: if one person is miserable, in all likelihood the other is, too. Why did so many men offer such paltry explanations for their wives' desertions? They probably worried that too vehement a defense might lead to the church's returning their wives.

2 The Logistics of Divorce

Divorce in the courts then, as now, was often a drawn-out, costly, unpleasant process with lots of hurdles and pitfalls along the way. In large part, the church's function as "marriage counselor" was responsible for prolonging divorce proceedings.[1] In the later Middle Ages, the church was determined to show "that they meant business about the unbreakability of the marriage bond."[2] The church doggedly guarded the sanctity of the marital union, reconciling couples whenever there seemed to be the slightest glimmer of hope. Only after repeated efforts at reconciliation failed was the church ready to consider alternatives that were more permanent. Subsequently, in many ways, the divorce process shaped the plaintiff: only the truly strong-minded were able to undertake and persist in such a degrading and unsettling experience. Self-divorce, which evaded the courtroom altogether, was no less irksome. In order to avoid detection, an individual had to be prepared to relocate. In a world where family played such a central role in one's life, and wealth was tied to land, this was not an easy thing to do, although geographic mobility in general was a much more ordinary feature of medieval existence than is often believed.[3] Because of the economic vulnerability of wives, in particular, divorce was an intimidating option. It is hard to imagine that many women were able to abandon their husbands without some assistance. Who were these women? To whom did they turn for help? What obstacles did they face in the process? The records shed ample light on the dissolution of medieval marriages in order to answer these fundamental questions about the kind of person who undertook a divorce and the logistics of the divorce process.

WHO DIVORCED?

Divorce happened at every level of society. Even men and women from the most well-known families across England sometimes divorced; although for those at the upper ranks of society, where families initiated marriages to cement political alliances and those marriages involved substantial property, the consequences of divorce were weighty. In addition, self-divorce, which required a degree of anonymity, was generally unthinkable for the upper ranks. If a wealthy Englishwoman hoped to bypass the church courts, knowing insufficient grounds for divorce existed, the best she might hope for was an unobserved period of illicit separation. Granted, given the itinerant lifestyles of many nobles and gentry, engaged in diplomacy, high politics, war and the administration of multiple estates, many affluent women did not even have to abandon their husbands to reside independently. Long separations within marriage were also typical of those slightly lower down on the social scale: the occupations of "soldier, sailor, merchant, architect, and builder" all required travel and absences of a lengthy duration.[4] Despite the grave consequences, some high-ranking women showed this kind of initiative. To give some examples: the register of the archbishop of York from the year 1286 includes a mandate to compel Margery, wife of Sir German de la Hay, knight, to live with her husband.[5] A record from the bishop of Worcester in 1278 notes the case of Agnes, wife of Sir James de Etyndon, knight, said to have been abducted by Henry Fown, who then "publicly detained her in adultery" for five years.[6] At the lower ranks of society, an individual's precise socio-economic status can sometimes be difficult to assess. Cases of ravishment—that is, the taking of wife and goods, a popular suit initiated by husbands and sued against those who assisted in a wife's departure—provide valuable insight into social standing. If those allegations can be believed, many other wives who deserted their husbands were fairly well off. Henry Hauke claimed John Bokke made off with his wife and goods worth 10 marks; from John Metheu de Tamall, Walter Hankocke and others supposedly ravished his wife and goods worth 20 marks; Agnes, wife of Robert Smyth de Kelstern, was said to have been abducted along with goods worth 100*s*.[7] Some other women clearly were born into money, but the records do not indicate how much. For example, Katherine atte Borwe, cited before the dean of Salisbury for not consorting with her husband, Philip, was accused also of refusing to "share any of her goods with him."[8] Because cases of husband desertion frequently revolved around money and the division of property, it is not surprising that women from the land-owning class appear in these records. However, a cursory examination of husbands whose occupations are mentioned in the documentation supports the hypothesis that divorce affected every spectrum of society.[9] Runaway wives are reported as being married to farmers, millers, yeomen, merchants, masons, coopers, goldsmiths and even butchers and cottagers. Indeed, these records reveal that all classes failed to properly instruct women on tolerating unhappy marriages.

DIVORCE EXPENSES

Self-divorce was probably as common as it was only partly because a couple feared the court might deny them a divorce. Rather, because the costs of getting a divorce were so prohibitive, it was not an option for most medieval couples. Lawyers working for the church courts did not work cheaply. Their clients paid for the preparation of each document and for every court appearance. A matrimonial cause from Lichfield in 1473 reportedly cost 26*s.* 8*d.*, but unfortunately the record does not break down how that total was determined.[10] A testamentary cause in the diocese of Canterbury from 1498 provides more detail: the plaintiff's total expenses were 22*s.* 5*d.*, and in the itemization of the costs, each proctor charged 6*d.* for every court appearance.[11] Because of the length of time and number of court appearances involved in a case of divorce, the expenses could be significantly higher. The plaintiff also had to be prepared to pay the costs of both litigants, as the outcome of the case determined who would pay the bills.[12]

Those expenses, however, were just the beginning. Because only diocesan and provincial courts had the power to dissolve marriages, unless the individual seeking a divorce was fortunate enough to live close by, travel costs were an additional burden. Time off was sufficient challenge for many medieval men and women. Paying for food on the road and accommodations, especially when an individual resided some distance from the court, was more than many lower-ranking individuals could manage. Moreover, successful litigation necessitated at least two reputable witnesses who could speak with familiarity concerning the reasons why a divorce was needed. If the case was at all complicated, a plaintiff needed even more witnesses. To offer some examples of cases with a profusion of witnesses: in the 1345–46 marital dispute at the court of York between Agnes Huntington and Simon Munkton, Agnes produced eleven witnesses.[13] In Marrays *c.* Rowclif, also at York in 1345, John Marrays brought twenty-three witnesses to court.[14] With good reason, witnesses expected the plaintiff to foot the bill for their travel expenses as well. Even for those devout couples who wanted to act honestly and procure a lawful divorce, the added costs imposed by distance often prohibited them from doing so.

A fifteenth-century petition to the chancellor provides insight into just how expensive the process might be. Drafted in the hopes of recovering a loan granted to Dame Jane Curson when divorcing her husband, the petition reveals that Jane borrowed 40 marks to pay for the process of divorce.[15] This amount must represent not only the sum of the court costs but the necessary expenditures to support herself during the process of litigation. For a woman of Jane's stature, with a household and a reputation to maintain, daily living was expensive. Although this figure corresponds to the upper limit of a wife's expenses, her experience is nonetheless common. All wives needed to find alternate means of support during the process of divorce. At times, the church intervened, ordering husbands to pay for their wives' living expenses until the court finalized the divorce. For example, in 1497, Peter Floyde entered into a recognizance agreeing to pay his wife an annuity of 46*s.* 8*d.* until the church awarded a lawful divorce. The recognizance even stipulated how the annuity was to be paid out: 26*s.* 8*d.* at the Annunciation and 20*s.* at Easter.[16] Sadly, in reality, for many couples the process was very messy, complete with unpaid expenses, missed court appearances and sordid allegations bandied about, sullying individuals' good names. When Margery, wife of Alexander de Hoo, appeared before the bishop of Salisbury in November 1316 to sue for divorce, she leveled a number of weighty and disreputable accusations against her husband: she alleged he had beaten her inhumanely, failed to provide her with necessary sustenance and alienated their joint goods. Alexander's response turned the tables, painting himself as the victim in this marriage. He denied vehemently the abuse, asserting instead that Margery had refused him conjugal rights. The bishop charged the couple to attempt reconciliation. If the parties failed, they were to reappear before him at a later date. Until that time, Alexander was obliged to pay all of Margery's legal costs, as well as 2*s.* per week in alimony. In December and again in January, the two appeared before the bishop. Reconciliation had failed, reportedly because of Alexander's contumacious behavior. Also, his proctor neglected to answer Margery's plea for legal costs and alimony, resulting in the proctor's excommunication. The entry in the register for January 20 repeats the court's demand that Alexander pay Margery 2*s.* weekly for the duration of the trial. By May, after the court's official had remitted an inhibition against Alexander's proctor, he appeared in court one more time to plead that his master was incapable of paying Margery's maintenance. Because he was unable to substantiate this contention, the court ordered both Alexander and his proctor once more to satisfy the debt to Margery under pain of excommunication. The bishop then appointed a day in mid-June for producing witnesses in a case of judicial separation between the two. Unfortunately, the legal paperwork documenting their quarrel ends here, so we have no way of knowing whether the divorce was awarded or whether Alexander eventually paid Margery what the court determined she was owed.[17] Margery's experience, however, not only highlights the sordid nature of medieval divorces but also points to the likelihood that even with the backing of the church, a wife still had to fend for herself during court proceedings.

PREPARATION FOR A DIVORCE

Given the expense of divorce proceedings, before embarking on the process of divorce, a shrewd individual would review the canonical rules of marriage to be certain that she had a chance of winning her case. Although canon law is often thought to have been the preserve of the elite, pragmatism alone meant that Englishmen and -women learned at least enough to grasp what constituted a valid marriage. In his examination of the York cause papers, Frederik Pedersen concludes that litigants "sometimes displayed a surprisingly informed knowledge of the canon laws rules of marriage." The laity "knew the canon law rules of marriage," and these rules "were used to initiate, legalize, and sometimes dissolve marriages among the laity." What is more, there was "a clear understanding even among those members of the laity we would least expect to know canon law." Maud Schipyn, a rural woman of lower social standing, knew exactly what it took to claim Robert Smyth as her husband.[18] Charles Donahue, Jr. has drawn a similar conclusion in his analysis of patterns in marital litigation in medieval England. He notes that "the witnesses know what it is that they have to say." Even more importantly, he observes that "this knowledge, not surprisingly, seems to increase as the Middle Ages go on."[19]

Although some litigants undoubtedly acquired their expertise through paid counsel, popular knowledge of canon law was relatively widespread and derived from a variety of sources. The church itself earnestly disseminated the information in an attempt to stem the tides of marital litigation. For example, the archbishop of Canterbury in May 1455 sent a monition to parish clergy throughout the province, warning them to publish the stipulation of "contracting marriage before two or three witnesses," noting that "the necessity of at least two witnesses for successful suits in the courts Christian is to be emphasized."[20] English synodal statutes "laid great stress on priest and parishioner interaction" in the educational process. The church required parish clergy "to give instruction 'frequently' and in their 'native tongue.'"[21] The rules of marriage were a recurrent and evolving subject of English ecclesiastical legislation. Bishops disseminated copies of diocesan statutes to all pastors, and statutes were read aloud at all synods to the attending clergy.[22] The legislation itself often included statements concerning how the clergy were to share the knowledge with parishioners. For example, the Statutes of Salisbury (1217–19) attempt to govern many aspects of marriage. Among others, they announce that "marriages be celebrated with honor and reverence, not with laughter and jokes, not in taverns, with public drinking or feasting." Officials saw the requirements concerning how marriage should be initiated as such vital knowledge that they ordered that "this statute be officially announced to the people every Sunday."[23] Statute 86, which addresses the dangers of hiding impediments to a marriage, was also considered serious enough that it "be repeated frequently in every single parish."[24] Manuals for parish priests suggest that disseminating information about marriage and the marriage process was an essential part of a priest's job. For example, John Myrc's *Instructions for a Parish Priest* not only emphasizes the importance of informing parishioners about the dangers of incest but provides a detailed list of "cousins by baptism" and "cousins by confirmation," avoiding the possibility of error through misunderstanding.[25] Thus, in this manner, even illiterate clergy were able to play a critical role in the process of teaching their parishioners about marriage, not only through direct instruction but also through the correction of behavior. David D'Avray also underscores the role of the friars in preaching about marriage in their sermons.[26] Wives pondering the idea of divorce might draw on a wide corpus of popular knowledge about marriage.

THE ROLE OF THE FAMILY

Although many wives avoided divorce, believing their families would not support them, the records themselves suggest just the opposite. Many wives returned to live with their natal families pending the decision of the court. When Margaret de Nerford was going through a divorce initiated in 1378, the king delivered her into the guardianship of her grandmother.[27] Agnes Huntington lived with her uncle during divorce proceedings in 1345–46.[28] Separated wives must have behaved much like single women in their living arrangements. As Cordelia Beattie has argued, "[l]iving with kin was probably a common residential strategy for women without husbands."[29] Given the significant role played by families in the making of marriage, it should come as no surprise that they also played an active role in the breaking of marriage. The records themselves illustrate a measured reaction by families in supervising marital tensions. Divorce was not the solution to the first (or even the second, or the third) instance of violence within a marriage. A family expected to play an active role arbitrating a couple's disputes, unless the level of violence surpassed the control of the family and greater community. The petition of John Baker of London to the chancellor at the very beginning of the sixteenth century underscores a family's cautious response to marital disharmony. As his bill recounts, when John Baker of London became aware that his sister was suffering abuse at the hands of her husband, he found himself drawn into a situation that quickly turned against him:

> [o]ne Thomas St. Nicholas have married the sister of your said Orator between whom now of late fell great unkindness in so much that the said Thomas St. Nicholas for a matter of small substance did beat his wife so grievously that it was thought she would die and your said Orator hearing of the said misdemeanor of the said Thomas St. Nicholas came unto him in good manner and entreated him with good words to be good and kind lover unto his sister and no more to demean himself after such manner and he would be unto the said Thomas as good a friend as he had been in times past and the said Thomas St. Nicholas answered your said Orator that he would punish his wife at his pleasure and the more for his . . . [saying it] and then in a great fury departed from your said Orator and so it is good and gracious lord that your said Orator came to London for such business as he had there to do and the said Thomas St. Nicholas thereof knowing sent to London one William St. Nicholas brother of the said Thomas and desired him only for vexation and trouble to attach your said Orator upon suspicion of felony and so the said William hath now your said Orator upon the said feigned surmise in the compter in London and there hath continued by the space of sixteen days and more.

John's petition concludes with a heartfelt plea to the chancellor to consider his circumstances and accordingly to grant him a writ of *corpus cum causa* to release him from his unjust imprisonment.[30]

John describes the beating inflicted upon his sister as being of a grave nature. His intervention was that of a concerned brother wishing to prevent a recurrence of this abusive behavior. That he chose to confront his brother-in-law rather than remove his sister altogether from a harmful environment is instructive. If the first known instance of abuse was serious enough to endanger her life and the reason for the abuse was reportedly "a matter of small substance" (as opposed to a grave argument spiraling out of control), to a modern audience, separation was the reasonable answer. John's decision not to aid his sister in pursuing this route supports the argument that there was an established process of intervention, and family involvement was merely the first stage. Moreover, John's allusion to this episode as justification for his actions demonstrates that a forceful *tête-à-tête* with his ill-mannered brother-in-law was fully expected. Unfortunately, the record reveals little about John's response to Thomas's frank assertion that he "would punish his wife at his pleasure." Nevertheless, that was not the intention of this comment. It is included in his petition in order to make a point about the flawed nature of his brother-in-law's character, in the hopes that this flagrant disregard for social ethics portrays the latter as not only a wretched husband but also a disagreeable person.

John's petition to chancery seems oddly incomplete. The request for a writ of *corpus cum causa* to release him from jail is appropriate and predictable. However, one would expect to see a secondary request to have Thomas and his brother, William, brought before the chancellor and compelled into good behavior. Without an explicit reproach of Thomas and William's shady involvement in John's current predicament, there was no reason for them to discontinue their dogged harassment of John and his sister. An appearance in court before the chancellor supplemented by a demand for sureties would have eliminated the source of both problems (John's imprisonment and the endangerment to his sister's life). The omission of such a request invites an obvious conclusion. John did not appeal to the chancellor for help in his sister's domestic situation, because it was not the appropriate venue. Thomas and William's behavior was a communal problem best dealt with informally or before the manor court; only John's imprisonment might not be resolved so easily. His failure to address the issue of spousal mistreatment suggests that Thomas's actions had not yet surpassed communal controls, even though Thomas "did beat his wife so grievously that it was thought she would die."[31]

Even so, when it became necessary, families assumed an active role in the divorce process. Their participation ranged from merely refusing to cooperate to assisting a wife in packing up her goods and leaving her husband's home. For example, the bishop of Rochester in 1332 cited Margery Brightyld for preventing her son, John, and his wife, Agnes, from living together.

How active was her intervention? Moreover, what was her reasoning? Our best insight into this part of the process comes from a rather unusual source. More often than not, in cases of husband desertion, husbands were less concerned about retrieving their wives than they were about reclaiming the goods she took with her. A suit of trespassory ravishment (that is, abduction) in the common law courts was the ideal solution. When a husband sued a plea in court for the ravishment of his wife, it was purely an economic plea made in the hopes of recovering the value of the goods taken with her rather than the wife herself.[32] Sue Sheridan Walker uses the term "consensual abduction" to describe the actions of these women: "[t]he wives in question were probably not only willing but had their portable possessions packed awaiting the arrival of their abductors."[33] This legal fiction was recognized and accommodated by the royal courts of medieval England. Consequently, in a suit of ravishment, the plaintiff might ask for an award of damages, but the suitable writ could not also order the restoration of one's wife. This was an explicit "extension of control by women over their lives and marriages"; by allowing themselves to be abducted, unhappy wives were consciously acting out a wish to end their marriages.[34] The fact that many of these abducted wives were involved simultaneously in cases of judicial separation in the church courts confirms that the abduction was, in fact, a variation on the theme of spousal desertion. Sometimes the ravisher was the wife's lover; other cases of ravishment reveal that the abductor was anyone from a father helping his daughter out of an adulterous marriage to a brother rescuing his sister from a coerced marriage.[35] Most plaintiffs who appeared in the royal courts with pleas of ravishment, then, were persons who had abandoned all hope of repairing the marriage and who sought only compensation for the loss of goods and chattels taken during the abduction. Cases of ravishment in the king's court are an ideal lens to explore the involvement of the family in the divorce process. The legal fiction of abduction, however, is problematic, because it forced plaintiffs to reshape the circumstances to fit the statute's requirements, thus seriously misrepresenting what actually transpired. The records generally make no mention of the wife's consent, and her rescuers become her "abductors" or "rapists," as the court records' use of the verb *rapere* for both offences make distinguishing between the two quite difficult at times.[36]

Family members at all levels were supportive of wives who left their husbands. The late-fifteenth-century petition of Philip Cabull, a dyer of Bristol, reveals just how active a family's involvement might be. When Philip married Margaret, widow of Philip Barthelmewe of Bristol, he suddenly found himself moving up in the world, but only for a short time. His wife's abrupt desertion after a short period of marriage implies that social mobility was his only reason for marrying the widow Margaret. This fact may have become quickly apparent to his new bride. It is also possible that Philip was abusive or that he had deceived her about his own wealth and the truth had only come out after their wedding day. Whatever the reason, Margaret was unwilling to remain in his household. While he was away in London, Margaret's sons from her previous marriage, William and John, stepped into action. With their mother's full "consent and agreement," they took her and goods and chattels reported to belong to her husband "of great value the extent whereof the said orator knows not." They carried her away to the city of London, where she had been in residence for a year prior to the petition. Since then, Philip had been unable to neither "speak with the said Margaret nor have any part of his said good." Her sons, "by coven and craft between them," allegedly sued numerous false actions of debt against Philip in court, "contrary to all right and conscience" and egged on "by the procuring and steering of the said Margaret." Moreover, "intending utterly to undo her said husband," Philip reported that Margaret had two obligations drawn up for her sons in the sums of £20 and £100 respectively, falsely bearing a date before their spousals had taken place. Philip's request to the chancellor, however, reveals that there was more to the story than he wished to admit. Instead of a simple demand of reparation for the goods stolen from him by his two vigilante stepsons, he requests that a writ of *subpoena* be directed to them, requiring them to appear in court before the chancellor bearing the false obligations, and then that an injunction be provided against them, preventing them from bringing further actions against the petitioner in court. If the stepsons had indeed abducted their mother and taken goods belonging to the petitioner as he asserted, he should have demanded damages or compensation for the value of the goods. The accusation of false documents is an indication that Margaret's motivation in escaping Philip was an attempt to safeguard her sons' inheritance before Philip spent it.[37]

Whether the actions sued against Philip were legitimate, Margaret's two sons probably had reasonable concerns about their inheritance and about their mother's happiness. At the very least, Philip had the decency not to protest his own innocence in the matter overtly, as does Richard Ores in his petition before the court. According to the latter's bill of complaint, he had endured many inequities at the hands of William Harryson. Ores had been defamed, compelled to perform public penance for a sin that he had not committed and had false suits brought against him in court. Moreover, Harryson had compounded his sins against Ores by carrying away his wife and goods from his home. Despite Harryson's allegations, with a clear conscience Ores was able to assert that he was "as guiltless therein as the child born this night."[38] It is unlikely that many of the petitioners who appeared before the chancellor were as virtuous as Ores claimed to be. Complainants resorted to the courts as a means of both redress and coercion when a marital dispute escalated in nature. Both parties employed this tactic. Many complainants in chancery were already facing suits against them in the courts of common law. Still, while the king's courts proved to be useful weapons in domestic warfare, the English court of Chancery was a more powerful weapon. In bringing his case before chancery, Ores could hope to receive compensation for his multiple losses.

In the case of Margaret Barthelmewe and her two sons, the circumstances of her abduction show all too clearly how very misleading the term "abduction" could be in cases of this type. William and John Barthelmewe were not abducting their mother for nefarious purposes; they were rescuing her from a marriage she saw as unsatisfactory. Although Walker is content to describe this as "consensual abduction," "assisted spousal desertion" is a more accurate description of a woman's agency. These women chose to leave their husbands but needed the support of loved ones in order to carry out their plans (or more accurately, carry out their goods in the moving process). Once again, the intervention by Margaret's two sons confirms that family members were the obvious choice. Similarly, when the daughter of William Morton of Bilburgh (*Yorks.*) chose to leave her husband, her father "abducted" her from her husband's home.[39] To call these cases "abduction" rather than "desertion" makes a very powerful point: these men were not holding their wives legally responsible for their actions, nor could they. Historians have studied the difficulties married women faced because of the rules of coverture in a variety of contexts, from property rights to civil liberties. However, they have sometimes overlooked the reality that husbands suffered similar restrictions. They, too, were incapable of initiating suits against their wives, because a suit against one's wife was essentially a suit against one's self. In the context of spousal desertion, a husband's powerlessness when faced with coverture becomes most apparent. Even though it is evident in all cases that the respondent merely abetted the wife in a plan of her own design, the husband was required to hold the wife's lover, family member or friend accountable. He could not sue his own wife for damages, because, legally, a wife was incapable of stealing from her husband—the law viewed them as one person, and it is simply not possible to steal from one's self. This is one situation where the law of coverture benefited wives.

Even in cases where the bill does not couch the wife's desertion in terms of abduction, the same language of consensual abduction permeates the record. When Alice, wife of John Matheu de Tamall (*Corn.*), decided that she no longer wished the "fellowship nor governance" of her husband, she deserted him and took with her goods and chattels belonging to her husband. Matheu heartily believed that she had been encouraged in her decision by the "counsel and wicked excitation" of two men, Walter Hankocke and Richard Martyn of St. Cue (*Corn.*). Since then, she had not only come to despise her husband but also refused to "obey his governance" and kept his property from him. Moreover, both Hankocke and Martyn "daily vex[ed] and trouble[d]" Matheu by "menaces and threatening in losing of his life," so that he might not comfortably "come in the fellowship of his wife." In his petition to chancery, Matheu directs his suit against Hankocke and Martyn, blaming them for "inducing" his wife to withhold his goods and chattels.[40] Similarly, Nicholas Dobson's wife was also incited to leave her husband by the "inordinate demeaning" of Richard Wymond, grocer of London. Richard caused Nicholas's wife "to be of no good rule" and "to absent her from her husband"; he had since "affirmed an untrue and a feigned action of trespass" against Nicholas, for which he had been arrested and imprisoned.[41]

The language employed in the complaints of both Nicholas Dobson and John Matheu reflects contemporary perspectives of late medieval ideals of family dynamics. In each, the petitioners carefully describe the problem as an issue of "poor governance" or "ill rule," which was a linguistic development of the late fourteenth century: "the introduction of 'governance' implies a change in expectations for individual behavior. A person of 'ill repute' gains his or her bad reputation only by external labeling, but a community condemnation of 'bad governance' implies that a person should know better."[42] Governance was not merely about personal conduct, however: being a man in late medieval society meant taking responsibility for the behavior of social inferiors as well as one's own conduct.[43] Because governance was intimately related to submission to a superior male authority, the situations of these women help to shed some light on the meaning of governance in this context. As the records describe it, both Nicholas Dobson's wife and Alice, wife of John Matheu, seem to have had very little control over their own ability "to be governed," having both been led astray by evil men. Their situations reveal that in late medieval England, a woman was of good rule if her husband ruled her; a woman was of ill rule if a man other than her husband (especially a lover) ruled her. In this equation, female independence was simply not an option; any man who permitted his wife to govern her own behavior was a poor excuse for a husband and a man. Not surprisingly, few men would have willingly appeared in court and confessed to being utter failures as men. Better to pin the blame for his wife's conduct on another man than to admit being married to an independent woman.

Of course, not all families were supportive of members' individual marital choices, and family members themselves were sometimes part of the problem in a marriage. Mary Assheby of Lincolnshire's petition to Parliament in 1421 recounts that she was married "by law of Holy Church" to John Thymelby, son of Thomas Thymelby, but her husband's father had since turned on the marriage. He "has separated them, and is holding John prisoner in his house," to prevent them from reuniting. She requests that the lords have Thomas summoned before the king's council to answer for his actions.[44] When the pope annulled Joan of Kent's marriage to William Montacute and ordered her back to her first husband, Thomas Holland, Joan's mother stood in the way. A mandate to the archbishop of Canterbury notes that Margaret, Joan's mother, had arranged for the second marriage while Thomas was away fighting in Prussia, because she "opposed Thomas in recovering his conjugal rights."[45] These cases, though, are miniscule in comparisons with the myriad instances of family who supported individuals throughout the divorce process.

THE ROLE OF THE CLERGY

If a woman had no family or lover to rescue her from an abusive relationship, who better than the local priest, dedicated to the care of souls, to fill this role? Numerous examples of this nature have survived from the records of the royal court. Husband deserters were assisted by clergymen drawn from a wide variety of positions, from parsons and chaplains, to a vicar, an archdeacon and even a monk.[46] With the lecherous reputations of clergy in late medieval England, some may also have been the women's lovers (although the documentation generally does not recognize this).[47] Some others were family members.[48] These cases confirm that marital disharmony had an impact on numerous people within a community, not just the couple. In the case of Thomas Gwyn *vs.* Thomas Colle, parson of the church of Combe Merton (*Devon*), Gwyn accused Colle of frequenting the family home in order to spirit away his wife. After four years of friendship with the couple, Colle came to the house of Thomas Gwyn and "took away Joan the wife of your said beseecher all his goods it there keep." These actions had, in keeping with the requirements of the court of Chancery, "brought [the petitioner] in so great poverty that he hath nothing to sue him by the common law."[49] Moreover, the parson had "by untrue means feigned actions" against the petitioner and "hath so labored against your foresaid beseecher [that] he dare not come into his country and thus utterly proposes to undo him." Impoverished and harassed, Gwyn turned to England's chancellor for assistance.[50]

Gwyn's case offers little insight into the actual state of affairs between him and his wife; thus, it is only possible to speculate about the reasons why Colle felt it necessary to intervene in their marriage. For example, it is entirely possible that Colle was Joanna's lover; priestly vestments were certainly no bar to sexual relationships in the medieval period.[51] Colle might also have been acting in his capacity as a spiritual advisor, intervening in a violent or adulterous marriage. Of course, it is also possible that this was simply an unhappy relationship and that Joanna chose to strike out against her husband in a way that would hurt him most: by targeting his purse.

Henry Ansgar Kelly has made a similar point in his analysis of the charges of ravishment leveled against Henry Wakefield, the bishop of Worcester, in 1387. The court accused Wakefield of feloniously ravishing the wife and daughter of John Henley as well as a number of their goods (namely, woolen and linen cloths and other household utensils to the value of 40*s*.). Although traditionally scholars have viewed Wakefield as a "rapist," Kelly supposes that this case points instead to "some sort of domestic strife. The bishop or his court may have helped to rescue Joan and Katherine from an abusive household, perhaps effecting a legal separation of Katherine for *sevitia* [cruelty] . . . or an annulment because of an impediment to marriage."[52] Other clergymen would have been carrying out similar curial duties, caring for the troubled souls of their parishioners.[53]

Generally, the records are no help in deciphering whether a cleric's intervention in a marriage was self-interested or whether he was acting in his role as arbitrator in a disintegrating marriage. When Joan, wife of Hamon Sirich, and her husband fought over a rumor that Hamon had heard concerning his wife and Stephen de Beck, described here as a beneficed clerk, "fearing that her aforesaid husband would have done her evil," Joan left her husband's house and went to stay with another man (relationship unspecified) in the same vill. The record does not clarify exactly what the rumor was or its truthfulness; it only hints that Stephen had some sort of prior relationship with Joan. Upon hearing what had happened to Joan, Stephen ordered two of his servants to go get her, "because she had frequently suffered so many injuries because of [her husband]." She soon came back with Stephen's servants, but not voluntarily. When asked if she went to Stephen's house of her own free will, the jurors replied that she did not, "for they say that she told the aforesaid servants that she would rather return to her husband and take the punishment which he would inflict on her than go with them." Not surprisingly, Hamon sued a case of ravishment against the priest.[54] Was Stephen a former lover? Or was he merely overly enthusiastic in playing the role of marriage counselor?

The tendency of husbands to interpret the actions of an ecclesiastical official as personal attacks rather than institutional intervention was probably a common feature in cases of ecclesiastical arbitration in later medieval England. The petition of John Carvare, clerk chancellor to the archbishop of York, substantiates this conjecture. In his bill of complaint, John recounts the story of Joanna, wife of Guy Dawny, esquire. When she requested a separation from the archbishop of York because of her husband's cruelty, she claimed that her life was in imminent danger. Her testimony to the court alleged that her husband had "menaced and threatened her to mayhem" and that he had tried to slay her. Given the volatility of the situation, the court ruled that it was in the best interests of both parties for Joanna to be sequestered from her husband within the city of York for the duration of the suit, as was often the custom in applications for judicial separation.[55] Irrespective of the court's ruling, Guy decided to take matters into his own hands. Using the language of the common law courts in which a claim of violent trespass had to include the allegation of "force and arms" (*vi et armis*),[56] John recounts how with force and arms Guy came to the place where Joanna was staying: "against her will with great violence [he] took and set [Joanna] into a cart and carried [her] away and the same Joanna then making thereof a great exclamation that a multitude of people came and retained the said cart." Once again, the community summoned the archbishop to arbitrate. He decided that Joanna should return to her place of residence in the city of York until the suit was determined and ordered Guy to leave his wife alone. The court appointed John Carvare, clerk to the archbishop, to escort Joanna back to her home in York. His intervention so enraged Joanna's husband that Guy sued an action of trespass against Carvare and "intends by might and power that he has in the same city to contempt your said beseecher in great cost and damage to his great hurt and loss." Facing imprisonment and unable to turn to his superior (the archbishop having recently died), Carvare found himself in a dodgy situation.[57]

In using the royal courts as a weapon to harass the church's officials, men like Guy Dawny hoped to discourage any further prying into their matrimonial affairs. Given the very low number of cases of judicial separations on the grounds of cruelty, this was probably an effective strategy.[58] More to the point, the hostility that Guy exhibited to ecclesiastical intervention speaks to the resentment felt by some concerning the church's encroachment into marriage. The underlying tensions between priests and the male laity are grounded in the domestic milieu. As R.N. Swanson has argued:

> [t]he collusion between clerics and women to civilize and Christianize medieval lay men could easily be interpreted as a conspiracy against male control over the family and domestic life: the clergy could be attacked as having too close attachments to women, encouraging their spirituality and acts of charity without reference to their husbands, thereby undermining male power.[59]

Guy's reaction likely represents a more general belief that marital disharmony was an issue best left to real men.

The case of a man named Horncastre from the eyre of 1271–72 presents a similar situation in which the husband very much resented a priest's meddling in his affairs, even though the priest was merely carrying out his office. The record tells us that Horncastre beat his wife so that she seemed about to die, and then he fled. Soon after, the parish priest arrived to administer last rites to Horncastre's wife; Horncastre returned while the priest was performing the ceremony. Immediately angry, Horncastre called the priest a thief and drove him from his home. Brandishing a knife, Horncastre chased the priest into town, at which point the greater community got involved. While neighbors raised the hue and cry, the priest's nephew attempted to mediate a truce between the two and was stabbed in the process. The townsmen then chased Horncastre and detained him. Horncastre responded by suing the townsmen for breaking the doors of his home, beating and wounding him and imprisoning him. Well informed of what really happened, Horncastre's version of events did not persuade the jury.[60]

Not all priests sided with the wives. In fact, the appeals of some wives include complaints alleging that certain court officials allied too closely with their husbands. Anne Malverne of London's 1464 appeal to the pope in a suit of divorce against John Jakis of London argues that Thomas Wynterburne, a clerk in the employ of the archbishop of Canterbury, was preventing her from a fair hearing. She felt she was "unduly aggrieved by the said Thomas because he placed her in such strict sequestration that she could not speak with her advocate and proctor for the defense of the cause, and because, although often requested on her behalf, he refused to promulgate sentence and do her justice."[61] Margaret Lucy of the diocese of Lincoln makes a similar complaint in her papal petition against the bishop of Lincoln. The bishop had "inflicted" several "grievances" on her, "including public excommunication for her alleged contumacy in not appearing in an unsafe and distant place, to which she dared not go on account of the power of the said Thomas [her husband] and his friends."[62] Because the clergy played such an active role in the supervision of marriages at both a local and a more formal level as judges, it was inevitable that they would become targets of complaints by both husbands and wives. Although some clergy were working out of self-interest, many others were simply doing their jobs.

SECURITY DURING DIVORCE PROCEEDINGS

Many husbands expressed their anger best through absence and evasion; regrettably, most wives were not that fortunate. The threat posed by vengeful husbands meant that many wives legitimately needed protection during the process of divorce. Naturally, the most detailed records of court-mandated protection come from the divorces of well-heeled wives who could depend on the king to step in to assist them. The king's personal communications reveal that he played a remarkably active role in sheltering wives from outraged husbands. When Joan, widow of John Fitz James, embarked on a suit of divorce against Thomas Fulbroke in 1384, the king ordered him on pain of £100 not to hinder Joan in her suit, "nor do or procure any hurt or harm to the said Joan in person, her men, servants, or friends." The king also dictated that Thomas must pay Joan's maintenance; until the church made a final decision, the king required Thomas to pay Joan half the rents and profits of all her lands occupied by him.[63] The king also awarded royal protection to Margery, widow of William Lord Ros of Helmsley, when she was divorcing her third husband, John Avenel, in 1355. The king's measures responded to her "fears that during the suit damage and peril will result to her and her men, household, advocates, proctors, attorneys and others by the said John and his favorers and accomplices."[64] Margery's concern for her well-being was justified: John's violent behavior landed him in prison only a few months after the award. Although the details for his imprisonment are scanty, the king guaranteed John's appearance in Margery's suit, granting license to him to leave prison only for the purposes of attending the church court.[65]

Much like the clergy, royal officials also ran the risk of being implicated while protecting a wife during the process of divorce. In 1377, when Alice, widow of Thomas Gerberge, was kidnapped, raped, imprisoned and forced into marriage by Stephen Worlyk (or Wolryk), she enlisted the assistance of John Brewes, sheriff of Norfolk, and William Curson, sheriff of Suffolk, while she sued a divorce before the Court of Arches.[66] Her "husband" retaliated by petitioning the king to assist him in persecuting the sheriffs. He claimed that Brewes and Curson "forcibly abducted" her, an abduction that was ongoing, as she was now residing with Curson (most likely for protection). Moreover, "[t]hey had incited her to sue an appeal of rape against her husband, her father and others who were at her wedding, and have indicted them of felony." William Curson had also reportedly sued for a divorce between Alice and Stephen, drawing up "false notorial documents to this end." Stephen respectively requested that his wife be returned, that he receive damages for his troubles and that the perpetrators be summoned to Parliament to answer for their actions.[67] Stephen's impassioned letter did not convince the king: a memorandum from May 1377 states that Stephen Wolryk of Skothowe, among many others, "shall not do or procure any hurt or hindrance to Alice who was wife of Thomas Gerberge knight nor any of her counsel or her servants in prosecuting her business in diverse king's courts and elsewhere."[68] It is noteworthy that the sheriff of Suffolk's decision to have Alice reside with him during the court process was not exceptional. For example, when Margery Sheppard was involved in a marriage dispute with Richard Tymond before the consistory court of London in 1487, the court awarded Margery's custody to Richard Spencer, the court's registrar.[69] Sequestration of this nature suggests the existence of an imminent threat to the litigator; thus, it was only logical to take precautionary measures to remove the woman from harm.

Not only did the king's officials risk harassment and imprisonment in the protection of divorcing wives, with some officials even playing the role of personal bodyguard, but the entire process might occupy much of their time over an extended duration. The experience of Margery de Nerford, heiress of John and Agnes de Nerford, illustrates the vulnerability of wives and the need for responsive, swift enforcement during the process of divorce. Entrusted to the guardianship of Peter Brewes at the age of five, Margery married Peter's son, John, as a teenager against her will.[70] Three years later, Margery sued for a divorce, presumably on the grounds of coercion. After a nasty confrontation with her husband and his men, she turned to the king for oversight. On June 26, 1378, the king commanded protection for Margery, her proctors, servants and all her goods for one year while she sued an appeal to the Holy See.[71] On the same date, the king issued orders to arrest her husband as well as his uncle, Robert Howard, and acquaintances John le Heyr and Richard "that was the lady's cook Nevill" and imprison them at Newgate jail (London).[72] Their crime was abduction in the hopes of deterring Margery from pursuing a divorce. Further requests for the arrests of John Brewes and John le Heyr from the following month (July 8 and July 28) indicate they were still at large.[73] By October, Margery was in the personal care of the sheriff of Norfolk, implying that the threat to Margery's well-being had accelerated, requiring more extensive security measures.[74] A letter from late October 1378, drafted by Dame Alice Neville, baroness through her third marriage to John Lord Neville of Essex, and also Margery's grandmother, clarifies exactly what had happened. She writes:

> John Brewes and other malefactors broke into her lodging in London and forcibly abducted Margery, daughter of John de Nerford her son, whom they found there, and took her to the Bishop of Norwich's lodging, where Robert Howard received and hid her, with the intention of resisting an appeal pending in the papal court, in Margery's suit to annul her contract of marriage with John Brewes. The court remanded Robert Howard to the Tower of London, to remain there until the council might bring Margery before it. However, the Council later released him, provided he made every effort to bring Margery before the Council in London . . . or to surrender himself to the Tower at that date, on pain of paying £1000 to the king. He pledged himself to do this, but has not done so; she requests that he be sent again to the Tower, and the £1000 paid to the king.[75]

Further letters patently reveal that Dame Alice played an instrumental role in conveying information to the king's officials and prompting the king into action. In December, at her request, the king delivered Margery into the guardianship of her grandmother. Soon after, the king once again released Robert Howard and John Mareschall from the Tower of London, both of them imprisoned for their involvement in Margery's abduction. On pain of £1,000, they undertook a promise that "they shall not eloign the said Margery from the company of the said Alice, nor procure that to be done by others, nor offer nor procure her hurt, violence, or grievance."[76] This time, they seem to have taken the king's threat seriously, submitting Margery to no further acts of violence.

Margery's experience reveals just how long it could take to win a suit of divorce. In July 1379, the king renewed Margery's protection for another year, as the appeal was still undecided.[77] In July 1380, he renewed it again; the final renewal was in July 1381.[78] Although the pope's sentence has not survived, Margery's divorce was eventually successful. In May 1383, Margery took a vow of chastity before the bishop of London, entering into a lifestyle of "calm domesticity," surely a welcome change after her time spent with the Brewes family.[79] Her surviving will makes it clear that she died with her property intact.[80]

With extensive landed estates in her own right and a connection to the baron of Essex, Margery de Nerford was admittedly an exceptional woman. As Gwen Seabourne has argued, the unusual level of royal involvement in this case was undoubtedly a result of her "grandmother's insistence on action and powerful connections."[81] The violence acted out against Margery, however, was not exceptional. Abduction and assault were typical weapons in the divorce wars, wielded by husbands determined to hold on to their marital properties (if not their wives). The divorce of Joan, daughter of Richard de Coutenhale, was remarkably similar to that of Margery de Nerford. When Joan's guardian, Walter de Soutenhales, learned that the marriage he had arranged for her with a London vintner named William Sharpyng had gone unconsummated, he encouraged her to sue for a divorce. To shield her from harm during the proceedings, Walter entered into a bond with William for £100 on the premise that William not hinder but assist his wife in obtaining an annulment on the grounds of impotence. The bond dated to February 1370. In June of the same year, while Joan was on her way to consult with her lawyer, her husband and six others assaulted her so that she did not dare keep her appointment. William spent some time in prison for his participation in this assault.[82] Delays likes this dragged out the proceedings; in February 1373, once again William "molested" Joan on her way to see her lawyer so that she had to take refuge in the home of her former guardian. In 1374, her guardian sued for debt on the bond that William had never paid. William's response to the suit brought the entire proceedings to a halt; not only did William claim that he had passed his test of virility with the ecclesiastical court (invalidating all grounds for a divorce), but on Christmas Eve in 1369, he and his wife had reconciled.[83] Although it is hard to imagine that all subsequent records were a sham perpetuated by Joan's guardian, if William had indeed overcome his impotence, the church would not have granted the divorce anyway.

What was perhaps most frustrating for medieval wives was that the need for protection did not vanish altogether once the court awarded a divorce. Humiliation, vengeance and even denial prompted some husbands to persist in harassing their wives. In 1385, Elizabeth Bretoun, daughter and heiress of Thomas Bretoun (*Essex*), won her divorce against her husband, Robert Persoun, taverner of London.[84] Soon after, "by his own authority," Robert "took her and kept her in irons in a house" at Pater Noster row in London. In answer to a complaint made by Roger Barre and "other friends," the court released Elizabeth. Robert did not cease his harassment; he then sued her rescuer for ravishment. Because he was going to Calais on the king's service, Roger Barre had a royal protection entitling him not to answer civil pleas, causing Robert's suit to fail.[85]

Although marital dissolution was common to all ranks of medieval English society, an individual's socio-economic status very much shaped his or her divorce experience. As the stories of many of the women in this chapter imply, a courtroom divorce was best suited to women of means: the expense of the proceedings, the need for financial support during that time, and round the clock protection from vengeful husbands are all factors that necessitate access to money. A number of these cases also underscore the protracted nature of divorce proceedings. The church took five years to award the divorce of Margery de Nerford and Peter Brews; Joan de Coutenhale and William Sharpyng's divorce took four years before the proceedings were quashed. Not many people were capable of putting their lives on hold for four or five years while the church decided their fates. Given the costs and the duration of formal proceedings, for most medieval individuals, self-divorce was not only cheap and relatively effortless but the only realistic option.

In particular, the stories of these couples speak to the experience of marital breakdown in medieval England, revealing that marriage was an exceedingly public institution. Couples anticipated their family, friends and communities would play active roles not only in the selection of a spouse and the negotiations leading to a marriage but also in the supervision and counseling of troubled spouses. In return, both the church and local communities expected couples to work through their problems, very much seeing divorce as a last resort. When tensions escalated, however, families and clergymen stepped up to assist wives in establishing separate households. The scope and diversity of support offered to wives in the divorce process reveal that medieval Englishmen and -women were not as disparaging of divorce as many couples believed they might be. The assistance of family and friends was vital in making divorce a viable alternative for medieval wives: without financial or legal independence, wives were only capable of abandoning their marriages when their family and friends supported them.

3 The Risk Factor

Today, many women stay married to incompatible or even abusive men, because they fear the alternative: economic vulnerability, custody disputes and even social or familial ostracism, despite the fact that we live in a world where divorce is available at law and is a common occurrence in our society. For women in medieval England, the stakes were much higher. Although alimony did exist in this period and examples of maintenance agreements do survive, enforcing those agreements was not easy, and most women could not have relied on alimony for full support.

Women had much to lose when they divorced. Among other considerations, a wife's position in the social hierarchy may have provided enough satisfaction to make a bad marriage tolerable. Just being married made a woman someone important. As Judith Bennett and Amy Froide have argued, "*marital status* shaped women's lives . . . [w]ives were assumed to be better governed than other women . . . [and] wives could exercise some informal political power through their husbands."[1] Indeed, "wife" was such a title of pride for older women that some women retained the title even after the deaths of their husbands.[2] Natalie Zemon Davis's celebrated case study of identity theft in sixteenth-century rural France reveals just how powerfully marriage influenced a woman's social standing and sense of self. When her husband abandoned her, Bertrande de Rols returned home to live with her parents: "Neither wife nor widow, she was under the same roof with her mother again. Neither wife nor widow, she had to face the other women at the mill, the well, the tileworks, and at the harvest."[3] Certainly, not all separated wives reverted to the dependent status of a daughter; as Cordelia Beattie has emphasized, life cycle had much to do with popular perceptions and social position.[4] A young separated wife was far more likely to live in a position of dependence than was an older woman.[5] Nonetheless, because marriage was such a significant rite of passage, fear of losing one's social adulthood may have been sufficient justification to stay in an unhappy marriage.

Desertion also had significant spiritual risks. The English church courts presented a united front, dedicated to keeping marriages together. By the early thirteenth century, the medieval church undertook the mission of declaring marriage a sacrament; thus church courts firmly upheld the biblical directive of "what God has joined together, let no man put asunder."[6] A woman who left her husband without first obtaining an annulment or a court-approved separation (neither of which was very easy to acquire) put herself in spiritual jeopardy.[7] The unwillingness of wives to divorce often stemmed from a perception of marriage as something sacred and inviolable, clear evidence of victory in the church's campaign to construct marriage as a sacrament. The chancery bill of Agnes, daughter of John Terry, from the years 1452–54 reveals the extent to which some wives upheld oppressive marriages out of respect for the institution. In her bill, she complains of the illicit behavior of her former guardian. As sole heiress to her parents' sizeable estate, she was entrusted into the care of John Bicombe, a family friend, at a "right tender age." Since that time, Bicombe's misuse of his guardianship had been blatant. The waste and destruction of her property amounted to at least £20; he had sold lands and tenements, thus alienating them from her; worst of all, he had imprisoned her in a small chamber for forty weeks until she was so "enfeebled in brain" that she consented to marry a man of his choosing. As her husband, the unnamed suitor gained control of Agnes's property. Making matters worse, he entered into a recognizance before the mayor of Oxford with Bicombe for £100, stating that he would abide the award, rule and judgment of Bicombe in all things and causes. Only when her husband lay on his deathbed did Agnes discover that nothing of her inheritance remained to her. After her husband's death, she determined to set things right by taking her former guardian to court for the mismanagement of her affairs.[8]

Agnes's story reveals the hazards of a culture that valued marriage inherently for the opportunities it might afford to climb the social ladder. What is most remarkable about Agnes's experience is the simple fact that she seems never to have contemplated the possibility of divorce, despite having more than ample grounds to prove it. Agnes's aversion to divorce exposes a deeply founded reverence for the sacrament of marriage. Many other women of this era echoed this dedication to one's spouse, no matter how the relationship was initiated. The peculiar experience of Elizabeth Venor, a fifteenth-century gentlewoman from Lancashire, made pregnant by her rapist, John Worth, and then coerced into marriage, articulates skillfully the sacred bond many women believed marriage to be. To avoid penalty for his actions, John escaped into sanctuary at Westminster, bringing his new bride with him. Although she had many opportunities to flee, Elizabeth remained with her husband in sanctuary, even after the king dispatched royal officials to counsel her, making certain she was aware that by staying with him, she risked her inheritance. She responded by saying that "she had made a promise that she would keep, and not for all her goods or lands would she lose her soul." Elizabeth did eventually leave sanctuary, although the records do not explain what prompted her decision. She sued (and won) a divorce at the consistory court of the archbishop of Canterbury and then proceeded in a lawsuit against her rapist. Her pregnancy presented a serious obstacle to her case, however, as conception was thought to occur only with consensual sex.[9] Her explanation for this was also revealing: "she said that her flesh was in a manner agreed," but "in her soul she never assented, that is, in all her entire will in her soul, so that she was not at ease" until she had left his presence.[10] Elizabeth's strong sense of devotion to this sham of a marriage substantiates that many women sided with the church in believing that even the worst marriages should be permanent.

Despite these factors, many women pursued divorce both officially and unofficially. Along with family and friends who chose to abet them, these women risked excommunication, imprisonment, public humiliation, weighty fines and even the threat of death to rebel against the permanence of marriage. The defiance of these women and the willingness of others to assist strongly suggest that, although the church regarded marriage as a binding contract between husband and wife, the English people were not as willing to embrace this point of view. Although this group of women was a small minority in medieval English society, their existence at least suggests that not all wives were desperate housewives.

THE RISKS OF SELF-DIVORCE

Although divorce was a difficult proposition for all medieval wives, the greatest risks were borne by those who self-divorced. As chapter 2 indicates, the centrality of family and friends in guiding medieval marriages played a pivotal role in opening up divorce as a possibility for wives. This same group, however, also presented a serious challenge to those individuals who refused to be steered by the morals of the communities, deciding independently to self-divorce before their families, friends and neighbors felt that circumstances necessitated it. Shannon McSheffrey has emphasized the moral guardianship village men asserted over its constituents, sometimes leading local patriarchs to burst into homes in the middle of the night to prevent sinful activities from transpiring.[11] Karen Jones argues that "fear that divine retribution might descend on a community that tolerated sexual misbehaviour probably played some part in efforts to eradicate it."[12] A 1486 case of trespass from the Common Bench clarifies not only that community elites believed they were entitled to unlimited access to the homes of their neighbors in order to supervise local values but that some municipalities even encouraged it. According to the defendant, he was only doing his civic duty when he broke into the plaintiff's home. He defended his actions by stating that when information reached the constable's ear concerning a woman's adultery, London custom required men from the parish to accompany the constable to the home to remove the man. In this case, the man did not passively accept the discipline of these self-appointed moral policemen: he responded by suing a trespass for assault, battery and imprisonment.[13]

The existence of such active friends and neighbors unavoidably complicated self-divorce. If the parting was by mutual consent and one or both individuals relocated away from the prying eyes of familiar neighbors tasked with safeguarding communal respectability, avoiding detection by the law was possible.[14] Yet relocation was no guarantee. In 1329 when Alice Grene, wife of John de Gaysham of Blechingley (*Sy.*), deserted her husband, she moved from Winchester diocese, where she lived with her husband, back to Worcester diocese, where she grew up (Salisbury diocese was nicely sandwiched in between). Because her husband remained behind, his single lifestyle soon came to the attention of the church. The bishop summoned him to explain their failure to cohabit as a married couple should. John not only shifted the blame entirely to Alice but also told the bishop exactly where she was living. When the bishop of Worcester investigated further, Alice contended that she had moved to Droitwich (*Worcs.*) with her husband's permission and was "ready to receive him as her husband with proper obedience." Nonetheless, her adamant refusal to return to live in Blechingley "for fear of death and disinheritance" indicates that there may have been more to the story than Alice was willing to admit.[15]

When self-divorce was not by mutual consent, individuals ran great risk of being reconciled against their will. For those spouses with financial backing, lawsuits initiated in the church court for the enforcement of the marital contract or restitution of conjugal rights were potential methods of returning one's delinquent partner to the marital home. Lawsuits belonged to *instance* jurisdiction; bishops also exercised *ex officio* jurisdiction, fulfilling their responsibility to oversee the morality of those Christians living within the diocese. In this situation, bishops acted on information brought to the court or even "promoted" by an individual involved in the offence. For example, a wife might instigate a case *ex officio* by personally informing the bishop of her husband's desertion, thus having the situation resolved without needing to pay legal fees. *Ex officio* cases revolving around issues of non-cohabitation or failure to pay the conjugal debt were also fundamental to the reconciliation of many medieval marriages. What is critical to recognize is that the medieval church had serious weapons at its disposal in order to convince couples into reconciling, despite their obvious distaste for doing so.

The threat of excommunication to coerce neglectful spouses into returning to their marriages was one of the church's most powerful weapons. For some, the threat itself was sufficient.[16] Others avoided the risk by responding in kind: the bishop of Rochester in 1324 observed that Henry atte Swan, who refused to appear in court to respond to his wife's suit for restitution of conjugal rights, had managed to steer clear of excommunication only because he bullied the executor of the sentence.[17] Many spouses, however, did not appear in court to submit to this kind of intimidation. Women like Emma Herevay persisted in spite of the warning. In 1336, when the court of the dean and chapter of Lincoln summoned Emma before it and told her to adhere to her husband under pain of excommunication, she was adamant in her refusal, saying that she would not return.[18] For wives like Emma Herevay, the intimidation tactics moved beyond being singled out to having sentences of excommunication carried out against them. The church imposed varying degrees of excommunication. In June 1463, when Katherine Kyrton failed to appear in court on charges of refusing to cohabit with her husband, John Kyrton, the dean of Wisbech suspended her.[19] In May 1409, when Isabel Cras of Lechelade (*Glos.*) failed to answer a summons to appear in court for non-cohabitation, she was also suspended.[20] Suspension was a minor form of excommunication, requiring exclusion only from the Eucharist and the sacraments. Thus, it was an expulsion from the church but still permitted inclusion in the wider community. Suspension alone was not enough to intimidate all runaway wives into returning to their houses. For example, when Nan Hoper of London was suspended in 1493 for refusing to return to her husband, Thomas Polard, she publicly declared, "curse and bliss, I set not a straw by the cursing there."[21]

Probably because of this attitude, the church did not treat most cases with such lenience. Christine Verner, cited in 1388 by the bishop of Salisbury for not consorting with her husband, was just one of many women who experienced major excommunication for her contumacy.[22] Major excommunication required full social exclusion—Christians were bound to avoid any contact or interaction with an excommunicate. Excommunicates also existed outside secular law: they could not sue in civil litigation or accuse in criminal trials and thus suffered a serious legal disability. The church also well publicized an individual's excommunicate state. When the bishop of Hereford excommunicated Roger Wyche and Alice Maidestone for failing to appear in court to respond to an appeal of divorce brought by Alice Orchard, the bishop not only published this news in the cathedral and St. Peter's church but also sent word to the king.[23]

Because major excommunication was such a weighty penalty, the church courts imposed it only when it became clear that nothing else would convince the sinner to commence the penitential process. An entry from December 1311 concerning John de Warenne, earl of Surrey, in the bishop of Worcester's register emphasizes the church's graduated approach to excommunication:

> The said earl at the instigation of the devil has dismissed his lawful wife and is living in adultery with a certain Matilda, wife of Symon de Dryby, within our jurisdiction, and ministering to her the necessaries of life as if she were his lawful wife, whereby a grave scandal has arisen against him through the whole of England. We summoned him to appear before us, and waited several days beyond the term set, but he neither appeared nor sent any excuse. We then pronounced him contumacious and suspended him from entering church. Of the kindness of our court we appointed him a second term, and, when he did not come, we passed sentence of greater excommunication on him,

> yet we appointed a third term, and when, with growing contumacy, he contemptuously refused to appear, we decreed that the sentence of excommunication be proclaimed throughout our whole province on Sundays and Feast days at mass with bell sounded and candle lit, until he comes humbly seeking the commands of the church and ours. We inhibit everyone from communicating with the said lord, except in a case permitted by law; and the names of any who do communicate with him are to be diligently sought and they are to be warned to desist from his communion, and, if they do not, they are to be excommunicated by name.[24]

The bishop of Salisbury followed up on this process by citing those who "consorted" with the earl during his excommunication.[25] Not surprisingly, John Warenne did return to the church the following year; his absolution was as well publicized as his excommunication.[26] He also sued for a divorce five years later, although the church did not award it.[27]

As the mandate above suggests, excommunication was a temporary state until the sinner came to his or her senses and began the penitential process. Few Christians were willing to remain excommunicated for all that long. On June 27, 1326, Pleasaunce Ovenhille, wife of John de Davy of Aylesford (*Kent*), was sentenced to excommunication for refusing to return to her husband. She appeared in court thirty-two days later to purge herself for adultery with the local vicar, ready to reconcile with her husband.[28] In those cases where the excommunicate remained obstinate, after forty days, the church mobilized the secular arm of the law to arrest and imprison the excommunicate until he or she declared a willingness to submit to ecclesiastic jurisdiction. Cases of desertion show that the courts did not shy away from calling in the local bailiff to collect stubbornly excommunicate spouses. In March 1419, the archbishop of Canterbury requested assistance from the secular arm in the capture of Lady Margery of Longford (*Staffs.*), a woman of very comfortable means. The archbishop had excommunicated Margery for her continued refusal to obey orders for restitution of conjugal rights.[29] The bishop of Durham made a similar request in the year 1417 to the lord of the liberty of Tynedale for assistance in the arrest of Joan Buntyng, excommunicated for more than forty days for neglecting to adhere or cohabit with her husband, Alexander.[30] Mabel de Survedal appeared in the king's court to fight an order for her caption, claiming she was in the midst of a suit of divorce against her husband, Peter de Frothingham, and the church had permitted her the right to live separately during the proceedings.[31] Caption was not just for runaway wives: in 1413, the bishop of Salisbury requested that secular authorities arrest William Godfray of Potterne (*Wilts.*), who had been excommunicated for forty days in a matrimonial case with his wife, Agnes atte Nesshe of Potterne.[32] The church's willingness to impose the full weight of the law on these individuals demonstrates that it perceived desertion to be a grave matter and was determined to make an example of delinquent spouses. It also underscores the danger of deserting one's spouse: excommunication and imprisonment were serious penalties.

For most individuals, probably the greatest risk was a forced return to an unhappy marriage.[33] For those who did consent to return to their spouses, often they did so with a threat hanging over their heads of future penance should they fail to become model spouses. For example, in June 1412, Katherine, wife of John atte Mulle, who not only left her husband but also wasted his goods, swore to stay and look after him on pain of 100*s.* and six beatings through the marketplace.[34] In July 1347, Isabel, wife of Robert atte Kyrk, guilty of both desertion and adultery with the local chaplain, agreed to cohabit with her husband and "to treat him peacefully and quietly and to humbly obey him and not provoke his anger," on pain of six beatings around the marketplace of Grantham and six around the church of Skelinton, dressed only in a nightshirt.[35] When the church summoned Hamo Corbyl of Kent for adultery and spousal mistreatment, the couple were reconciled. For treating his wife poorly, Hamo submitted to seven floggings in the neighboring markets; for the adultery, he was flogged five times through Romney Market, five times through Hythe Market and six times around the parish church.[36] These were typical monitions, imposed for a variety of other penances, from fornication to adultery to a cleric's breaking his vow of celibacy.

For wayward wives who did not know their place, the church was attentive especially to the need to reinstate the marital hierarchy. The humble pledge of Isabel, wife of Robert atte Kyrk, to obey her husband was typical.[37] To offer a number of other examples: the bishop of Carlisle instructed Emma, wife of Nicholas Swayn, specifically to "obey her husband in conjugal duties" when they were reconciled in the fourteenth century.[38] Before he would allow the newly reunited couple to return home, the bishop of Lincoln also required Agnes Curteys of Est Deping to promise to obey her husband.[39] In a mandate to the dean of Worcester in 1275 regarding the complaint of Richard Caylott that his wife, Christiana atte Wode, was not obedient, the bishop of Worcester expresses clearly the church's position: "[T]here is a natural order of mankind that women should serve their husbands . . . [thus] the dean is ordered to warn the said Christiana, and induce her to be obedient to her husband in all lawful and honest matters, and treat him with wifely affection."[40] Even more remarkable is the story of Isabel, wife of Thomas Kyrkeham. When she failed in her suit for a separation on the grounds of cruelty, the judge forced her to seek her husband's pardon on bended knee.[41] With the very real threat of further penance hanging over her head if she failed in her wifely duty, a reunited wife must have been all too conscious of the simple fact that her recently estranged husband would be the final judge of whether she had fulfilled her promises.

The church courts' judgments were usually effective immediately, even though some of these separations had been lengthy. As an example, when

Joan, mistress of John Comyn, appeared before the court to hear accusations of adultery and husband abandonment, it had been six years since her desertion.[42] When the diocese of Lincoln cited Joanna Apulbe for failing to cohabit with her husband, they had not been living together for four years.[43] William and Batilda Baker had been separated for sixteen years when the bishop of Norwich ordered them to resume cohabitation in the year 1509.[44] After such a protracted interlude of estrangement, it might have been difficult for couples to get used to the idea of being reunited. Occasionally, the church showed some compassion by giving them time to prepare for the transition. For example, the court awarded Emma, wife of Nicholas Swayn, eight days with which to return to her marriage; Isabel Poterne had three weeks.[45] The more common sentiment, however, was as expressed to Margaret, wife of John Cutte of Drayton (*Bucks.*): resume her marriage "without delay."[46]

RISKS TO THOSE WHO ASSISTED DIVORCES

Some families may have shied away from assisting a wife in leaving her husband simply because of the risks involved. Because a husband was capable of suing for ravishment—that is, the taking of wife and goods—those who sheltered a wife were personally liable. The goal of a suit of ravishment was the return of the goods taken with the wife, not the wife herself. Because marriage is a sacrament, royal justices considered a husband and wife's relationship to be in the hands of the bishop. In cases of ravishment, the issue at stake was consent. Whether the wife consented (either before or after) to her abduction was not a vital concern. If the act was contrary to her husband's consent, however, he might sue the abduction as a case of trespassory ravishment.[47] Husbands frequently pleaded ravishment against men whose actions could hardly be seen as offensive. In a 1504 suit, a man interpreted ravishment as giving his wife a ride to Westminster so that she could sue a divorce.[48] Sometimes husbands construed ravishment as offering a runaway wife a place to stay. When Isabel, wife of Bartholomew Ware, discovered that she was more closely related to her recently espoused mate than she had believed, "in order to avoid the peril of sin in salvation of her soul and her Christianity," she sued for an annulment, which the church eventually granted. While the process was pending, the archdeacon of the monastery of Westminster decreed that Isabel should live outside the company of her husband until the case was fully resolved, so she divided her time between the homes of her adult son and daughter from a previous marriage. Both her son and her daughter's husband soon found themselves accused of ravishment.[49]

Ravishment suits pleaded at common law were a common tactic to discourage anyone from assisting a wife intent on gaining a divorce. What is impressive is the number of families and friends who defied the law to assist a woman in her desertion. There are abundant examples of fathers, uncles, sons and sons-in-law who stood accused of ravishment when helping wives leave their spouses.[50] When Isabel, wife of Robert Bull, "returned of her own free will" to her father's home after a short period of marriage in which her husband was caught "misbehaving with other women," her father presently found himself up on charges of ravishment as a trespass in the king's courts.[51] Beatrice, daughter of Sabina Herring, similarly endangered her family. Although she had been forced into marriage "against her will" by Henry le Welye while she was under-age, Henry still felt confident enough in his position to plead a suit of ravishment against Beatrice's mother and uncle for aiding in her escape.[52] Even servants were accountable, although one might think their bonds of obedience should excuse their actions. When Elizabeth Blount left her husband, Matthew de Clyveton, in 1359, he sued a writ of ravishment against the servant who helped her move her goods out of Matthew's home.[53]

Cases of ravishment also appeared in the manorial courts. For the abandoned husband, this was a far superior venue. The common law courts did "not provide quick, simple and accessible justice in minor local disputes"; the manorial courts did.[54] No costly writs were involved, and the litigants were not required to travel or pay the costs for their witnesses' journey. The manorial courts also did not require the involvement of significant sums of money, whereas those suits brought to the king's court usually did.[55] Thus, John Werkman of Earls Colne manor (*Essex*) was capable of winning his suit against John Crudde for entering his enclosure during Pentecost of 1402 and abducting only his wife—he did not also have to assert the theft of goods or chattels.[56] A jury of one's peers, equipped with a more intimate knowledge of the various personalities involved in the case, might have been more inclined to sympathy than a group of strangers. This may well explain why John Werkman won damages of 6*s.* 8*d.* A suit of abduction in the local court may also have functioned as a mechanism to apply pressure for return. For example, in 1307, the servant of Nicholas, parish chaplain of Wakefield, abducted Alice, wife of John Hyde, with the woman's consent. Her husband was concerned chiefly because she took with her 11*d.* from her husband's purse, three gold rings worth 18*d.*, a cup or mazer worth 12*d.*, a napkin worth 12*d.*, a towel worth 6*d.*, a gown worth 6*s.* 8*d.*, and a new hood worth 12*d.* The record tells us nothing about what happened to the chaplain's servant, but it notes that Alice returned to her husband.[57]

Manorial courts also offered the added perquisite that coverture need not apply. Although the common law courts insisted that suits of ravishment be sued against the "abductor" precisely because of the legal difficulties a husband encountered trying to sue his wife under the rules of coverture, in the manorial courts the wife might also find herself in trouble with the law, arrested for stealing from her husband. A tourn at the manor of Wakefield (*Yorks.*) in 1286 notes, "John son of Sybbe and Cicely wife of Adam the Miller, carried off the said Adam's goods in the night. They are to be arrested."[58] Emma, wife of Luke Grain d'Avoine of the Channel Islands, found herself in a similar situation in 1309: she was also indicted for taking away the goods of her husband against his will.[59]

Conviction in manorial courts generally resulted in a fine, usually the equivalent of the goods allegedly stolen from the husband in addition to damages; the common law courts took the same approach in trespassory ravishment. At times, the amounts awarded were substantial. For example, the court ordered Robert de Heydon, the former apprentice of Stephen de Upton, accused of ravishing Stephen's wife, to pay £60 for the goods and chattels he "maliciously carried away." After damages, his total bill came to £126 13*s.* 4*d.*[60] If he was not capable of paying this bill, he risked being imprisoned coercively until he was able to do so.

Although this process was certainly embarrassing, financially taxing and frustrating to those women and their families who, no doubt, saw those "stolen goods" as rightfully belonging to the wives, trespasses of ravishment generally inflicted no additional damages. A conviction in either court also resulted in no physical penalties. Much more dangerous were those cases where husbands instead chose to plead their wives' "abductions" as a felony of rape with the much greater penalty of death. Felonious suits of ravishment in the king's courts fell into the same category as cases of rape and, in fact, were often indistinguishable from them. As Emma Hawkes notes, "medieval legal records generally blurred the two crimes together."[61] Because the term "rape" was so ill defined in the medieval period, jurors had to be careful in the wording of indictments to distinguish between cases of rape in which sexual assault seemed to have been the primary offence and cases of ravishment, or abduction, where the wife was often a willing participant.[62] The statute of Westminster II (1285) attempts to standardize the vocabulary of ravishment by combining the term "rape" with a qualifying term, such as "abduct" (*rapuit et abduxit*). For a sexual assault, a jury would employ the verb "rape" (*rapuit*) on its own. Although many modern historians have been "repelled by the ambiguities and vagueness of the statutes and by the inconsistencies in the prosecution of these laws," medieval juries were diligent enough in the use of conjunctive vocabulary that many cases of ravishment can be found among the felony suits of the records of the king's courts.[63] For example, when Roger de Harleston, archdeacon of Cambridge, and Henry de Bongheye came to Walden Abbey in June 1349, the records note they feloniously raped and abducted (*felonice rapuerunt et abduxerunt*) Katherine, wife of Hugh Veysee, and feloniously carried away goods of the said Hugh to the value of £40.[64] Some juries went to extremes in their wish to clarify the nature of the offence. For example, when Thomas Walsshman, a tailor, entered the home of Stephen Irish, he is said to have taken and abducted and raped (*cepit et abduxit et rapuit*) both Stephen's wife, Alice, and his goods to a value of £40. To underscore the ravishment even further, Thomas is said to have taken both Stephen's wife and the goods far from Coventry (*ac de villa Couentre longe duxit*).[65]

At other times, the record omits the term "rape" altogether, most likely because juries knew how confusing it could be. When William Beverel, chaplain, entered the close of Matthew Gardrobier in the vill of Plessis (*Essex*) and abducted the Matthew's wife as well as goods worth 10*s*., he was said to have taken and abducted her against the peace (*contra pacem cepit et abduxit*).[66] When Matthew Pye de Crauncewyk came to the home of John Fissher at Watton (*Yorks.*), the scribe reported that he had merely "led away" (*minavit*) John's wife.[67]

The use of these qualifying terms ensured that trial juries knew exactly what had happened, and thus it should come as no surprise that they were unwilling to convict any of the "rapists" in situations where the crime was clearly a case of ravishment. Quite simply, death did not seem a fitting punishment for a man whose guilt lay in helping or seducing a consenting woman. Even without the death penalty looming over a man's head, the impact on the accused would have been substantial. Damage to one's reputation from the indictment was sufficiently injurious. Add to that the arrest, imprisonment while awaiting trial for probably a year or more, which meant living in unpleasant conditions and not being there to help family members support themselves, as well as paying the travel costs of any necessary witnesses. With such high stakes, it is remarkable that anyone was willing to assist those unhappy wives and thereby risk being labeled a "rapist." To add insult to injury, after dealing with the kerfuffle of the royal courts, the well-meaning rescuer of an unhappy wife might also find himself in trouble with the church. For example, the register of the Palatinate of Durham from the year 1339 includes a case of wife robbery. In response to Richard de Hyd's complaint that William, then of Gourtone, had robbed him of his wife of thirteen years, the bishop issued a mandate to the official of Alverton demanding that justice be attained for Richard.[68] This was not the only case of spousal abduction to appear in the ecclesiastical courts.[69] England's multiple and often complementary judicial systems were usually an asset to Englishmen and -women hoping to find justice. As Frederik Pedersen has argued, "[w]ith such a plethora of legal systems it should not be surprising that medieval people used the courts with a considerable amount of cunning."[70] For runaway wives, however, multiple courts merely provided multiple means of penalizing those who had assisted her in her desertion.

When individuals sheltered wives from abusive husbands, the risk was infinitely greater. A bill of complaint written to chancery by Isabel, widow of Richard Vergeons, at the end of the fifteenth century illustrates how a wife's rescuer seriously endangered himself and his household in the process. Six months before the writing of the petition, the wife of Thomas Hyll, the wiremonger of London, approached the petitioner's husband to beg for "succor and safeguard of her life." She was driven to this request only after "diverse variances and discords between her and the said Thomas her husband and for great fear and jeopardy that the said Thomas put to her of her life." When Richard happened upon her, Thomas was chasing her, wielding a dagger. Seeing "the ungodly and hasty disposition of the said Thomas and the great fear of his said wife," Richard decided to take matters into his own hands. He received Thomas's wife into his home and then confronted Thomas about his actions, hoping to reason with him and convince him to treat his wife appropriately. This soon proved to be a fatal error. According to the plaintiff:

> Richard entreated and desired the said Thomas to take his said wife to him again and to guide her and chastise her under a due manner and not to draw his dagger to her and the said Thomas answered if he might meet with his said wife he would utterly slay her; and the said Richard, seeing his ungodly disposition, kept her in his house till anon. After, by the false and mischievous labor and procurement of the said Thomas, the said Richard, then husband unto your said oratrice, was slain at his own door in London.

Richard's death only strengthened Isabel's conviction to shelter Thomas's wife from her brutish husband. Isabel locked her home and refused to allow Thomas near his wife, but he was not so easily dissuaded. Thomas made repeated threats on Isabel's life and then quite shrewdly turned to the courts to continue his assault. He sued a plea of trespass against Isabel and arranged with the sheriff of London to hold an inquest into the action. Fearing imprisonment or worse, the newly widowed Isabel threw herself on the mercy of the chancellor.[71]

Because no sentence survives for this case, we have no idea of how it resolved. Yet a degree of fiction is apparent in the case of Isabel Vergeons and Thomas Hyll. If witnesses could prove that Thomas Hyll had assaulted and slain Richard Vergeons, or even that he was likely to have done so, a coroner almost certainly would have ordered his arrest, making Hyll unable to sue a case of trespass against his victim's wife. That he was not arrested diminishes the reliability of Isabel's story. It is possible that Richard's death was an unwitnessed assault that Isabel believed related to the hostility between Thomas and her husband, yet she had no proof of his involvement. The fact that she was merely requesting a grant of *certiorari* to have her case heard before chancery rather than the local sheriff also reveals that her evidence of Thomas's villainous actions was weak and unconvincing. If the petitioner's story is to be believed, then, Thomas's suit in court against her was possibly an attempt to silence his victim's wife before she had the opportunity to finger him. Although it is clear there is more to this story than meets the eye, it is also unlikely that her story represents pure invention. A cursory investigation of coroners' rolls for the city of London by the court's officials would easily uncover the known facts concerning her husband's death. Isabel's narrative, then, would have to conform to this report in order to remain within the realm of credibility.

This particular petition offers abundant insight into the inherent tensions in medieval society that led to marital breakdown and the danger it presented to those who assisted runaway wives. The very language of Isabel's petition points to a tenuous balance between discipline and abuse in marriage, while simultaneously illuminating contemporary expectations of gendered behavior. When Thomas pursued his wife through the streets of London with a dagger in hand, Richard willingly stepped in to put an end to this "ungodly" behavior. His request that Thomas take his wife home and "guide her and chastise her under a due manner" invites a number of interesting conclusions. First, Richard explicitly acknowledged Thomas's right to correct his wife, if only in the name of chastisement, but that right had identifiable limits that did not include attempted homicide. Second, Isabel, as a woman in a similar position, also recognized Thomas's claim to use physical force with his wife. In fact, she appears to have agreed wholeheartedly with her husband's request that Thomas curb the degree of force rather than eliminate it altogether. This suggests that, at least when they were trying to get a trespass case removed to chancery, "chastisement" as a form of physical discipline for one's wife was socially approved and internalized by both genders in the medieval community.

Unfortunately, Isabel's husband was not the only Good Samaritan who lost his life trying to protect a wife from her husband. When Margery, wife of Walter Rake of Wislingham, fled to the home of her husband's sister, Alice Sely, during an altercation with her husband, Walter stabbed his sister accidentally while trying to kill his wife.[72] A similar situation happened in the death of Peter Peyteun. Richard le Marchant of East Merton was beating his wife, Clarice, when Clarice's brother Peter happened to appear at their home. Angered at what had happened to his sister, he entered Richard's home. Richard claimed that Peter was trying to kill him, and, out of self-defense, he stabbed him. Richard fled, and the court eventually outlawed him.[73] The list goes on: John Smalrod wanted to beat his wife, but his father's wife, Joanna intervened to stop him. She was hit with an arrow and died; John fled to a church and abjured the realm.[74]

ESCALATION OF VIOLENCE

In response to a "public outcry," the bishop of Salisbury in 1392 demanded an investigation into the marriage of Nicholas Portlond, mason of Salisbury, and his wife, Lucy. The story, as it was recounted to the bishop, noted that the two had been married for twenty years, during which time they produced more than twelve children. After all that time, Nicholas repudiated Lucy and engaged in an adulterous affair with Margaret, daughter of John Kentbury, producing an illegitimate child. When Lucy "grumbled a little as far as she dared," Nicholas reacted by imprisoning Lucy "for a long time in iron fetters within a narrow room, without [sufficient] food and other necessities." Outraged, the bishop appointed the chaplains of St. Martin's Salisbury to look into the matter of Nicholas's incorrigibility immediately.[75]

Lucy Portlond's fate is emblematic of abusive wives who preferred to stay in their marriages rather than risk escalating the violence. Surely, Lucy did not sue for divorce because she feared her husband's reaction; the outcome, however, establishes that she would have been wise to approach authorities sooner. Nonetheless, the surviving documentation echoes Lucy's initial instinct: not only did the degree of violence intensify after a spouse left the home environment, it also evolved and mutated, sometimes taking on new forms entirely. What is most striking, though, is the confidence and agency of wives newly separated from their husbands. Under the direction and even assistance of those wives, the same families and friends who participated in removing wives from their homes sometimes also helped stalk, terrorize and even assault abandoned husbands. Agnes, wife of John atte Pole, and her lover, Stephen Sutor, teamed up to attack and beat John, in due course leading to the arrest of both Agnes and Stephen.[76] Joan Lylle and her "adherents" had her husband "fearing daily to be in jeopardy of his life" and ultimately drove him to the chancellor, begging for their arrest.[77] Some wives went to extremes in the harassment of the husbands they abandoned. In the late-fifteenth-century case of John Haket, a long time before his petition came before the court of Chancery, Nicholas Montgomery of Wiltshire had abducted Haket's wife, Alice. Consensual abduction, however, was only the first step in his wife's decision to take control of the situation. According to Haket, since the abduction:

> Nicholas and Alice have procured strange persons to lie in wait for the said supplicant and to slay him for the which cause he has purchased a writ of menace against him and now it is so full gracious lord that the said Nicholas has waged four unknown persons nonsufficient which are of him for a noble in deceit of our sovereign liege lord the king and his court to become mainpernours for the said Nicholas and Alice in the said court wherefore liketh to your gracious lordship to charge the court that if any such mainpernours come into the said court to undertake for the said Nicholas and Alice that are sufficient more be known and if they be found deceivable in that party that they may be punished after your wise discretion and example of other for God's love and in work of charity.[78]

Attempted homicide and legal harassment were crimes not easily prosecuted in the medieval courts of common law; and so, the English court of Chancery was indeed the appropriate forum for the resolution of Haket's problems. In the absence of any further details, it is difficult to surmise the exact circumstances of the abduction. A possible scenario is that an unhappy relationship ended because of Alice's adulterous affair with

Nicholas Montgomery. Only after she had achieved distance from her husband and had secured Nicholas's support did she decide to strike back.

The courts themselves provided jilted spouses with considerably powerful weapons to harass their absent spouses. Suits of trespassory ravishment against family members or friends were just one example of the ways the courts functioned in matrimonial battles. The early-fourteenth-century divorce of Lucy Twenge and William le Latimer reveals one of the most profligate examples of a war manned by sheriffs and lawyers. On the surface, the match of these two high-powered individuals seemed to have been a good one. Lucy was the heiress to the Brus of Skelton family estates and a royal ward; William was the son of a knight to the royal household, who had also accompanied King Edward I on crusade. Like his father, William also became a knight of the royal household and spent much of his career in Scotland fighting on behalf of the king. The marriage took place in the year 1294, when Lucy was only fifteen years old. The early years of their marriage were beleaguered with doubts relating to the paternity of her son, born just four months after the wedding. Although the courts ultimately deemed him legitimate, this rocky start did not bode well for the marriage. In 1303, while William was off campaigning in Scotland with the king, Lucy moved out of the couple's home.[79] The king's letter to the sheriff of York makes it clear that William had used all his resources to convince the king to assist him in finding his missing wife. The letter ordered the sheriff

> to enquire by all means that he shall see fit where Lucy, wife of William le Latimer, the younger, may be found in his bailiwick, and to cause her to be arrested and taken back, by force if necessary, to William's manor of Brunne, in that county, and to cause her to be delivered to William's attorney or attorneys, to dwell there under safe and suitable custody, as the king learns from William that certain evilly disposed persons have taken Lucy from the said manor, where he had left her to stay during his absence in Scotland in the king's service, by force and arms against his will, with certain of his goods found there, and that they detain her.[80]

It is hard to imagine that force and arms were necessary for this abduction. Lucy's departure was contrary to William's will; Lucy, though, had been very willing indeed. Nonetheless, William sued a writ of ravishment against Robert Conestable and his wife for abducting Lucy and his goods. The Year Books report that Robert literally threw down his gauntlet, demanding a wager of battle; although William wanted to respond to his challenge, justices decided it was unnecessary. The writ had named Robert's wife also as defendant; this was problematic because of the sexual connotations of ravishment. A woman could not ravish another woman. This technicality was sufficient to quash the case.[81]

In the meantime, Lucy took her first venture into the curial arena, suing a divorce on the grounds of consanguinity before the dean and chapter of York. Hindered by the sheriff's mandate to arrest her and those helping her, Lucy directly petitioned the king in June 1305 to request that he rescind that order, so that she might plead her suit in the court Christian.[82] The archbishop of York sent a letter in support of Lucy's request, detailing how the king's command was not only delaying her suit but also jeopardizing her soul.[83] The king complied. Pending the decision, the court permitted Lucy to live apart from William at William's expense.

Rather than return to her husband, Lucy pursued an adulterous affair with Nicholas de Meynell of Whorlton, a knight and distant relation.[84] In 1306, William charged Nicholas with procuring men to slay him. As he told the story, he was on his way to consult with Lucy in the hopes of convincing her to reconcile, when three men hired by Nicholas lay in wait to kill him. William just barely escaped with his life. Officials arrested the three hired men; they immediately confessed to their part in the attack. Under cross-examination, however, the whole case fell apart when the ringleader, Robert de Bordesden, admitted that William had hired him for 50 marks and a promise of impunity to say that Nicholas had paid him to kill William.[85] Bordesden's petition to the king and council for satisfaction makes it clear that he was not a compliant participant. In it, he recounts how Thomas de Boulton "came in deceit and collusion by the procurement of William le Latimer and ordered him to bring Bordesden from his house to speak with Latimer at his manor in Scampston, where Boulton" and others, "by force and arms, took Bordesden and beat and badly treated him against the peace and imprisoned him, and brought him before the justices at York."[86] Only at that point was Bordesden willing to lie for William, and he was most likely quite glad to have the opportunity to rat him out. How the king appeased Bordesden is not clear, but William seems to have suffered no harm from his participation in this enterprise.

In the hopes of defeating Lucy's suit for a divorce, William went over the heads of the York officials, sending an appeal to Rome. His excommunication in 1305, however, undermined his influence in the church. The excommunication was at Lucy's request, after repeated failures to receive alimony from William.[87] Presumably, in response to his newly excommunicate state, William informed the court about Lucy and Nicholas's affair. By 1307, the archbishop of York tasked the dean of Cleveland with investigating the allegations. Lucy took her time responding to the court summons.[88] In 1309, Lucy finally appeared to purge herself of adultery and incest with Nicholas.[89] She was ordered to "take up her abode in Watton priory," where she was to undergo penance for her adultery; oddly enough, Lucy could not be found when it was time to begin her penance.[90] William was also responsible for informing the king about Lucy's adultery. Because Lucy had been a royal ward, in 1305 the king's escheator confiscated part of her inheritance—namely, the manors of Yarm, Brunne, Skirmingrove and Brotton (all in *N. Yorks.*); the church fined Nicholas 40*s.* for his involvement.[91] In January 1310, the relationship between Lucy and Nicholas that had produced at least one child (also named Nicholas) concluded. To purge their sins, they each paid £40 towards the fabric of York Minster; the court fined Nicholas an additional £10 for the dominant role he played in the affair.[92] Her divorce must have come through soon after; by 1312, she had moved on to her next husband, Robert de Everingham. The lengthy and sometimes sordid experience of the divorce between Lucy and William established that William le Latimer was a mastermind of legal strategy, with a hand in every court. Although he did not succeed in holding onto Lucy (although it is still unclear why he would have wanted to do so), he did get to keep much of her land. In 1311, the king confiscated Danby-in-Cleveland (*N. Yorks.*) and Bozeat (*Northants.*), regranting them solely to William; in 1312, Lucy granted William the manor of Sinnington (*N. Yorks.*).[93]

Lucy Twenge was no match for her husband's legal strategizing; but this was merely her first marriage. The enduring court battle between an experienced matron, Margery of Longford, daughter of the knight Alfred Sulney, and her husband, Richard of Clitheroe, esquire, emphasizes the difference that age and experience could make in winning a war waged primarily in the courts. Before wedding Richard, Margery had been married twice before, first to Lord Nicholas Longford; the two were married for twenty-eight years before he died. This solid union produced five sons and two daughters. [94] Her second union was not as fruitful: she married Robert Legh of Cheshire, who died merely seven years after Nicholas' passing. By the time she married Richard of Clitheroe in 1410, she was skilled in both marriage and marriage negotiations; she was also appreciably wealthy in terms of her dower lands and as co-heiress to her brother's estates;[95] and she had adult sons whom she freely called upon for assistance. The documentation portrays Margery as having been a confident, self-possessed woman, unwilling to tolerate much nonsense. When exactly she deserted Richard is not entirely clear, but a failure to obey the archbishop of Canterbury's orders to return to her husband in a suit for restitution of conjugal rights led to her excommunication in March 1419. After letting Margery spend forty days as an excommunicate, the archbishop mobilized the secular arm to arrest her.[96] Presumably, she returned to live with Richard for some time after this experience, but by 1425, she had abandoned him once more. Given his earlier success, Richard turned again to the courts in an attempt to retrieve the goods Margery took with her, although this time, he was less concerned with recovering Margery also. He appealed first to the church courts, complaining to the bishop of Durham about the theft of precious articles stolen from his home; the bishop issued a monition against those who participated in the theft, warning them on pain of excommunication to appear before the court.[97] When the bishop's monition failed, Richard petitioned the chancellor, claiming that Margery had been carried off against his will. He contended that four men and one woman, armed and arrayed as if for war, arrived at his home over the feast of Corpus Christi, attacking Richard and his servants and destroying much of his home, in order to abduct Margery and Richard's goods. The instigator behind the abduction was Ralph Longford, one of Margery's five sons.[98] Margery herself materialized in chancery soon after, with the purpose of enlisting the chancellor in making suitable arrangements for a divorce. She explained that she had left Richard and was pursuing a judicial separation in the church courts on the grounds of cruelty, because "she was sore afraid of her said husband." The degree of violence she reported, however, was a far cry from the severity necessary to attain a divorce. Although she alluded to "great variance and debate" between them, the violence she described was not physical so much as proprietary. Richard had alienated some of her dower lands without her consent, and she wanted them back. After complaining to Sir Henry Pierrepoint, father-in-law to her son Nicholas,[99] on his counsel and that of Robert the Prior of Calwick (*Staffs.*) and others, Margery left her husband. Her petition clarifies that she believed a divorce should also sever her husband's governance over her property; she requests that the chancellor approve her plan to retrieve her property, leaving Richard with a yearly maintenance of £40. Margery's petition concludes with an oath that her "tale is true" and is accompanied by the depositions of Henry of the Both and Robert the prior of Calwick.[100]

What happened to Richard and Margery? Did the church award them a divorce? Did the chancellor and Richard find this compromise acceptable? Because the legal trail ends here, we have no way of knowing what happened next. For someone of Richard's standing, though, £40 a year was a pittance that he may well have considered an insult. An order from the parliamentary rolls for November 1407 records a grant of £2,668 by the treasurer to "Richard Cliderhowe, former admiral of the seas towards the west and the south," due him for the time he was admiral. The king did not intend the sum for Richard's profit alone; the king expected him also to pay the men in his retinue for their expeditions.[101] Assuming that this was the same Richard, he probably would not have been content with a mere £40 a year. What we do know is that, in the end, Margery got what she wanted: Richard's will reveals that he died six years later. Margery acted as Richard's executor and throughout is referred to as his widow.[102]

Heiresses and widows, like Lucy Twenge and Margery of Longford, were prime targets for marriage proposals motivated entirely out of a desire to merge estates. The lengths to which their estranged husbands went to control their property even after their marriages were essentially over mirror the size of their inheritances. Lucy and Margery were fortunate to have the support of family and friends in defending the aggressive maneuvers of their husbands both in and outside the courts. Not all women were that lucky. When Mary, daughter of Thomas Felton, married Geoffrey de Worsley (or Workesley) in 1376, like Margery and Lucy, she was also an heiress; her father's marriage had produced three daughters, all of whom would eventually share in his estate. According to Mary, after the death of her father in 1381, Geoffrey won an annulment from the church; Mary became a recluse in the Abbey of St. Clare without Aldgate (London), and Geoffrey remarried.[103] Geoffrey's second marriage to Isabel, daughter and heiress to Sir Thomas de Lathom, did not last long; shortly after his daughter Elizabeth's first birthday, he died. A 1385 royal order to the king's sergeant-at-arms to arrest Mary de Felton, "an apostate minoress," and deliver her to the abbess for punishment reveals Mary's forceful reaction to Geoffrey's death.[104] Freed from intimidation, she blamed Geoffrey for compelling her into religious orders, established the validity of her marriage to Geoffrey and blocked his infant daughter from her inheritance. She also remarried; her husband, John de Curson, was instrumental in preventing Elizabeth's guardian from laying claim to her inheritance.[105]

If we take Mary's story at face value, it confirms that marital abuse was multi-faceted and might even involve compelling a wife into religious orders to keep her quiet. Mary's return to the world after Geoffrey's death to reclaim her status as wife (or widow), and thus entitled to a third of Geoffrey's lands, seems positively triumphant. However, Geoffrey's 1381 petition to the king undermines somewhat Mary's version of events. In this letter, he states that the Spanish had only recently released him after his imprisonment while fighting for the king abroad. During his incarceration, his servant, Thomas Pulle, who was assigned to attend upon his wife while Geoffrey was away, had been "false and traitorous to his master and dishonored his wife in his absence." Even worse, he had "roused the wife to falsely make a divorce, by which falseness and treason Geoffrey had lost his advancement, marriage and a great heritage." Geoffrey and Thomas had met at a council at Reading, and a dispute "[had] erupted between them in which Thomas was wounded." Since that time, Thomas and Mary had wedded, but Thomas had died, and "his friends wish to impeach Geoffrey that he died from the said injury."[106]

Did Geoffrey fabricate his story? It is hard to imagine. The truth certainly lies somewhere between these two accounts. Nonetheless, Geoffrey's letter is telling; he makes it clear that his marriage to Mary was predicated entirely on "his advancement." Moreover, Thomas Pulle's death after an altercation with Geoffrey certainly implies that Geoffrey was prone to violence and thus was probably intimidating, as Mary claimed. Did he force her into religious orders? Did she enter into religious orders herself rashly after Thomas's death? Although we will never know exactly how the events unfolded, Mary's example uncovers the key to success in matrimonial war. The medieval English were not fools: they knew well that marriage was a political game in which women (especially heiresses and widows) were pawns, manipulated for the social and financial standing of both individuals and their families. They knew that women were the victims in all of this. Mary's tale of woe played aptly upon those expectations. Regardless of whether she really was the victim, she played the role expertly, obtaining a release from her vows, negotiating her own second marriage and taking revenge upon her first husband. Mary Felton made it clear that even pawns might aspire to be queens.

Making the decision to leave one's husband was not easy in the medieval context. Wives had much to fear: from excommunication to imprisonment to forced reunion. Because those who assisted a deserter risked imprisonment, penance, weighty fines and death (although the latter seems to have been in theory rather than in practice), many families and friends must have been dogged in their determination to keep married couples together, if only to save their own purses and reputations (and sometimes even their lives!). A wife eager to abandon her husband had good reason to believe she might have difficulty in finding supporters among her family and friends. Yet even when facing formidable adversaries, women like Mary Felton, Margery of Longford and Lucy Twenge did choose to lead separate lives, and some of their families and friends supported them. In light of the resolve of these bold women who surmounted huge obstacles to separate from their husbands, the traditional ideal of the passive and compliant medieval wife falls flat.

4 Whose Property Is Whose?

Historians have identified the 1581 case of Mary Walgrave *c.* Arthur Goldinge as a turning point in the law of marital property. When Mary wedded Arthur, she was a wealthy heiress in her own right. Her marriage to Arthur was not a happy one, however. His abusive behavior towards his wife soon led to a judicial separation, and Mary abruptly found herself in need of financial support. Thus, she turned to the court of Chancery, petitioning to have the property she brought into the marriage revert back to her name now that she was required to maintain herself. Her request found sympathy with the chancellor. Although coverture prevented him from choosing this precise course of action, her appeal to justice may well have influenced the tenor of chancery's decision. The court ordered that all the lands from her inheritance be sold and that the proceeds be put into a trust for Walgrave in order to guarantee her separate maintenance, setting a guiding precedent for future wives in need of support.[1]

The decision of the Elizabethan chancery to allow a divorced wife some control over the property she brought into the marriage was a vast departure from earlier practice. Before the success of this case, there existed no clear-cut method of determining how to divide property in the event of a divorce. One would think that the courts would define their approach by the nature of the divorce: in the case of an annulment, because the marriage had never been valid, a wife should leave the marriage with everything she brought to it; in the case of a judicial separation, because the court still deemed the couple married, a husband's responsibility to provide his wife with the necessities of life afforded by his means seemingly should continue, regardless of whether he was living with her. Nevertheless, no guidelines existed to clarify this process, and in practice, alimony and property settlements varied tremendously in both kinds of divorce.

This chapter seeks to understand how issues of marital property were resolved during instances of marital dissolution, beginning first with the dicier situation of separated wives. Was alimony guaranteed both during the legal process and after the award of a separation? How did alimony payments work? Was there a guiding ideology employed in determining the proper amount to be paid as maintenance? In the case of an annulment, did the courts enforce the return of a wife's property? And, finally, what happened to the wedding gifts?

A SEPARATED WIFE'S RIGHT TO SUPPORT

The question of a separated wife's entitlement to support is an important one for a number of reasons. First, the rules of coverture greatly undermined a woman's economic independence. Not only did coverture prevent a wife during the time of her marriage from controlling all real and moveable property (including chattels real) as well as the profits accruing from them, she was also prevented from drawing up contracts, taking a loan or suing a civil plaint in the king's courts in the absence of her husband.[2] Because of the economic limitations imposed on wives during marriage, without an enforceable maintenance agreement, separation was simply not a practical alternative for medieval wives who might otherwise have remained in abusive relationships. For many hapless wives, life with violent husbands was preferable to trying to scrape by on their own as single women in a breadwinner economy. Second, informally divorced wives also needed support that was enforceable without requiring the intervention of the church courts. If a husband wished to continue in his divorce, it was in his best interests to support his former wife and make sure that she did not feel the need to inform the courts of their living situation.

Secular law addressed two distinct scenarios concerning the support of separated wives, both of which strongly implied that the separation must be amiable and that the wife must conduct herself honorably in order to lay claim to maintenance. In discussing a husband's responsibilities for his wife's debts, a Norwich custumal of *c.*1340 speaks to the situation of couples who lived separately. The custumal notes that a husband was accountable for his separated wife's debts, providing "the wife of the said man is cohabiting with her husband at the time when the debt was made, *or living separate by his assent and good-will*" and "she does not . . . wrongfully separate herself from her husband by her own wilfulness, and that she does not separate herself to make mischief."[3] The wife's good conduct seemingly was also a key issue in the second aspect of a separated wife's maintenance addressed by secular law: the right of a separated wife to claim dower. In this respect, the legal treatises are particularly insightful, although they do not present a coherent perspective. *Glanvill* (*c.* 1187–89) boldly states, "if a man's wife is separated from him during his lifetime because of some shameful act, she cannot have any claim to dower."[4] The original *Glanvill* does not elaborate on the meaning of "shameful act," but the revised edition, written in the year 1261, glosses *turpitudo* as fornication or blasphemy.[5] *Bracton*, which distinguishes much more carefully between annulments and judicial separations, makes it clear that an annulment extinguishes a wife's right to dower, but a separation from bed and board does not.[6] The treatise does not focus on a wife's shameful acts, however. *Britton* is much less ambiguous. If the marriage ceased to be a reality—that is, if the couple no longer shared a bed—then a widow's "action to demand dower is extinguished."[7]

Glanvill and *Britton* cast a shadow of doubt on the feasibility of a separated wife's claim to dower. *Britton*, especially, seems to suggest that a wife's place was in her husband's bed; if she forfeited this role, the court would deprive her of the benefits attached to being a wife. Both Joseph Biancalana's and Paul Brand's research into actual cases of refuted dower claims in the medieval English courts confirm that common law justices believed a wife "earned" the right to dower through copulation.[8] Biancalana notes that being old enough to bear children was a "minimum requirement" to claim dower, because dower "was characterized as compensation for the pains and burdens of motherhood."[9] More recently, Brand has established that an ability to "earn" dower through sexual intercourse was a condition of common law practice from roughly the middle of the thirteenth century onwards. During this phase, "there was a significant shift away from seeing dower as an automatic entitlement arising out of any valid marriage to seeing it instead as a 'reward' for service rendered by the wife during the marriage."[10] Certainly, conclusions drawn about a woman's rights to dower should not be over-generalized; however, it is only a small leap in logic to assume that a separated wife may have been equated with an under-aged one where finances were concerned: neither one of them "earned" the right to support.

Both versions of *Glanvill* intimate that a woman's dishonest behavior during a separation quashed any right she once had to claim dower. Statute law reflects this moralizing attitude. According to the second Statute of Westminster (1285), an adulteress was ineligible to claim dower rights after the death of her husband unless he had forgiven her and the two were reconciled at the time of his death.[11] Almost a century later, Richard II's lawmakers reaffirmed these sentiments. A statute of 1382 remarks that if a wife was raped and consented afterwards, she was prohibited from all rights to dower or jointure after the death of her husband.[12] It is hard to know whether, in practice, royal justices endorsed this perspective. Certainly, some rivals for dower lands manipulated this plea to their benefit, making allegations of adultery against some widows.[13] A 1369 dispute over dower in Common Bench reveals the case of a woman whose right to dower was challenged because she was living with her lover, unreconciled to her husband up until the point of his death. She responded that the man described as her lover had actually abducted her from her home against her will, stabbing her husband in the process; her husband died four days later because of the assault, while she was still imprisoned (thus, technically "unreconciled"). The court was sympathetic: it granted her rights to dower, but the challenge itself suggests that a shrewd litigant might have exploited this technicality to the detriment of women.[14]

A dialogue recorded between justices and pleaders in the Year Books suggests that justices were less concerned about a wife's behavior than her marital status. Discussing a writ of dower brought by Joan, formerly the wife of Walter Curtes, before justices of Common Bench in 1336, one justice astutely noted, "[i]n some cases divorce revoked matrimony, and in some cases not." Although an annulment voided a wife's right to dower, in a judicial separation, "matrimony was not revoked, and consequently the wife not ousted of dower."[15] A writ of novel disseisin sued in 1325 before justices of King's Bench also made this point. Hoping to appropriate their nephews' inheritance, John le Joeven and his brother Richard claimed their other brother's tenements and lands upon his death, noting that he had long before divorced their nephews' mother. In this instance, the nephews themselves knew their rights, asserting "that the wife in this case would have dower and the sons heritage because this was not a case of consanguinity" but merely a divorce from bed and board. The judges agreed.[16]

Once again, statements about dower are not a reliable indicator of a separated wife's right to support while her husband was still alive; yet, it is conceivable that a separated wife who brought shame or dishonor on her husband might have received comparable treatment. Collectively, the sources point to the likelihood that a wife's support was of necessity not a right but an ethical decision influenced by the particular circumstances of a case.[17]

ALIMONY IN THE CHURCH COURTS

Canon lawyers also failed to adopt a unified position on the necessity of supporting separated wives. By the early fourteenth century, some canonical writers, such as Giovanni d'Andrea in his *Additio* to William Durand's *Speculum iudiciale*, argued that separated wives were at liberty to demand support payments from abusive husbands.[18] Nonetheless, a discussion of the nature of support or division of marital property is absent from the writings of d'Andrea and his fellow canon lawyers. Despite this muddled canonical perspective, in practice the English church courts recognized the vulnerability of wives in financial terms and were determined to do something about it. For example, the fifteenth-century deanery of Wisbech held Robert Grey responsible when he neglected his wife "so that she has become a beggar." [19] Court officials took it upon themselves to charge husbands with the maintenance of their separated wives and even enforced payment. Financial support existed in two distinct forms. Alimony *pendente lite* (pending litigation) was only a temporary form of support. In this circumstance, the court separated husband and wife provisionally while officials investigated allegations of cruelty or other claims of marital misconduct that might endanger the safety of either spouse. During this period, it was usual for the wife to be sequestered in the home of a relative or friend approved by the court; sometimes, but certainly not always or even frequently, husbands were expected to foot the bill.[20]

Alimony also assumed a more permanent form. At times, court officials required husbands to provide their separated wives with financial assistance for the duration of their lives. Only occasionally do the rulings in cases of judicial separation include particulars about maintenance agreements, such as the amounts to be paid or the payment schedules. Because most records focused on alimony are requests by the separated wife for the enforcement of a support agreement (rather than the actual contract that created the agreement), it may not have seemed necessary to include these ostensibly insignificant details. For example, a letter to the official of the bishop of London in October 1365 describes a dispute between Adam de Brabazon and his wife, Margery, over maintenance. The letter describes Margery as being deprived of her alimony and necessary expenses by her husband but adds that "mutual friends" settled the issue in the presence of the bishop. Both spouses agreed to the arrangement, but the bishop had reason to believe that Adam's obduracy might prevent him from carrying through his end of the deal. Thus, the bishop cited Adam to appear in the church of Farnham the following month, apparently to verify that he was indeed making payments to his wife.[21] Such a record provides invaluable evidence into the settlement of alimony disputes and the role played by the church in the enforcement of these payments. This case highlights not only the resolve and good judgment of the bishop but also the participation of friends and neighbors in the settlement of marital disputes. Regrettably, it offers no clues about the nature of the settlement; in particular, the record neglects to describe how much the bishop expected Adam to pay his wife and the regularity of the disbursement.[22]

Where cases do discuss the finer points of support agreements, a yearly payment of a fixed sum of money seems to have been an easy and popular route. Most likely, Englishmen and -women were accustomed to the practice through the support of widows.[23] Church officials settled alimony on an individual basis, reflecting the husband's socio-economic status. As a result, annuities varied greatly in amount. At the upper ranks, the amounts were substantial. John de Warrene, earl of Surrey, entered into a recognizance to pay his wife, Joan, £200 per year in sustenance until their divorce came through, with the additional stipulation that when the divorce was official, he would also deliver to her land worth 740 marks yearly.[24] In a deed enrolled before the king's courts, Sir Thomas de Burgo vowed to pay his wife £20 yearly for the term of her life.[25] When Richard Mervyn and Joan Dencourt separated in 1394, Richard agreed to pay Joan the sum of 5 marks sterling each year until the end of her life; but when Robert Tebold and Maud Copiltyk separated in 1422, Robert was required to pay only 6*s.* 8*d.* yearly for maintenance.[26] When the church awarded John and Joan Blare a judicial separation, after John had expelled his wife from the family home and deprived her of sustenance, the court asked him to pay her 26*s.* 8*d.* every year for a period of four years, at which point his obligation ended.[27] An annuity was not the only means of providing for one's wife. The records present at least four cases in which husbands were compelled to pay their separated wives a weekly support fee. In the case of Margery, wife of Alexander de la Hoo, the court set a price of 2*s.*[28] This was substantially higher than other arrangements. John Cok de Holyngham was obliged to pay his wife 12*d.* per week; the wife of William Bergh was to receive only 6*d.* per week from her husband.[29] The church did not always require men of high rank to foot the highest bills. For example, William fitz Weryn, lord of Upton, was required to pay his wife 7*d.* per week, at the four quarter-days in equal installments.[30] In this particular case, one possibility is that William's wife was wealthy in her own right and had taken over governance of her lands; thus, a considerable alimony was unnecessary.

Alimony was not always monetary; the courts sometimes ordered husbands to pay it in kind. Richard and Alice Torif were divorced in July 1343; by November 1345, the court summoned Richard to remind him of his obligations. The court warned him that, on pain of major excommunication, he had promised to support his wife for as long as he should live. Their agreement stipulated yearly gifts—namely, six bushels of food stuff (two of corn, two of pottage, and two of rye)—to be paid in equal portions at the feasts of St, Michael, the nativity of the Lord, and Easter. The court also reminded him that he needed to return two trunks and other utensils to Alice within the next 15 days.[31]

A formal division of marital property was a much more practical solution for a variety of reasons. First, separate management of property avoided the pitfalls of a delinquent or miserly husband, guaranteeing court officials that they would not waste time coercing husbands into holding up their end of the bargain. Second, such an agreement was more functional, because it did not reinforce the power relationship by necessitating close communication between spouses. If the wife was a genuine victim of ill treatment, she probably feared a continued relationship with her abuser. Weekly or even yearly alimony payments might well entail gentle reminders on her behalf to ensure delivery of funds; a division of property, on the other hand, effectively severed all ties between the two. Thus, it is not surprising that some spouses chose the less personal route. Such was the case with Richard Wilkynson and his wife, Margaret. In 1420, when the couple approached the court to request a separation, to which both parties unanimously consented, they divided the property equally between them, and four arbitrators, two chosen by each party, carried out the division itself.[32] The case of Henry de Leck (*Glos.*) and his wife suggests that equitable division of property was an appropriate alternative in cases of affluence. Although the archbishop's register does not specifically describe the Gloucestershire case as a judicial separation, the register notes that it pleased them to lead chaste lives apart from one another.[33] Henry's obligation to support his wife, however, remained intact, and goods held jointly by the couple were to be divided equally between them. The court permitted Henry's wife to retain her complete inheritance, comprising two acres of land, and Henry was asked peaceably to give her one dress worth 20*s*. every two years, or the value of a dress in cash. Undoubtedly, Henry's wife was a woman of some affluence, and the court did not feel that she deserved to lose her standing as the result of a failed marriage. Nonetheless, it is striking that, despite her personal wealth, the court should have upheld Henry's obligation to support her. If her inheritance was more than sufficient to provide her with maintenance, why require an equitable division of goods held jointly or the biennial gift of clothing? The resolution of this case would seem to argue that even when a man married a well-to-do woman, medieval society expected him to "act like a man" and support his wife. Taken on their own, these two cases insinuate that this kind of equity was only achievable in amicable settlements, in which the participants (rather than the court) set the terms. The evidence of a fourteenth-century Lincolnshire case undermines this conclusion, however. When William Chipgold staunchly refused to cohabit with his wife, Isabella, he soon found himself in court before the dean and chapter of Lincolnshire. The reason for his obstinacy was that his son refused to live in the same house with his bride, and consequently his loyalties to his son outweighed those to his wife. In dealing with this case, the court presented William with an alternative: he must either treat Isabella as his wife in bed and board or else give her a sum of money representing half his wealth.[34] Although three cases are certainly not enough to build a strong case for equitable division of property, they do provide an indication that the church courts of medieval England supported such a division where the judge thought it appropriate, principally when the joint wealth of the couple was significant.

If the couple wished to sever all future ties, a one-time only payment of support, such as that proposed by Margery of Longford for her husband, was a practical form of alimony. Some husbands also adopted this approach to wife maintenance. For example, when Henry atte Pette and his wife, Joan, divorced in the year 1321, he entered into a promise before the bishop of Rochester to pay her £10 sterling within a year from the date the divorce was celebrated.[35]

The English church earnestly supported the right of a separated wife to maintenance. A case from the year 1300 in the register of Archbishop Thomas of Corbridge best demonstrates this. The court's official warned Henry Leue of Walkeringham (*Notts.*) to treat his wife with marital affection and to provide her with necessities. Moreover, the court required him to pay his wife 5*s*. annually for her maintenance, even though the church had not awarded the couple a separation and required the two to resume cohabitation. Why should a court expect a man to pay maintenance when he lived with his wife? It seems probable that Henry Leue was a repeat offender; having proven his unreliability in the past, the court's patience had run out. The archbishop of Canterbury took the same approach with John de Pendeford in 1283, summoned to court to respond to allegations that he neglected his wife; the court ordered John to pay his wife 40*s.* for food and clothing, even though the court expected them to cohabit.[36] In these situations, a fixed payment documented and enforceable in court erased the need for regular supervision and frequent citations. At the very worst, the archbishop's officials would see him in court once a year. In the face of contumacious husbands, this approach may have been the most effective, even where formal separation was not the goal. For example, a sentence against Sir William le Poer, knight, from the register of Bishop Godfrey Giffard demands the payment of alimony to the Lady Margaret, his wife. According to Margaret, William failed to treat her with marital affection and no longer resided with her. The register notes that if William would take back his wife and treat her appropriately, all requirements for payments of alimony would cease.[37]

A SEPARATED WIFE'S RIGHT TO HER OWN PROPERTY

Some petitioners assumed that separated wives retained rights to the real property they brought into marriage. This perspective was not unusual for the period. A wife never relinquished ownership of that property to her husband, even though he actually controlled that property during the marriage. Common law deemed that he held title only "in right of his wife."[38] Medieval English law and society still considered all real property hers, even if in practice the management of any dowry or inherited lands rested entirely in the hands of her husband. Some separated wives believed that the termination of marital relations should also halt their husbands' marital property rights. In asking to support herself out of her dowry and dower lands pending litigation with her second husband, Sir Thomas Lengleys, Alice, widow of Walter de Kirkbride, certainly seemed to believe she was within her rights to resume independent control of her pre-marital estate.[39] Thomasina de Fornivall's 1383 petition to the king similarly implies a right to resume her properties, although Thomasina announces her entitlement much more delicately. Her letter states that

> on her marriage she brought her husband rents and possessions to the value of 100 marks annually, with other money and goods and chattels to the value of 4000 marks, but that through his cruelty and harshness she had been unable to live with him for fear of her life, as is well known, although no blame attaches to her for this. She has often humbly requested her sustenance from him, as he was adjudged by law of Holy Church to give her £100 annually, but he has refused to do anything. Therefore she asks that a remedy might be ordained for her, so that she might be able to have sufficient security of peace, and a suitable maintenance.[40]

Knowing the extent of the property Thomasina brought to the marriage, the church's decision to award her only £100 yearly seems highly inappropriate. Undoubtedly, the formation of this impression was Thomasina's goal. She had been the ideal wife; the blame for their botched marriage, "as is well known," belonged to her husband; and even though she had "humbly" requested support, he continued to fail in his duty to support her. Thomasina intended her diplomatic letter detailing her worth to suggest the ideal solution: the king should return her property to her.

Lady Margery of Longford (*Staffs.*) was much more candid in her request. When she decided to divorce her third husband, Richard of Clitheroe, she went first to the court of Chancery in the hopes that the chancellor and his officials might assist her in creating an equitable division of property. Her petition makes it clear that she wished her pre-marital rights to real property to remain intact: her interpretation of "equitable" was to grant her husband the right to curtesy should she die as well as an immediate grant to him of £40.[41] In both of these cases, the records provide no indications of how the various courts proceeded in response. The rarity of these cases points to the likelihood that a woman's property rights continued to function within the limitations of marriage even after a separation; however, their very sense of entitlement underscores the difficulties associated with women's married property rights. For heiresses or women of affluence, the legal fiction of unity of person meant that non-consensual separation was never really a practical option.

Margery's suggestion of curtesy for her husband forces us to examine an aspect of post-marital support that the legal record rarely addresses: husband maintenance. A widower could only claim curtesy if "issue capable of inheriting had been born of the marriage."[42] Although Margery's petition does not address children, the issue of curtesy strongly suggests that one had been born (although it was not necessary for the child to still be alive). Because this is one of the few cases of husband maintenance to survive, it is unfortunate that the chancellor's final judgment remains a mystery. What his decision might have been in this matter is difficult to discern. At the very least, Lady Margery believed that hers was the just course of action and that she had every right to keep her property.

Margaret de Boslingthorp's petition to the pope in 1363 while her divorce was still pending makes it clear that she shared Margery's belief that some form of maintenance should be sufficient to support her estranged husband. Her petition makes it clear that her husband was untrustworthy. Roger Hannsard had taken out his anger with his wife on her property. He

> seized her personal property, lands, and possessions, of inheritance and of dower alike, to the value of 400 marks, and holds them, and has destroyed fair manors and buildings, and has thrown down the stones, tiles, and timber of the said manors, and has sold her lands and

> possessions, alienating and transferring them to her adversaries, and has committed dilapidations of her goods and hereditaments.

Anxious to thwart further destruction to her lands and goods, Margaret begged the pope to intercede, asking specifically that he order the bishop of Lincoln "to sequestrate the said lands, possessions, and manors, and to cause a fair proportion to be allowed from them to the said Roger for his sustentation pending the suit." [43] Once again, the pope's pronouncement on this matter has not survived: these two requests, however, leave us wondering just how common husband maintenance was. Both Margery of Longford and Margaret de Boslingthorp remind us that, despite the rules of coverture that gave husbands governance of their wives' property during marriage, the law did nothing to dull a married woman's keen sense of ownership and responsibility for her lands.

ENFORCEMENT OF ALIMONY AGREEMENTS

Respecting a woman's right to alimony was only half the battle; enforcing it was another matter altogether. It is important to bear in mind that wives who sought judicial separations from ecclesiastical authorities alleged to be the victims of cruel physical treatment at the hands of their husbands and/or his repeated sexual infidelities.[44] Thus, then, as is often the case now, separated couples sometimes harbored a good deal of resentment and pent-up hostility towards each other that may have impeded amicable financial settlements. Further, a husband who felt betrayed or mistreated by his wife's desertion may even have believed that her behavior exempted her from any expectation of support.

Given that most of these women appeared in the records only because their husbands defaulted on payments, we can certainly draw the conclusion that the system was not foolproof. The church lacked adequate weapons to compel effectively the payment of alimony. Penance, fines and public humiliation were only useful if a husband chose to cooperate with the court; but if a separated husband were accommodating by nature and spiritually conscientious, he probably would not have defaulted on his payments in the first place. Even the threat of excommunication, the church's most powerful weapon, failed to rouse fears of social exclusion and eternal damnation for many late medieval delinquent husbands. Repeated appeals, failed appearances, recalcitrance, and even judicial inadequacy abound in the alimony suits of the late medieval English courts. With many cases, there is little indication that the wife ever received her due.

The pursuit of alimony was a lengthy and expensive endeavor. Alice, wife of Thomas de Neuton, spent at least four years pursuing support in a variety of ecclesiastical courts. She first appeared before the bishop of Carlisle on April 3, 1354. At this time, she recounted how her husband had removed her from his household and refused to provide her with necessities. Her husband admitted that all of this was accurate, but his debts were such that he simply could not afford to support her. The court ordered the two to resume cohabitation within eight days; Thomas was also required to treat his wife with conjugal affection and support her according to his means under pain of excommunication. Thomas reappeared before the bishop on October 14, 1355, after Alice complained yet again. Apparently, he had not readmitted Alice into his home, nor had he made any effort to maintain her. Thomas swore that he was in the midst of negotiations with the knight, William Dacre, to direct a portion of his pay annually to Alice's keep. Thomas then requested a stay in the proceedings until he had completed his negotiations. By January 1358, Alice had given up on both her husband and the bishop's court altogether. She was now suing for divorce before the archbishop of York. The archbishop requested all supporting documentation from the bishop's archives, which he sent along with a note "asking him to favor Alice in this business, [because] the bishop has learnt that she has not been fairly treated."[45]

The case of Alan Plokenet, a knight of some economic prosperity who owned lands throughout England, and his wife, Sybil, perhaps demonstrates contumacy at its worst. The couple first appeared in the surviving records of the church in April 1321. In what appears to be a case for restitution of conjugal rights, Sybil initiated a suit against her husband, complaining that he failed to show her marital affection or treat her as his legitimate wife (meaning that he had deserted her) and that he denied her proper sustenance. Sybil respectfully requested that the bishop of Salisbury order Alan to pay all court costs, support her during the hearing of the case and furnish her with alimony of 40*s.* annually; the bishop without delay complied with this request.[46] By May, the couple made another appearance in the records. Alan appealed to the court of Arches in Canterbury, protesting the actions of the bishop of Salisbury, who reportedly rejected Alan's request to postpone an alimony hearing until he had engaged an advocate, behavior that Alan interpreted as evidence of preferential treatment. The court cited Sybil to appear in the church of St. Mary Aldermary (London) on the first court day after Trinity Sunday, which she did, presumably indicating her readiness to carry on with the case.[47] *Her* willingness, however, was not the problem. An incomplete commission to the chapter of Salisbury from September 1322, citing a mandate of the official of Canterbury, explains that the bishop failed to proceed with Sybil's suit against her husband. Moreover, it states that Alan neither reimbursed Sybil for her court costs nor paid her the 40*s.* in alimony pledged before the bishop more than a year earlier. Frustrated, she appealed yet again for the court's assistance; the dean of Salisbury summoned the couple once more, although Alan failed to appear.[48] A certificate to the court of Arches from October of the same year notes that the court was incapable of locating Alan. Without a defendant, the dean could not proceed with the suit, nor could he enforce the payment of alimony.[49] A fresh citation failed to produce Sybil's husband, and it was determined that he was no longer living in his home at Longford, which had since been seized by the king.[50] By December, the dean transferred the case to the provincial court at Canterbury.[51] The case makes a final appearance in the surviving records of the church in June 1323. A mandate of the court of Canterbury instructs the bishop to pronounce sentence of excommunication against Alan Plokenet, citing that he contumaciously refused to pay certain moneys assigned by the court to Lady Sybil.[52]

Alan Plokenet was a man of considerable means. His lands in Somerset boasted a yearly value of £52 12*s.* 0.5*d.*; in Dorset, £26; in Hereford, two properties worth £20 13*s.* 6*d.*, and 33*s.*, respectively; in Gloucester, £19 15*s.* 8.5*d.*; in Wiltshire, £6 13*s.* 4*d.*; in Southampton, two properties worth £10 10*s.*, and 23*s.* 8*d.*, respectively; and in Berkshire, 52*s.*[53] The administration of these various properties doubtless necessitated a broad network of personal staff, including many stewards or bailiffs responsible for supervising village affairs and collecting his revenue. Plokenet must have been in close contact with all of these men in order to guarantee an efficient and productive management. How is it possible for a man of this stature simply to disappear? The church's officials searched Alan's home in Longford; if it had had greater resources available, a subsequent investigation of his staff's homes in other counties surely would have assisted in locating the errant knight. Such an extensive enquiry, however, was understandably beyond the resources of the court. Sybil was the regrettable victim. Even after Alan's death, sometime between the months of August and October 1325,[54] Sibyl's predicament continued, as she attempted to claim dower lands. The Close Rolls document repeats orders by the king on Sybil's behalf over the course of the next four years, requesting various escheators to deliver to Sybil lands and profits rightfully due her as dowager.[55]

Although ecclesiastical courts expressed concern for the well-being of separated wives, overseeing the logistics of separation (sequestration, payment scheduling and so forth) was not their forte. When Alice, widow of Walter de Kirkbride, made the decision to sue her husband, Sir Thomas Lengleys,[56] for a judicial separation on the grounds of cruelty in 1342, the decision was probably long overdue. Thomas had already appeared in the church courts twice to defend his reputation as an upstanding patriarch. He appeared first before the bishop of Carlisle, demanding the punishment of those whose malicious allegations had "gravely harmed" his reputation. The mandate states that several unknown persons alleged that "he cut hair off the head of Alice, his wife, with some skin; when she was pregnant, he so injured her that he killed the child in her womb; and he broke the back of another of her children."[57] Alice also appeared in court, accusing her husband of maliciously cutting off her hair. An inquiry by the bishop into the matter elicited a confession from Alice that her charges were indeed false, at which point she asked her husband for forgiveness, and the two were reconciled.[58] Was her confession genuine or extracted through intimidation?

Thomas was certainly a violent character: in March 1339, in consideration for his service in Scotland and elsewhere, the king granted Thomas a pardon for "all homicides, felonies, robberies, receiving of felons and thieves, rapes of women and other trespasses and of any consequent outlawries."[59] The king did not grant pardons of this nature without reason. It is no surprise, then, that the court took seriously Alice's renewed allegations of cruelty in 1342: she was awarded a temporary separation. The court allowed Alice to reside at the home of an honest matron in Carlisle for the duration of the trial. Alice requested that her stay be paid for jointly (with her guardian) and that she be permitted control over the goods that she had brought into the marriage in order to pay her share of the expenses. However, the bishop failed to make any specific arrangements with Thomas for her support. Since then, the case had been passed on to the prior and archdeacon of Carlisle, who also neglected the issue, although they had reportedly kept the case in suspense for a long time and simply ignored Alice's repeated requests for maintenance. Thus, Alice turned to the court at York, pleading for assistance. The court of York sent the bishop an order to give Alice justice in this action. Once again, the bishop did not address the case, and it devolved to the audience of the court of York. When the bishop of Carlisle finally responded, he explained that he had committed the case to the prior and archdeacon some time before this; the notary had simply been too preoccupied with other business to write the process into a proper form for transmission. The record ends with a demand by the official at York for the bishop to send records of the entire process; if the bishop failed to do so, he risked proceedings against him for contempt.[60] Whether Alice was indeed the victim of inefficiency and exhausted resources rather than deliberate subversion of her cause is impossible to determine from the records. Yet her plight was not extraordinary. Although the church recognized the necessity for support, enforcement of these payments, in light of the animosity between parties (especially during litigation) and the seemingly inadequate resources of the church, was never an easy undertaking.

In some cases, a husband's obstinacy with respect to support payments may have sprung from a sense of moral superiority. The existence of legislation demanding that adulteresses forfeit all rights to their dower raises the question of whether a wife's culpability entered into the court's decisions when determining a man's responsibility to provide alimony. If the court (or the husband, for that matter) considered the wife primarily responsible for the separation, might she realistically expect financial support? The records reveal that even sexual infidelity was not inevitably grounds for a husband to abandon his responsibilities. A Lincolnshire case from the year 1340 describes the plight of Simon Smith, presented for failing to treat his wife appropriately. He replied that she had committed adultery with three different men, including John Penser, who was related to Simon within the third degree. Simon's wife, Cecilia, appeared before the court and confessed to her adultery and incest. Simon then demanded a separation, which the court granted; nonetheless, the court warned him to provide his wife with all the necessities of life.[61] Along the same lines, the records of the bishop's court at London offer a rare case of judicial separation granted because of the wife's cruelty. William Alpe appeared before the bishop's officials and adamantly repeated his refusal to live with his wife, Joan. He argued that his wife was insane and that he could not live with her out of fear for his life. His wife did not reply to those allegations. The court awarded the separation, but not before William agreed to pay Joan the sum of 10*s.* per year to afford her food and clothing.[62]

The cases of Simon and William are very instructive; none of the censorious or righteous attitude evident in the works of *Glanvill* or *Britton*, or even in the practice of the royal courts, is apparent in the church's decisions. This discrepancy may be indicative of a broader disparity in the interpretation of marital obligations. Separated wives might have felt more confident of their claims to alimony than dower, simply because church officials, not royal justices, judged their worthiness; and in the eyes of the church, the couple were still married, no matter how many years or miles between them. Although royal justices may have believed that a wife's adultery or disloyalty signaled an end to a husband's obligations, clergymen knew better: what God had joined together, no man might put asunder. Admittedly, with only two cases, this hypothesis remains tentative. Certainly, more research is necessary in order to discern the discrepancies in approach between royal and ecclesiastical courts with respect to the support of separated wives; however, the court orders for both Simon Smith and William Alpe suggest that a wife's failure to live up to contemporary expectations had little to do with a man's responsibility as a husband.

An insightful discussion between justices and pleaders in a Year Book from 1315 reinforces this viewpoint. Examining the claim of Lucy, widow of William Devereux, to dower lands, the courtroom confronted the situation of a wife who spent her husband's last years living in adultery. Pleader for the defendant stated the case clearly: she was not entitled to dower, "for we tell you that she deserted her husband and went to the manor of Tasley in the county of Oxford, and there abode in adultery with one Master Walter, without being reconciled in the life-time of her husband." The situation was not so straightforward, however. Pleader for the plaintiff responded that, yes,

> she went away to Tasley, etc., but he cannot for that reason bar her from her dower, for we tell you that the manor of Tasley was the joint purchase of this same woman who is now claiming dower and also of her husband for the term of their two lives. And we ask for judgment whether, seeing that she lived nowhere but in her husband's manor, of which they were joint purchasers, you can, on such grounds, bar her from her dower.

Although adultery normally invalidated a wife's claim to dower, "when a wife is living in her husband's house she cannot be said to have left him."

Justices concluded that this was a private, rather than a legal, issue: "and it is the husband's business to keep an eye on his guests."[63]

Society expected husbands to support their separated wives. When James Mawncy of London crippled his wife, Agnes Bawdewyn, and then deserted her for more than a year, Thomas Thornton, a clergyman, felt obligated as a chaplain to assist her in her time of need. In total, Thomas spent 20 marks to feed and shelter Agnes during her husband's absence and was enraged when James finally returned and refused to repay "any penny" of the 20 marks to Thomas. The situation quickly degenerated. Not only did James allegedly enter Thomas's home in London with "force and arms and made assault upon the said Agnes his wife," he also falsely sued an action of trespass against Thomas, for which the sheriff arrested and imprisoned Thomas. The chaplain's request to the chancellor, then, was for a writ of *corpus cum causa* in order to have him released from prison, but also for a *subpoena* directed to James, requiring him to appear in court where he might be compelled to pay Thomas the money he was owed for Agnes's support.[64]

Agnes's priest was secure in his rights to compensation. Maintenance of an abandoned wife was not a charitable matter. Maintenance agreements for separated wives existed for exactly this reason: communities did not wish to assume the responsibilities of the husband simply because the marriage had gone sour. James was fully responsible for his wife's support, even if he no longer resided with her. Thomas's sense of entitlement in this issue is remarkable. If Thomas's was a well-founded expectation, it is likely that, despite a formal arrangement renouncing any future support, a husband was still responsible for his separated wife's maintenance. In short, this was what being a husband was about in the medieval context.

ALIMONY OUTSIDE THE COURTS

Given the centrality of a maintenance agreement to the future prosperity of a separated wife, it is striking that provisions for alimony are seldom mentioned in cases of judicial separation appearing before the archbishops' court for either York or Canterbury, even where rulings have survived. This omission leads us to a number of conclusions. Many separated women may have simply moved in with their parents or other family members and consequently were not concerned with enforcing payments of financial support from a tight-fisted curmudgeon. It is also possible, however, that support for wives was so ingrained in the minds of late medieval Englishmen that it was often not necessary for the courts to address the issue. Negotiations for maintenance may have taken place outside the legal setting. An entry for the borough court of Colchester in 1311 bolsters this suspicion:

> William de Hetha, chaplain, complains of Roger Cartar that he forcibly entered his house at La Hethe, in the suburb of Colchester, and

> searched for the wife of Peter de Aseton, and even entered the said William's chamber and looked for her there, and accused him of keeping her with him, and of other enormities, whereas the said William had made arrangement with the said Peter that he would support the latter's wife at his table for the whole of that year for 3 marks, but on account of this accusation and defamation the said Peter refused to keep to the agreement, to the loss of the said William of 40*s.*, and thereto produces suit.[65]

Whether the relationship between Peter's wife and William the chaplain was sexual in nature or purely economic, it is apparent that this arrangement was a form of maintenance agreement in order to provide for Peter's wife now that she no longer shared a dwelling with her husband. Without Roger's invasion of William's property, this contract would not have left a trace in the legal record. This kind of informal understanding may have been much more common than the surviving documentation permits us to discover. For example, Thomas Leylond of Norfolk chose to care for his wife through enfeoffment. He granted the use of a messuage of land in Cley (*Norf.*) to another man on the condition that he provided meat, drink and clothing for Thomas's wife, Agnes. However, the feoffee failed to live up to his side of the bargain, and the court of Chancery was asked to step in when Thomas refused to pay for Agnes's support.[66] Despite the failure of common law courts to recognize uses, enfeoffment to use was a standard procedure in this period for all sorts of purposes. In fact, many marriage settlements at this time stipulated the creation of a use to provide for a wife, whether separated or not.[67] The fact that meat and drink were part of the maintenance required for Agnes would seem to indicate that she and Thomas Leylond were no longer co-residing; however, it is also possible that Thomas was a businessman who traveled frequently. In 1336, when William Bonde and his wife, Alice, were no longer happily married, William apparently returned her to her father, with the agreement that he might hold her goods and chattels in return for supporting her.[68]

A petition to chancery on a related matter bolsters the contention that extra-legal separation agreements may have been a familiar feature of late medieval life. According to the petitioner, after her daughter Margaret had been married to John Glover for the space of a year, "variance and debate fell between" them to such a degree that, out of fear for her own life and that of her newborn child, Margaret did not dare remain living with her husband. Thus, in need of support, Margaret turned to John's father, "trusting by his means to have had accord between them." The petition notes, however, that John's father found all attempts to reason with his son fruitless. With her father-in-law's encouragement, Margaret turned to the bishop of Hereford for assistance. The bishop awarded Margaret's mother guardianship over Margaret and her baby pending litigation, and the case was removed to the jurisdiction of the deanery of Bridgenorth (*Shrops.*). Believing Margaret's mother was holding her against her will, John's angry response was an allegedly false action of detinue against Margaret's mother, demanding damages of 40 marks. As a foreigner, and knowing that John was said to be "in service with one of the bailiffs of Bridgenorth," Margaret's mother feared partiality; she sought assistance from the chancellor, hoping to solve the matter before John's action led to her arrest or imprisonment.[69] Once again, Margaret's plight found its way into the records of the king's court for reasons unconnected to the need for support. In approaching her father-in-law to act as intercessor between her and her husband, Margaret seems also to have hoped for an informal maintenance agreement.

A 1373 lawsuit from Common Bench also seemingly refers to an informal agreement for a wife's separate living. The defendant recounted how the plaintiff and his wife had a dispute, "upon which, by an agreement between their friends," the plaintiff assigned lands to his wife "for her sustenance." The defendant, who was the wife's bailiff, was now being sued for an account of those lands.[70]

An out-of-court settlement was the most practical tactic for separated wives to adopt. The services of a court proctor and repeated appearances in the bishop's court were a costly endeavor. Without assistance, most separated wives would have been incapable of amassing the funds necessary to utilize the resources of the church. Moreover, many wives may have preferred to avoid the church courts altogether. An appeal to the bishop might solicit an unwelcome response. For example, when Idonia, wife of Gilbert Kempe of Hadlow (*Kent*), sued her husband for alimony in 1326, her complaints were multiple. She argued that, abetted by a certain John ate Wolde, Gilbert failed to treat her with marital affection and had deprived her of sustenance. Despite the severity of the charges, she did not find the bishop's court as sympathetic as she had hoped. It requested Gilbert and Idonia to live peaceably together and to show each other marital affection (*affectio maritalis*) under pain of excommunication. Gilbert was required to provide her with necessities (also under pain of excommunication), and John ate Wolde was ordered not to encourage Gilbert in his poor behavior.[71]

Fear of a forced reconciliation was not the only deterrent keeping wives from approaching officials of the church. Even if the bishop believed a woman was justified in having deserted her husband, she might then be required to go through the formality of a judicial separation, making their marital difficulties public knowledge. Some women may have found this kind of publicity embarrassing; a judicial separation advertised marital inadequacy, and communities tended to lay blame as they saw fit. Opening themselves up to public scrutiny was probably more than many women had bargained for. Idonia's allegations of desertion and economic deprivation, as we have seen, were not exceptional. In most instances, the ecclesiastical court's response was a hasty reminder to the woman's husband of his manly obligations.

ANNULMENTS AND PROPERTY SETTLEMENTS

The medieval world was intensely aware of the centrality of property transfers to marriages and the potential risk of loss without return in the event of a divorce. English families worked hard to protect their investments through individual arrangements. Amy Erickson has argued that the strictures of coverture, in fact, acted as a catalyst for capitalism: "the peculiar English doctrine of coverture in marriage quite unintentionally stimulated financial awareness throughout the population and significantly contributed to the creation of the instruments to move capital."[72] English families with substantial estates frequently tried to safeguard property through pre-nuptial agreements. The agreements themselves tended to be weighted in favor of the husband, revealing a resolve to reap the profits of the marriage, whether the marriage endured or not. The earliest agreement of this nature appears in the patent rolls for October 1250 and belongs to the marriage of Margaret and John de Plessetis, earl of Warwick. The threatening nature of the agreement surely would have prompted an immediate confession if any legitimate impediment had existed: "if she should be lawfully convicted of having contracted with anyone matrimonially before John de Plessetis, earl of Warwick, took her to wife, her lands should be liable to the king forever." Furthermore, "if a divorce should be had between him and her, he shall have the said lands for his life, and after his decease they shall revert to the king or his heirs."[73] Similarly, the marriage charter of Nicholas Blundell and Margaret Scaresbrek from 1430 includes a pre-nuptial clause favoring the groom's family. It states specifically that if Margaret sued for a divorce, her estate would remain with her husband, although he promised to pay for it in increments over a five-year period.[74]

Written pre-nuptial agreements were the preserve of the wealthy; nonetheless, the impact of divorce on family property was a concern shared by all levels of society. Not only was the premise of marriage to acquire property, but individuals were then averse to relinquishing that property upon divorce. Much of the lawlessness evident in medieval divorces stemmed from a husband's desperation to retain his wife's property. The prospect of losing permanently the profits of landed estates was a powerful motivation for men, prompting them to work both in and outside the law to avoid any losses. Because of the disinclination of husbands to return their wives' property, some divorced women requested the involvement of the strong arm of the law. A justice's words recorded in a Year Book from 1465 refer to divorce specifically as "a conveyance"; more than anything else, the job of the courts involved dealing with the return or division of marital property.[75] Theoretically, because an annulment pronounced that the marriage had never been valid, both individuals should leave that marriage with what they brought to it. Pope Gregory IX specifically addresses this issue in his *Decretals*, requiring that a man return a woman's dowry upon divorce, and the two divide the goods they owned in common.[76] The English church also applied this approach in practice. When the church annulled the marriage of Avelina de la Legh and Alan Waldershare in May 1297 on the grounds of pre-contract, it commanded Alan to restore to Avelina all her property. The bishop also dispatched a mandate to the officials of the archdeacons of London and Oxford as well as the rural deans of Ongar (*Essex*), Henley (*Sy.?*), Guildford (*Sy.*), Elham (*Kent*) and Shoreham (*Ssx.*)—all areas where Avelina owned land in her own right—to publish the court's judgment and ensure it was enforced.[77] In the 1431 annulment of John, son of Gilbert de Alburgham, and Alice de Pynyngton on the grounds of consanguinity, a papal letter to the abbot of St. Mary's Norton (*Co. Durham*) declares that John must "restore to Alice all goods received by him from her by reason of the said marriage."[78]

Without a valid marriage, a man had as much legitimate claim to his former wife's goods and lands as he did to a stranger's; thus, obviously he should return everything upon divorce. Precisely because of this expectation, the legal documentation seldom includes mention of how to divide property in cases of annulment. The law in practice, though, demonstrates that the return of a wife's property upon divorce rarely worked out so neatly. The courts regularly interceded to oversee the conveyance of lands and goods. The affluence of the litigants did not dictate curial involvement; rather, court officials eagerly participated in the dissolution of marriages at all levels of society to ensure that wives would not go hungry. For those in the higher ranks, frequently the king was drawn into disputes, not only to assist his vassals as feudal lord but to safeguard the kingdom's best interests. In 1254, when Joan de Valura divorced Geoffrey de Doet of the diocese of Bordeaux, to prevent her lands from remaining in the hands of a foreigner, the king sent in his officials to confiscate them. Only after Joan had provided the king with sufficient written evidence of her divorce did he regrant those lands to Joan.[79] On a much lower level, in the 1305 dissolution of the marriage of Alice and William de Lyndesseye, Alice relied on the participation of the under-sheriff of London to retrieve goods worth £20 upon the awarding of her divorce.[80]

Common law recognized a wife's vulnerability in this respect, so much so that a writ existed explicitly for facilitating a wife's recovery of lands after a divorce. A writ of *cui ante divorcium* ("whom before the divorce") was intended for use by wives whose lands and tenements held in fee-simple, fee-tail, or for life, were alienated from her during her marriage. Justices focused primarily on the fact that a wife could not gainsay her husband during their marriage, even if she wanted to do so.[81] The very existence of this writ is significant: not only does it imply that divorce was a common occurrence (and thus the courts developed a regular method of addressing the experience), it also suggests that wives experienced difficulty retrieving what lawfully belonged to them. This process is essentially similar to that of a widow attempting to recover her dower lands after the death of her husband. The greatest challenge for the courts always was to discover whether a wife had indeed consented to her husband's conveyance of lands that properly belonged to her. Although officials regularly examined a wife separately to confirm her consent, the process did little to prevent coercion. If she had consented to the conveyance, then the action was binding. If her husband had coerced her consent, upon his death the law granted her the right to challenge those conveyances made without consent through a writ of *qui in vita* (essentially the widow's equivalent of *cui ante divorcium*).[82] However, just as widows often found it nearly impossible to eject those feoffees from the land, so, too, did divorced wives. A chancery bill from the 1460s highlights the great nuisance Alice, daughter of John Thorp, encountered after her divorce in recovering extensive lands spread across Surrey, Berkshire, Wiltshire and Buckinghamshire. Her former husband, Robert Osbern, had enfeoffed those lands to John Bourgchier and four co-feoffees. Not only had the feoffees refused to make account to Alice, but her former husband continued to receive the profits from those estates.[83] Alice's experience reveals that Robert and his cohort preferred to ignore the implications of the divorce altogether; a need for expediency led Alice to the chancellor to put an end to this unlawful situation.

The ignominious behavior of some husbands with respect to their former wives' property knew no limits. A petition on the behalf of William Saxmundham and his daughter Agnes complained of Alice's former husband, Thomas Wyther. Thomas had lodged with William in his household at Leystoft (*Herts.*) for several years. During that time, he and Agnes resolved to marry. Before approving the union, William insisted upon written proof that Thomas was indeed "a single man." Thomas returned to St. Albans (*Herts.*), where he had grown up, and had "forged a letter testimonial" certifying that he was a "good and virtuous and single" man. William granted his approval; Agnes and Thomas married, and they had a child. Soon after, Thomas's other wife arrived from St. Albans to claim her husband. "Shamed of his untrue being," Thomas went home to St. Albans, leaving everything from his marriage with Agnes behind him. However, through "subtle means," he plotted with a friend to recoup his marital goods. William reported that Thomas appeared before the chancellor, claiming he was enfeoffed in fee of nine acres of land and meadow with appurtenances in the town of St. Albans, of a yearly value of 20*s.*; the chancellor issued a *sub poena* for William and Agnes to appear in court at Westminster. The two endured the great expense of travel to Westminster; realizing he was about to be undone, Thomas sent thugs to confer with William and Agnes. Thomas's men promised them 20*s.* if they did not appear in court; but Thomas, of course, only paid William and Alice 6*s.* 8*d.* Despite his pledge to cease his "vexation," most recently Thomas's friend had taken an action of trespass against William and his daughter for false entry into lands in St. Albans. Irate and plainly exhausted, not having remedy for the vexation and with his daughter "deflowered," William begged the chancellor for support.[84] Thomas's own petition to the chancellor offered a very different story. He claimed that the land and meadows in St. Albans had originally belonged to his father and were entrusted into the guardianship of William Saxmundham. After his father's decease, William failed to make estate to Thomas; and Thomas was thus required to fall on the generous assistance of the chancellor.[85]

Was Thomas Wyther just a con man? Probably not. His background strongly suggests that he and his first wife self-divorced; he then relocated to Leystoft in the hopes of making a fresh start (why else would he be lodging with William rather than living with his own family?). It is unclear what prompted his first wife to retrieve him after such a long period of estrangement, but a threat of excommunication in the church courts may well be the answer. Regardless, Thomas may not have set out to marry Agnes with the intention of swindling her; certainly, they were together long enough to see the birth of a child. In terms of marriage strategies, however, his marriage to Agnes seems to have been significantly more profitable than his first marriage. The loss of that income was a strong motivation to manipulate the courts into regaining those lands.

A wife's repossession of landed estates was typically easier than recovering movables. Nonetheless, divorced wives were most intent on seeing their chattels returned. The dedication of women to recovering their movables most likely derived from two particular facets of medieval marriage. First, because parents typically endowed their daughters with goods upon marriage, a wife might be especially desirous to see those goods returned for sentimental reasons alone. Second, both canon law and common law underscored a woman's ownership of her *paraphernalia* if she outlived her husband. What that constituted was not always clear. *Bracton* defines them as being "especially things given and granted her for personal adornment, as robes and jewels, which may be said to be her own."[86] Custom in some region augmented a woman's portion: the province of York and the city of London also gave a woman her bed and a chest.[87] Canon law was decidedly more liberal in its interpretation, including not only a widow's clothes but also "the things she used about her person, her array."[88] Janet Loengard's study of wills drawn from the Prerogative Court of Canterbury emphasizes that husbands regularly stipulated bequests to their wives of not only their paraphernalia but also "all goods hers before she became my wife."[89] The list of those goods was generally long and varied, including such items as beds, pots, tablecloths, barrels, chairs, mass books and even the occasional handgun.[90] Knowing that a woman, by custom if not law, had ultimate ownership of household items may have had an impact on the way they viewed them. "[E]xpectation of ownership," Natasha Korda has argued, "led women to act as if their paraphernalia were their own even during coverture."[91]

Nonetheless, the frequency of spousal abandonment complicated the recovery of chattels. Often, in a vain attempt to locate their roving former spouses, abandoned wives turned to the chancellor. Margaret Grymmesby, a foreigner living in Strasbourg (HRE), who had little sense of the normal English means of locating a delinquent spouse and retrieving one's goods, appealed to the chancellor to champion her cause. The story she recounted was, unfortunately, all too familiar: she married the Englishman Reginald Cobham, esquire, on October 14, presumably of the year 1384, in her homeland. Reginald won her over not only with his charm but also with his persistent boasts that he was the son of the Lord Cobham and had an impressive inheritance in England. At the time of their wedding, he affirmed publicly "he had no other wife." By November 20 of the same year, they arrived in Tilbury (*Essex*) on the pretext of visiting his properties; away from the protective environment of her family in Strasbourg, he abandoned her, absconding with goods worth £200, saying, "he had another wife at home." Her request to the chancellor was that he commission a sergeant-at-arms to find Reginald and bring him to answer before the court.[92] Margaret's unwillingness to be victimized is admirable; left to her own devices in a strange land, it would have been very easy to turn tail and return home. The virtuous, assured tone of her plea makes it clear that she was aware Reginald's behavior was criminal. Despite her unfamiliarity with the land and the legal system, she was not going to tolerate the loss of her goods and her reputation.

Most court requests for assistance provide only the value of the goods taken, leaving us to speculate about their nature. The 1492 petition of Juliana North in the court of Requests offers much more detail. In her bill, she recounts that she was a widow with substantial dower lands when she married Thomas Northe of Dorking (*Sy.*). She soon decided that Thomas had married her only for the "rule, order, and governance of the lands tenements and goods of" Juliana. She divorced him shortly after, but he unlawfully retained her lands, tenements, rents, goods and chattels. "Without friends, goods or substance to maintain herself and her poor fatherless children," she was turning to the chancellor for help in locating her delinquent ex-husband and recovering her property. A list of her chattels still in Thomas's possession and appended to the bill expresses just how determined she was to retrieve household items, many of which she probably brought to her first marriage as part of her dowry:

> five brass pots, one brass small pot, one brass chaffer pot, five brass pans, one cauldron, three kettles, one skillet pan. Also, latin candlesticks, one latin basin, one chaffing dish, one latin colander, one latin laver, two skinning knives. Also, one basin with a pitcher, one great basin with three great platters, a posset basin, six plates, three pewter dishes with three pewter pottingers (*soup bowls*), one wine pot, and two ale pint pots, two saltcellars, two goblets, and six spoons of tin, a grate with a nail drain. Also, three spits, two cob-irons (*an iron on which a spit turns*), a brand iron, a trivet, a gutter shovel, a pair of tongs, a handsaw with a pair of pincers, and also a feather bed on bolsters, two

> pillows, a coverlet, a mantle, a canopy, three mattresses, five blankets, three pair of sheets with a draper towel. Also, four chests, three tubs, a barrel, a bolting-tun (*a barrel used for sifting*), three bowls, four wooden dishes, one pair of wool cards with a pair of drafts (*to attach beasts*) for a cart. Also, three bedsteads, a table, two trestles (*supports for a table)*, and a form. Also, a cupboard and a spade. Also, a dozen poultry. Also, one cow, one sow, and one mare.[93]

Thomasyn Rysley's joint petition to the chancellor emphasizes the sentimental nature of chattels. Thomasyn was daughter and heir of Richard Turvaunt, esquire. Supported by her second husband, John Rysley, she was suing her first husband, Richard Charlton, to repossess goods bequeathed to her by her grandmother. As the details of her petition confirm, she was substantially better off than Juliana Northe; nonetheless, she, too, offered a very detailed list of the cash and goods Richard still withheld: "six marks and a covered cup of five paris gold weighing 26 ounces of troy weight the value of £47 13*s.* 4*d.*, and a pair of beads of gold weighing 10 ounces the value of £24." Richard also retained gifts delivered to Thomasyn from her father, namely: "two basins of silver parcels thereof gilt with arms of 3 mullets, and a pair of azure the same weighing 109 ounces, and other goods," as she detailed in a list reportedly attached to the bill (but not surviving), and also 102 marks worth of bequeathed goods. She also reported that the divorce was Richard's idea: not being "content with the marriage," of late "by his own special labor," he sued for an annulment, which the church awarded, but Richard declined to give up Thomasyn's goods. After she remarried, her new husband applied himself to assisting her in the rescue of her goods. Following Richard's repeated refusals to cooperate, she turned to chancery for some legal muscle to back up her requests.[94] Although no sentence to the bill survives, Thomasyn was successful, but not in the way that she had hoped. Richard Charlton died in the Battle of Bosworth in 1485 in Richard III's armies. The crown confiscated his lands because of his status as a traitor. In 1487, Henry VII regranted them to his most trusted councilor, John Rysley, Thomasyn's husband.[95]

Not all annulments ended badly. An agreement between Gilbert de Clare, earl of Gloucester and Hertford, and Lady Alice de Marchia is one of the few chivalrous examples of marital dissolution. "In consideration of the nobility of her kin and being unwilling that for lack of suitable maintenance she should have cause of sadness," Gilbert granted her six manors for the duration of her life. His grant included the provision that "she do not attempt by herself or another anything to the damage or grievance of Gilbert's honor or profit by word or by deed, secretly or openly, so using and enjoying the manors and lands for her maintenance as aforesaid that alienation, mortgage, or enormous waste or destruction shall not happen to them."[96] Gilbert was trying to buy her silence; two years before the church awarded their divorce, he had already entered into negotiations with King

Edward to marry his daughter Johanna and applied for the necessary dispensation from the pope because the two were too closely related.[97] His act, nonetheless, does suggest that even in annulments, a husband may have felt some concern for his wife's future prosperity.

RELUCTANT WIVES

Men were not the only ones capable of exploiting the financial underside of marriage. The rules of coverture, which granted a husband full responsibility over marital property, certainly gave men an advantage in terms of marrying for property; but some women also played the marriage market. Much like what we saw with the husbands above who were averse to returning their wives' property, the legal documentation consistently portrays reluctant wives as charlatans out to steal from their new husbands. This portrait is no more reliable with wives than it was with reluctant husbands: many of those husbands may well have intended to engage in long-lasting marriages. Their scurrilous instincts surfaced only when they realized that the marriages were unworkable. The unkind depictions of wives in the legal record may also mask similar situations. When Thomas Caudrey married Katherine, she purported to be a widow. Thomas's clerical uncle kindly showered them with wedding gifts of a tenement in Smithfield (London), £20 in cash, and a silver cup, altogether worth 10 marks. In the petition Thomas's uncle brought before the chancellor to be remunerated for this generosity, he claims that it was only after the gifts were distributed that Katherine revealed a pre-contract with John Hampton. "By coven," she sued a divorce before the archbishop of Canterbury, who upheld the pre-contract and declared the union of Thomas and Katherine null and void. "Notwithstanding" the divorce, Katherine kept in her possession the tenement, money and cup; but more importantly, she also kept the evidences granting her legal right to that land. Although Thomas seemed content to put it all behind him, his uncle wanted his gifts back.[98]

How different would Katherine's side of the story be if her response had been written down? Katherine's widowed state was probably true. Was the pre-contract a fabrication, or had she reneged on a promise to John Hampton to which he was now intent to hold her? Either way, Katherine had no legal rights to keep the gifts from Thomas's uncle; but it is also undeniable that the uncle's story would elicit much more sympathy from the chancellor if she were indeed the swindler he purported her to be.

A certain degree of prevarication is evident in the chancery petition of Thomas Preest, a London goldsmith. It recounts that four years previously, he married Margaret Wyncote, daughter of John Anne of London, a saddler. The two kept a house in London together for more than a year and a half, but, as Thomas tells it, the entire marriage was a sham: during that time, Margaret was merely plotting to gain his goods. Through her "coven" with a man named John Ganne, Margaret and Thomas were enticed to leave their home and take up a chamber in John's house. John promised that "if [Thomas] would do so, the said chamber nor his board for his wife and him should never cost him no money" (double negatives aside, Thomas interpreted this as free rent and board). John sent his servant to fetch Thomas's goods from his house, to the value of £200. Within the month, John evicted Thomas, "saying he should have there neither wife nor goods." Thomas was suddenly homeless, with only two pennies in his purse with which to support himself, not even enough to hire a lawyer to recover his goods. Not long after the eviction, "it was proved that the said Margaret had two husbands yet alive." Thomas sued for divorce. John's "malicious appetite" was still not "satisfied." He took out a plaint of debt against Thomas in the sheriff's court of London, suing for the rent and board of the couple during that time. Even worse, because John was one of the "most common jurors in all London," Thomas feared he had no hope for an impartial verdict and lay himself on the mercy of the chancellor for assistance.[99]

If Thomas's story is to be believed and John Ganne and Margaret Wyncote were really con artists, they must have been rejoicing at the ease with which they duped Thomas. Even in such a Christian period of history, the very notion of free rent and board is unfathomable. What justification did John have to be that generous? His position as a regular juror in the sheriff's court suggests that he was a man of some means; but even if he could well afford it, why would any man undertake to support a couple financially if there was nothing in it for himself? Thomas's claim that Margaret had not one but two other husbands also smacks of hyperbole. What really happened to the marriage of Thomas and Margaret? The fact that John evicted Thomas but not Margaret indicates that she and John probably engaged in an adulterous affair. Evidence to suggest that her marriage to Thomas was a charade from the very start, however, is noticeably lacking.

One recurrent element is the determination of the plaintiff to ensure that his or her betrothed was, indeed, eligible for marriage. This uncertainty underscores the hazards of medieval marriage; the potential for ambiguity in the medieval spousals, the popularity of self-divorce and desertion followed by unlawful remarriage all complicated the decision to marry and put one's property in jeopardy. Responsible individuals needed to address this issue somehow. This matter was foremost in Thomas Deyncourt's mind when he entered into negotiations with two marriage brokers to wed Joan Brous. Eager to cut a deal, the brokers confidently declared that she was "clearly her own woman, unmarried to any man," although Thomas later claimed they knew all along that "she stood married and of long time had been to one John Broune, fuller," but they chose to keep that "secret" from Thomas. Before she would agree to marry Thomas, he was required to enter into an obligation to pay her a marriage gift of lands and tenements in Essex and Middlesex with a yearly value of £20 for the term of her life. Apparently, the ink was not yet dry on the obligation when John

Broune showed up declaring that Joan Brous was his lawful wife. Joan disappeared with her husband, and the marriage brokers vanished with the obligation, sending Thomas to beseech the chancellor for support in retrieving his land.[100]

WHAT TO DO WITH THE WEDDING GIFTS?

Western culture has transformed weddings into a great occasion for gift giving. Wedding gifts today play much the same role as they did in the Middle Ages: their purpose was to help a couple establish a life together, often by stocking a home with necessities. As many of the cases above suggest, upon divorce, the medieval English expected couples to divide their gifts appropriately. An uncle presumed his gift would stay with his nephew; a brother expected his to stay with his sister. When wedding gifts landed in the wrong hands, the court brought couples back together, however briefly, to resolve the issue. In an odd tale of deception, the Year Book of 1309 demonstrates just how dedicated some litigants were to repossess their wedding gifts. A man named Ellis, almost immediately after he exchanged vows with Alice, paid Isabel to claim him as her husband in a case of precontract before the court Christian. His ruse worked: the church declared his marriage with Alice was invalid. Since that time, Alice had appeared repeatedly at his door, asking for the gifts her father had given on their wedding day. The gifts were not inconsequential: gold, silver, oxen, cows and sheep, worth 40*s*. in total, were more than sufficient to motivate Alice into bringing a suit of detinue against her former husband. Justices sided with her; they also explicitly stated that the difficulty with keeping wedding gifts is that guests usually presented them in a very public setting, with great ceremony. What wedding guest would have trouble remembering the focal point of the wedding?[101] The courts were especially supportive when the gifts were of a landed nature. The Year Book for 1345 discusses a gift of tenements by a woman's father, given to her and her spouse when they married as children; upon reaching full age, her husband sued for a divorce, with her full consent. Rather than return the property, however, he ousted her entirely, causing her to appear before justices of assize with a writ of novel disseisin. The justices sided with her, and she recovered her land.[102]

Collectively, the financial agreements examined here contribute to a clearer understanding of the rights and responsibilities of both spouses upon the dissolution of a marriage. Chiefly, they demonstrate that the 1581 case of Mary Walgrave *c*. Arthur Goldinge was not a historic turning point after all. In judicial separations, despite the failure of either canon or common law to address the issue, some medieval wives expected to receive alimony payments and even defended this right in court. The maintenance agreements reached to care for wives in this situation may not have been as equitable in general as the Elizabethan example of Walgrave *c.* Goldinge that begins this discussion; nevertheless, the medieval courts demonstrated a strong sense of equity in dealing with these cases. The courts based their decisions on the merits and circumstances of each couple. Variety best characterized alimony agreements from late medieval England. There were no standard payment methods or schedules; even the degree of formality might vary tremendously. A legally enforceable maintenance agreement, however, was more important to some medieval wives than to others. The higher the stakes, the more likely a wife was to find herself in court demanding access to her husband's purse.

Despite all good intentions, the church courts were never capable of guaranteeing separated wives financial security. The cases of Sybil Plokenet and Alice Kirkebride are two dramatic examples, revealing that alimony litigation might be a lengthy and expensive undertaking with little hope of success. Quite simply, the church lacked the necessary resources to coerce deadbeat husbands into living up to their obligations. Moreover, common law practice reveals that some husbands may have believed they were no longer required to support a wife who had shown herself to be unfaithful. In the royal courts, an adulterous affair, and perhaps even a separation itself, endangered a wife's claim to dower; in the ecclesiastical courts, on the other hand, the records of this investigation provide no obvious parallels with separated wives' claims to alimony. The officials of the church awarded even adulterous or abusive wives maintenance. The English church advocated rigidly defined gender roles in marriage. Historians have examined the many burdens a medieval wife had to bear in light of Eve's famed indiscretion. In the church's perspective, the maintenance of a wife, even if she had not "earned" it, was one of the burdens medieval husbands had to bear.

In terms of annulments, the medieval courts expected husbands and wives to walk away from a marriage with the same goods and properties they brought to it. Nonetheless, court records demonstrate that divorced women faced many of the same obstacles as widows in pursuing the restoration of their property. The eagerness of husbands to retain their wives' property propelled divorced wives to seek the intervention of the courts to assist them in recovering what was theirs. The tenaciousness of these wives is evident in the fact that they pursued not only land but also movables, resolute to see each pan and spoon home, back in its proper place. In general, divorced wives found strong allies in both the royal and ecclesiastical courts. Although enforcement of property settlements was never an easy feat, both venues stood up for a divorced wife's rights, regardless of the grounds for the divorce.

5 What Happened to the Children?

The concern most regularly articulated by divorcing parents today is for the support and custody of their children. If truth be told, custody disputes have become a staging ground for vicious battles to control marital property, often leaving children in the hands of a parent whose primary objective is either to receive or avoid paying a monthly child-support payment. Given the centrality of child support and custody to modern disputes, what is most astonishing about the medieval records of divorce is that they do not echo these apprehensions: the court documentation rarely even acknowledges the existence of children. It would be misleading to presume that the omission of children from divorce documentation signifies that medieval parents and the church considered children inconsequential. Medieval canon law generally had much to say about children, but it focused on a more pressing matter for the era—that is, the marriages of young children. Canonists spilt much ink on the subject of child marriage, leading some historians to highlight the "medieval pedigree" of the "vocabulary of children's rights."[1] Although canon law did not address in any unified manner the rights of a child to support or a parent's obligations towards his or her children, canon law in its various incarnations was not silent on the matter. Gratian propounds that "absent or separated parents [must] furnish adequate support for their children."[2] Not providing for one's child was anti-Christian. The *Decretum* states, "[i]f anyone abandons his own children, and neither feeds them nor provides them with the necessities (which is the mark of piety), but, under the pretext of asceticism, thinks that they are to be neglected, let him be anathema."[3] As Gratian's meager foray into the arena of child support implies, in rhetoric (if not always in practice) the church championed the rights of these children, eager to prevent them from being affected negatively by their ignorant or selfish parents. The *Decretals of Gregory IX*, penned by Raymond de Penãfort in 1234, declares, "[d]o not prohibit the children of this man and the woman from succeeding to their paternal goods and from being supported by them. Do not suffer them to bear any annoyance or harm from anyone by reason of their parent's divorce."[4] The force of canonists in their statements led R.H. Helmholz in 1977 to write, "[t]he obligation to support adopted by the medieval canonists was a more extensive obligation than English or American law was to enforce subsequently."[5] Granted, the canonists had a much broader view of familial obligation than do the courts today. A parent's duty to support his or her children (either legitimate or illegitimate) was only one piece in a much larger puzzle. This obligation extended also to grandparents, aunts, uncles, stepchildren and so on.[6]

Canon law also expressed some preference for the mother as guardian to young children but inevitably focused on what was in the best interests of the child. Like much of medieval canon law, however, the ruling greatly depended on context, and jurists may have sometimes overlooked the relevancy of the law's statement on the matter. Pope Gregory asked to whom belonged the custody of children when one parent was an infidel and the other became a Christian. His response is very instructive:

> a certain man, having been led from the error of the Jewish blindness to Christ the true light, with his wife having remained in Judaism, petitioned the court that their son of four years be assigned to him, to be led to the Catholic faith, which he himself had taken up. To that [the wife] responds, that since the boy is still a child, because he needs more maternal comfort than paternal, and for her he is known to have been onerous before birth, caused pain in childbirth, and after childbirth was more troublesome, for this reason the legitimate union of male and female is called matrimony rather than patrimony, the aforesaid boy ought more fittingly to remain with her [rather than go with the father who has been newly brought to the Christian faith, or at least to follow neither one('s faith) before he comes of age . . .]. But since the son is in the power of the father, whose family he follows, and not that of the mother, and [he] is of such an age that he ought not remain with those persons, concerning whom there can be suspicion that they might threaten his safety or his life, and boys after the age of three ought to dwell with an upright father, and the mother of the boy, if it should happen that he remain with her, could lead him to the error of unbelief, we respond in favor of the most Christian faith, that the same boy be assigned to the father.[7]

This statement is the basis for the modern *Codex Iuris Canonici's* declaration that "[w]hen a separation has been effected, the children are to be educated under the care of the innocent party."[8] Unfortunately, we have no means to discern how the medieval jurists interpreted the *Decretals*' views of child custody and whether medieval English jurists considered the separation of Christian parents in the same light.

Although debates over child custody and support are absent from divorce proceedings, some of the couples who divorced must have had children and thus at some point addressed the difficult questions of where they would live and who would support them after a divorce. When Joan, daughter of

William Matheuson, pressed the court for a separation from her husband, Robert of Pontefract, on the grounds of cruelty, she told the court that they had five children together.[9] What happened to those children, and others like them, after their parents divorced? What concerns did parents convey about their children in the process of divorce? With whom did they live? In addition, who supported them? Admittedly, because divorce litigation itself rarely spoke to these questions, the evidence is necessarily peripheral and inconclusive; the findings, however, do confirm that parents and officials alike looked out for the welfare of children in the process of divorce.

MEDIEVAL ATTITUDES TOWARDS CHILDREN

Before attempting to answer these questions, it is essential to state that the omission of child-centered dialogues from medieval records of divorce is not a reflection of how parents felt about their children. The historical world finally has doused the raging fires on the debate concerning familial affection, fueled most infamously by Philippe Ariès and Lawrence Stone.[10] The existing documentation simply does not support the idea that parents failed to appreciate childhood as a distinct stage of life or love their children because of high mortality rates. That is not to suggest that human nature is unchanging and parental affection a given; certainly, cultural comparisons in the twenty-first century demonstrate that views of childhood and appropriate parent-child relations are geographically and chronologically contingent. In the last thirty years, the Western world alone has significantly transformed its perceptions of permissible parental discipline. Although "spare the rod and spoil the child" was an axiom that once held a great deal of meaning in the West, today corporal punishment is almost entirely absent from the education system, and a parent who spanks his or her child in a public setting might well be arrested for the offence. Naturally, with technological innovation, the protective eye of the welfare state, a well-defined human-rights discourse and the generally affluent lifestyles of its people, it is difficult for us today in the West to fathom a world where a child's labor was seen not as exploitative but in fact necessary to the subsistence of a household and to the formation of a self-supporting, respectable Christian. Releasing our own deeply entrenched cultural preconceptions of childhood is a vital first step in order to appreciate medieval values.

Proponents of the hypothesis that childhood is a modern invention work from an absence of documentation. The historical record lacks evidence of daily life in general, thus it must be flushed out of unusual sources. Given the vehemence of this debate, it is crucial to acknowledge that the legal record offers copious evidence that medieval society was concerned for the well-being of children and that parents cared for their children. The medieval coroners' rolls provide plentiful examples of parents who sacrificed themselves in the effort to save their children's lives. An Oxfordshire coroner's roll from the year 1298 relates the tragic story of a house set aflame by a forgotten candle left burning in the shop of John and Alice Trivaler while they slept. Although John and Alice escaped, Alice instantly realized they had forgotten Roger, her twenty-week-old son. Single-minded in her determination to rescue him, "she leapt back into the shop to seek him, and immediately when she entered was so overcome by the greatness of the fire and choked, so that she could not come out, and so she and the said boy were burnt to death."[11] The manner in which Alice Trivaler and her son died is a common trope, reflected also in a Northamptonshire coroner's roll relating the deaths of Alice, wife of William Stanford, and her son. The fire that consumed Alice's home began while her son, Richard, was sleeping in his cradle, and Alice was outside collecting laundry. She also rushed back into the house, "wishing to take him," but was suffocated by the smoke so that both mother and child were "totally cremated" in the fire.[12] Is it possible to imagine a more heroic demonstration of a mother's love? Even fathers, who were much less engaged in child rearing than were medieval mothers, exhibited formidable evidence of affection for their children. The accidental death of Simon, son of Warin Thurgod, a toddler who tumbled into a ditch and drowned, also provides insight into the depth of parental love: following soon after the account of Simon's death is the record of Warin's suicide.[13] Was Simon's father driven to suicide by guilt over his negligence as a parent? Moral treatises and sermons of the time cautioned bereaved parents against this kind of excessive grieving for dead children in the hopes of preventing deaths like Warin's.[14] Although love is not something that can easily be measured, the actions of these parents suggest heightened levels of concern for the welfare of their children. It is critical to recognize that church legislation also hoped to stave off accidental deaths by educating parishioners about the dangers of careless parenting. The Canon of Edmund, included in Lyndwood's *Provinciale* states specifically:

> Let women be monished that they nourish their children warely and that they lay not the younglings nigh to them in the night lest they oppress them. Also they may not leave them in their houses where is fire, or nigh hand to the water, alone without a keeper, and let this be shewed them every Sunday.[15]

Medieval parents were also fiercely protective of their children, actively seeking to penalize those who abused them. When one of John Stirlond's apprentices "sore beat" the five-year-old son of Margaret, wife of John Hilton, so that he died two days later, Stirlond allegedly took out a plaint of debt against Margaret at the London mayor's court precisely to intimidate her and thus prevent her from retaliating against him for the child's death.[16] His defensive behavior insinuates that the normal response of a parent in these circumstances was to sue a plaint against the aggressor.

Because the crown records of unnatural deaths include such paltry detail, generally omitting the age of the victim and often the events that led to the death, who knows how many children died in similar situations, propelling their parents into initiating lawsuits. The situation is complicated by medieval attitudes towards the castigation of children: disciplining a child was considered a necessary element in child rearing and in the formation of ethical human beings. But where do you draw the line between correction and abuse? John Stirlond's apprentice, in his inexperience and exuberance, clearly overstepped that boundary. How many others had difficulty negotiating that fine line?

A chaplain's fifteenth-century petition to the chancellor complaining about a lawsuit over the beating of a child in his care is very revealing in this respect. John Robertson protested that he "never hurt nor beat the said child, but as a child ought to be chastised for his learning." The child's father evidently disagreed on the level of acceptable chastisement; he was suing an action of trespass against the chaplain before the sheriff of London, and the chaplain was confident he was about to be convicted.[17] Because clergy played a central role in the education of children, it is significant to realize that they were punished for overzealous disciplining of their students. Regrettably, documented cases usually expose clerical behavior at its worst; but church officials were more likely to address minor infractions verbally than in written form. Nonetheless, the church plainly supervised clergy in their relations with children and intervened when necessary. For example, the register of the bishop of Bath and Wells for the year 1503 records a dispensation for John Wyllyams of the diocese of Salisbury: Wyllyams had been dismissed from his position after being charged with homicide for the discipline of a boy of ten or twelve, whom he locked in a room in cold weather, finding the next morning that the child had died of hypothermia.[18] Presumably, the courts treated the child's death as accidental (thus, explaining why Wyllyams was not executed for felony); yet, the initial indictment on the grounds of homicide demonstrates intolerance for priests who abused their positions of authority. Clergymen were also anxious enough about their reputations to defend themselves when hounded by reports of cruelty. J. de Calneton appeared before the archbishop of York in 1287 to clear his name, because he was rumored to have beaten a child so severely that the child's back ruptured. After an investigation into the allegations, the archbishop of York pronounced the presbyter innocent.[19]

Although parents showed little patience for others who castigated their children too firmly, the church expected a good and pious father to discipline his children.[20] Yet as Barbara Hanawalt reminds us, "[d]iscipline [and] corporal punishment . . . did not imply tolerance of abuse or a lack of love for children." Rather, a medieval parent's "tough love" had the very real goal of promoting "survival in a harsh world."[21] Moreover, the law did not accord parents *carte blanche* in the scolding of their children's sins. There were limits to acceptable correction of a child, and punishment that led to a child's demise was not only deplorable but criminal and treated accordingly. The Northamptonshire eyre of 1329–30 reports that when Alexander Heved of Buckeby struck his son John with a staff in order to castigate him, inadvertently killing him, the county sheriff arrested and imprisoned him for homicide.[22] The York eyre of 1279–81 relates that Elias of Sutton, who killed his son while disciplining him for consorting with thieves, fled and was outlawed.[23] Flight is an immediate indication that parents expected the law to treat their behavior as felonious and did not assume they could defend their actions in any way. This condemnatory attitude also applied to guardians: when the wife of William de Wohnesworthy beat nine-year-old Matilda, daughter of Gilbert de Stokwyth, a child living in the custody of William and his wife, to death with a staff, she fled the scene of the crime on the supposition that the sheriff would seize her for homicide. The court waived her (waivery was the female equivalent of outlawry).[24]

The courts also freely denounced slipshod parenting that endangered the lives of children. Medieval justices or juries could do little to penalize neglect: English common law targeted active criminality rather than passive behavior that might lead to criminal ends. Nonetheless, public declarations that a child's death was the result of parental carelessness surely had a profound impact on a couple's standing in a community. The coroner's rolls regularly inserted pointed, yet meaningful, remarks about the absence of parents in child deaths. For example, when one-year-old John, son of Thomas Pyngel de Grinton, died in a house fire set by a hen in the year 1352, the record states specifically that it happened "because he was without custody."[25] When a house fire set by a candle burning consumed Alice Jeke's one-year-old daughter in 1351, the scribe noted that all of this transpired "in the absence of Alice."[26] Finally, when three-month-old Felicia, daughter of John Grocer de Jepewyce, died in her sleep because of a fire set by a hen, the record states specifically that she was "without the custody of her mother." It continues to say that the hen was only able to inflict such damage "because the mother of the child exited the home."[27] The church courts also adopted a firm stance on lax parenting: in 1418, John Ramett of Theddlethrope and his wife, Matilda, were excommunicated for their negligence in the drowning death of their daughter. The bishop of Lincoln eventually absolved them, and they began the penitential process.[28] If the church was willing to exercise its most potent weapon to encourage good parenting, we can rest assured that the medieval English valued children and sought to protect them from harm.

Perhaps the best evidence of parental affection comes from a legal record of an entirely different nature. Churches recorded the miracles at saints' shrines specifically with the goal of accumulating evidence for canonization trials. Those same miracle stories provide copious insight into parent-child relations. Parents of children who suffered illnesses or injuries were regular visitors to saints' shrines. As Eleanora Gordon has observed, the tragic tales of children are replete with parents "often beside themselves with grief, and their pleas for celestial aid were tearful and desperate."[29] Parents' prayers for intercession were replete with remorse over parental negligence, much like that played out in the suicide of Warin Thurgod above. Gordon recounts how one mother begged Thomas Becket to assist her five-year-old daughter, urging "[r]eturn my daughter to me, O Martyr Thomas. If anyone is guilty, I alone the mother, must bear the blame. I, who did not order supervision of her child wandering. I should have had a servant accompany my child, but I was blind."[30] The desperation of sobbing mothers moved Gordon to conclude that

> parents loved their offspring and were physically and emotionally close to them. They cuddled them and soothed them. Family members and neighbors banded together to sustain each other through the crises and shared their joy at the recovery. Clearly, then, children had a special and distinct place in their society.[31]

CHILD CUSTODY AND THE LAW

Divorce documentation most likely did not address child custody, because there was no need to do so. The medieval world viewed children as property; and, as with all property acquired during the course of a marriage, children inevitably belonged to the father. The common law's provisions for wards reiterate this stance. Under primogeniture, when a father owning freehold land died leaving a minor heir, the common law supplied a guardian for that heir. This protection related more to property than child welfare: if that heir had younger siblings, the court did not arrange for their guardianship. Nor was provision made for the children of the poor. The law only cared for those who stood to inherit. Even in the church courts, where one might expect greater compassion for the guardianship of minor children, Helmholz has noted, "the Church courts regularly provided guardians only for minors with rights, or at least potential rights, to part of a decedent's estate."[32] Medieval law defined an "orphan" as a fatherless child. In many of these instances, their mothers were alive and well and frequently hoped the court might appoint them as their guardians.

Appointing a mother guardian of her own children was certainly not out of the question. The later medieval world inherited a strong tradition of preference for the mother as guardian. The laws of Æthelberht of Kent (*ca.* 600), Hloþhere and Eadric (685–86) and Ine of Wessex (694) all stipulate that in the event of the death of the father, the child should remain with his or her mother.[33] The separation of the child from the father's property facilitated a mother's right to the guardianship of her children. Anglo-Saxon law provided a guardian from the paternal kin group to be responsible for the child's property until he reached the age of ten, what the Anglo-Saxon world deemed as the age of majority.[34] Under primogeniture, the bond between heir and property was not so easily broken. Consequently, some heirs were simply too valuable to be left in the custody of their mothers. As Sue Sheridan Walker has described it, "feudal wardship was a lucrative right."[35] The guardians of feudal wards (that is, for those in knight-service tenure) enjoyed both the profits of the ward's lands and the value of his or her marriage. Guardianship might also be prolonged, as the post-Conquest world deemed twenty-one a more fitting age to claim an inheritance.[36] Not surprisingly, rights to wardship were eagerly sought after in the later medieval period, leading to abuse and exploitation: the king auctioned off the wards of his tenants-in-chief to the highest bidders, guardians coerced their wards into marriages under-age and against their will and those who could not legitimately purchase wardship simply abducted the ward instead. Frederick Pollock and F.W. Maitland emphatically reject the idea that the king might award a mother the guardianship of her husband's heir. Paraphrasing a Norman lawyer, they outline the concerns of the era in a decidedly acerbic tone:

> A fatherless heir must be in ward to some one. Who shall be his guardian? His mother? No. Why not? She will take another husband and have sons by him, and they, greedy of the heritage, will slay their first-born brother, or the step-father will slay his step-son. Who then shall be the guardian? The child's blood relations? No. Why not? Lest, thirsting for his heritage, they destroy him.[37]

Better to see the child in the hands of his feudal superior than "to commit the care of a child to the custody of his expectant heir . . . set[ting] the wolf to guard the lamb."[38]

Despite Pollock and Maitland's distrustful view of family relations, even at this level, the courts made some preference for mothers. In fact, in his pledge to protect his baron's families after their demise, Henry I's Coronation Charter declares expressly a predilection for the mother, stating that in the absence of the father, "the wife or some other relative who has the best claim shall be guardian of the land and of the children."[39] Litigation over wardship reveals that the courts regularly appointed family members, "most often the widow of the late tenant," as guardians to their heirs.[40] A mother's guardianship was most appropriate when the child involved was young. The king's correspondence regarding wardship emphasizes this standpoint. In a mandate to the widow of Ralph, son of Bernard, demanding that she relinquish her husband's heirs, the king reminded her of a bond she had entered into at her husband's death, in which he awarded her custody only "because of their tender age."[41] The king also awarded Eleanor, countess of Ormond, custody of James, son and heir of James le Botiller, "on account of his tender age," reportedly "until he attain his full age."[42]

Lower down on the social scale, the guardianship of wards was much less scandalous and contentious, in good part because socage guardianship was not profitable. Rather, "[i]t is the prototype of the modern trustee-type of child custody in which the guardian derives no profit from the wardship and acts in the heir's interest as an accountable steward and protector of the heir's person and estate."[43] Even benefitting from the ward's marriage was off limits. Chapter 17 of the Statute of Marlborough (1267) states specifically that the guardian could marry off the ward or even sell the ward's marriage, providing it was to the heir's profit (not the guardian's). Both *Glanvill* and *Bracton* identify the mother as the ideal socage guardian, chiefly because she was not able to inherit from the heir.[44] The local courts, both manorial and borough, respected a mother's rights to her children. As Elaine Clark has noted, "mothers were thought the most capable of nurturing the young. Borough custumals never advocated removing small children from the care of a mother, nor did mayors place little boys and girls in the custody of neighbors without her consent. Municipal officials recognized the needs of mothers as did urban courts."[45] Thus, when Thomas of Kent, a bureller (a maker or seller of coarse woollen cloth), died in 1331, the mayor of London committed his two children—Richard, age five, and Juliana, age two—to their mother, Margery, newly remarried to Thomas of Canterbury.[46] An analysis of custody decisions in the mayor's court of London indicates that the courts acted on a powerful urge to keep children and their mothers united. A custody suit from April 1315 referred to the custom of the city, "whereby the nearest parents of children under age, to whom the property of the said children would not come by inheritance after their decease, should have the guardianship of such children."[47] Hanawalt's analysis of the Letter Books concludes that "the mother was the favored guardian; from 30 to 57 percent of the individual children were in the care of their mothers, either alone or with a stepfather."[48] In many of those cases where the mayor did not appoint the mother as custodian, he instead appointed her new husband. This decision still had the effect of recognizing a child's need for his mother. The court awarded these new husbands the custody of children of all ages. Isabella, widow of Henry de Coventre, and John de Whight (whose relationship is not identified) received wardship of her three children: John, age six; another son, age two; and a daughter, Johanna, age seven.[49] Isabella, widow of Thomas Goldyngham, became the independent guardian of her sons, William and Thomas, ages seventeen and thirteen, respectively.[50] In the absence of a mother, stepmothers sometimes filled the role of guardian. The mayor and alderman awarded the guardianship of Robert and Elizabeth, children of Henry Wodewey, to their stepmother, Mary, in 1416.[51] In some cases, the court limited the term of guardianship. For example, in 1444, Alice, mother of Matilda, the daughter of John Walter, became her daughter's guardian for a period of five years; in 1431, Elizabeth, mother of Henry, William and Elizabeth, the "orphans" of Ralph Skynnard, also became guardian for a "term of five years."[52] Whether this was a temporary guardianship or the court expected the children to reach their age of majority within that time is unclear; nevertheless, all of these cases plainly indicate a preference for mothers.

Although the king often exploited the prerogative of wardship, even he sometimes defended a mother's right to her children. In 1310, when the mayor and alderman committed Christiana, daughter of William de Hundesdiche, to a guardian other than her mother, William's widow and her new husband sought the backing of the king. The king responded with an order to the mayor and alderman to restore the child to her mother.[53] In an even more pointed case, the king intervened to return a child named Agnes to her mother, Matilda, and her new husband, Simon de Burgh, even though neighbors were apprehensive about their parenting abilities. Simon and Matilda were accused of "contriving to marry the aforesaid Agnes, who was eight years of age, and had property to the amount of 40 marks rent, to Thomas, a son of the aforesaid Simon, who was not yet eleven years old, and the banns of their marriage had been published, and the wedding garments and feast had been prepared." Yet, the king deemed the reason for removing Agnes from the custody of her mother was "insufficient."[54]

The recognition of an indestructible bond between mother and child, as posited by Clark above, is the basis for numerous tales in medieval literature. The story of Patient Griselda, most famously recounted in Chaucer's "The Clerk's Tale," was horrifying to medieval audiences precisely because Walter chose to test his wife's loyalty to him in the cruelest means imaginable: by taking her children away from her. This topos appears in literature all across medieval Europe. The Norse sagas even call attention to a mother's attachment to her child. In *Gunnlaugs saga ormstungu*, a wife whose husband instructed her to abandon their newborn daughter defies his request after looking lovingly upon her child; she sends the child to live with her sister-in-law instead.[55] Even those tales where mothers callously abandon their children for frivolous reasons emphasize the naturalness of this bond. When a mother pawns her son to a moneylender in the *Cántigas of Alfonso X of Castile*, prompting the Virgin Mary to intercede and save him, the audience is supposed to respond with horror: how could any mother behave in such a heartless fashion towards her children?[56] The medieval literature underscores how strongly medieval society believed a mother's place was with her child.

To return to the world of law, the medieval courts not only recognized a mother's ability to act as guardian to her child but lauded and encouraged her right to do so. Yet in all these cases, the mother's guardianship hinged on the fact that the father had died. Thus, the experience of Margaret de Heton, whose husband was mentally ill, is instructive. The 1354 inquisition into John de Heton's sanity recounts how Margaret and John's brother William had been caring jointly for John, his children with Margaret, and his financial affairs since he succumbed to illness in 1348; at that time, he had three children under the age of six. By 1352, the relationship between

William and Margaret had deteriorated, making the existing custody arrangements untenable: Margaret "would not dwell with her husband in the company of William de Heton, his brother, and the latter would not let his brother be away from his guardianship in that of his wife." Friends and neighbors assisted in negotiating new terms of custody: William assumed guardianship of the youngest two children and sufficient lands to support them; Margaret became guardian for her oldest son, John, and they lived on the remainder of the property.[57] Margaret's experience is edifying in two respects: first, it demonstrates the central role played by communities in brokering the terms of guardianship in informal custody agreements. Second, it highlights the active involvement of the mother in parenting in a situation of marital non-cohabitation.

Divorce (in which both parents were *compos mentis*) obviously presented a very different scenario. The over-riding assumption here is that there is no evidence of custody award in the event of a divorce, because custody automatically went to the father. The real question, then, is did fathers want the custody of their children? Certainly, in the case of an older son who might be capable of assisting his father in the field or in his craft, it is hard to imagine that the father would have permitted his former wife custody when it meant depriving himself of free labor. Fosterage, domestic service or apprenticeship were normal ways to spend one's teenage years and thus provided an easy solution to custody disputes involving older children. However, what about the custody of small children? Although some men could afford to hire nurses to look after their children, most could not, and changing diapers was not an especially manly activity. Childcare was women's work, and, as Mavis Mate has pointed out, "[m]en, whatever their social class, did not engage in tasks such as childcare."[58] The medieval records are also rife with cases of men denying paternity, suggesting that not all men were eager to take up the mantle of fatherhood. As the guardianship of fatherless children confirms, women were often enthusiastic for custody of their children; and there existed a distinct appreciation in the medieval world for the nurturing environment mothers provided the very young. Why would the father's continuing existence undermine any of these factors?

Cases of desertion in which husbands abandoned their children without maintenance bolster the assumption that wives normally cared for the young after a divorce. In her petition to the chancellor at the end of the Middle Ages, Juliana Northe specifically bewails the support and fate of her "fatherless children" after her divorced husband absconded with a substantial amount of her property.[59] The court generally took a firm stance on fathers who abandoned their children: a request to the bishop of Lincoln from 1308–9 ordered the denunciation of William Gamel of Middleton, excommunicated for having abandoned his wife, Elena de Fridaythorp, and their children before fleeing to Barlings Abbey (*Lincs.*). The court expresses its abhorrence of his action in the record, describing William as being contemptuous of the laws of marriage by refusing to adhere to his wife and denying his children nourishment.[60] A similar sense of manifest disapproval is evident in the record for the diocese of Hereford in 1397, which notes that Walter Kadyle maltreated his legitimate wife, Ivel, expelling her from the home, denying her food and clothing and refusing to maintain their child.[61] The archbishop of Canterbury's 1297 letter to the abbot of Langdon also expresses great dissatisfaction with the abbot's lone decision to permit John de Bacheford to enter the monastery and keep him there, even though John deserted his wife and children and left them with nothing to sustain themselves.[62] Just as medieval society held a man to the expectation that he must support his wife, a man must also provide for his children.

Although men who abandoned their families belong to a relatively familiar trope for both the medieval and the modern era, the same connection is not made between mothers and their children. The few documented cases in which medieval mothers abandoned children to the care of their fathers indicate an overwhelming degree of desperation. A Wiltshire eyre of 1281 recounts how Isabella de Bradefeud brought her one-year-old son to the home of his father, Robert Hudde, in the ville of Clyve Wanncy. When Robert refused to admit the child into his custody, she left the child at his door, assuming he could not ignore the cries of his own child. Robert did: the child died the next night from exposure. The court did not indict the parents for homicide; however, royal officials fined Robert, Isabella and the village itself for their negligence.[63] A record drawn from the diocese of Lincoln for the year 1519 tells a similar story: Thomas Leeke turned away a baby boy left at his door, even though the mother claimed he was the child's father. Thomas denied it. The baby was taken to different places and ill-treated before finally dying.[64] These few cases make it clear that, more often than not, mothers were the principle caretakers of their children, and efforts to transfer that responsibility to the father were not always successful.

Admittedly, the supposition that young children remained with their mothers after a divorce is speculative, built entirely on anecdotal evidence; but Pollock and Maitland express the problem so clearly: "[a] fatherless heir must be in ward to some one. Who shall be his guardian?"[65] Divorcing couples must have addressed the question of their children's custody. Although today courts are required to mediate in order to negotiate the rules and schedules of custody, the medieval courts did not play the same role, most likely because social expectations dictated where a child would live. Because mothers played such a formative role in the rearing of young children, logic alone indicates that they were the ideal custodians.

CHILD SUPPORT

Medieval church courts did not address the matter of child support in their written documentation. The simple, if somewhat cynical, explanation for this may be that because fathers traditionally paid child support only to the single mothers of illegitimate children, it was not useful as a bargaining tool to gain additional remuneration, and thus children were simply a non-issue. What is clear is that the courts did not consider how a husband and wife provided for the support of their children as a matter to be determined by the courts. Mothers would have been the usual recipients of child support. Although court-mandated child support did not exist for divorced wives, as the last chapter relates, alimony most certainly did. Variation in the amounts of alimony awarded by court officials probably reflects not only the socio-economic status of the individuals but also the number of children involved. Women phrased their requests for alimony as a right owed to them by their standing as wives, not as mothers. However, Matilda de Pembridge's undated petition to the archbishop of Canterbury overtly links those two familial roles: she asks that her husband, William de Brokbur, pay alimony for both her and her two children.[66] Matilda's remarkably explicit supplication seemingly resolves the mystery of how men provided for their children. In the modern West, the courts separate alimony from child support in recognition of a woman's very different roles as wife and mother. This approach speaks to a world where birth control is relatively affordable and abundant, and mothers regularly work outside the home; thus it is possible to discriminate between marriage and motherhood as separate responsibilities. Marriage in medieval England, however, inexorably led to motherhood for healthy women. Thus, it should come as no surprise that the medieval courts did not make that same distinction. Provisions for alimony by the medieval church recognized fully a woman's role as a wife, which unavoidably included her function as a mother.

Not all mothers were willing to place their trust in the church to enforce the payment of alimony. Some couples entered into bonds to guarantee the support of their children. The discovery of a Suffolkshire bond tying Richard Withermarsh by the Statute Merchant to Clement Spice in the penal sum of £100 from the year 1379 is particularly instructive here. Clement Spice was acting on behalf of Richard's wife, Christian, widow of John Peke. The conditions of the bond related to an upcoming annulment between Richard and Christian and addressed specifically the financial settlements of the marriage. Emphasizing the need for haste, the indenture stipulated that within fifteen days of the award, Richard must pay £33 6*s*. 8*d*. for Christian's support; a similar sum was due within six months. Although the payment of alimony would suggest that their divorce was a judicial separation, it was, in fact, an annulment. The condition that within eight days of the award Richard was to return the title to Christian's dower lands from her marriage to John Peke emphasizes this status. What is most striking is that Richard also entered into a separate bond for £40 in which he pledged "to provide for the children of the marriage and to indemnify Christian for life from the expense of the maintenance."[67] Richard's bond for child support is identifiable as such only because of all the other conditions relating to the divorce with his then wife. How many other men entered into bonds with their wives' protectors for child support without explicitly stating that was what they were doing?

Formal or informal agreements for child support only come to the attention of the historian when those agreements were breached. For example, the Year Book for 1469 discusses an informal contract on a lease violated by a man referred to as "B," who put his wife and son to board with "A" for a three-year period. "B" promised to pay "A" 6*s*. 11*d*. per week for room and board, and "A" clearly demonstrated that the wife and son were with him during that time. "B", however, declared that he had never leased a chamber; the contract, in his mind, was for board only.[68] Although the dispute does not explicitly address why the couple were living separately (divorce is one possibility, but he may also have been a mariner or a pilgrim), it does reveal that informal agreements for "putting at the borde," as one justice referred to it, were usual. At times, men intended their agreements for support of the child alone. A debt on an obligation from the year 1496 makes a similar complaint: the plaintiff argued that he had entered into an obligation with the defendant on the grounds that the defendant find "sufficient food, drink, and apparel" for an infant until he reached the age of twenty-one; if he failed to do so, the obligation was void. The plaintiff claimed that the defendant had not found the child sufficient apparel during that time; he voiced a concern that the defendant had also failed to secure sufficient food and drink, but as he feared "double-pleading," he chose not to take issue with that at this time. The court sided with the plaintiff.[69] Again, although the context of this agreement is not clear enough that we can definitively state this was an arrangement for child custody after a divorce, this model would certainly be viable in that situation.

BECOMING A BASTARD

The impact of divorce on a child's legitimacy took place of pride among parental concerns in the medieval documentation relating to marital dissolution. Unlike the central Middle Ages, when a bastard such as William the Conqueror could aspire to rule a kingdom, in the later medieval period, legitimacy was paramount for both inheritance and entrance into ecclesiastical orders. In fact, parents were so highly conscious of aspersions of illegitimacy that they even petitioned the pope for supporting documentation of truly legitimate children. The informality of the marriage process meant that gossip might wreak havoc on the family lives of medieval Englishmen and women. As David D'Avray has noted:

> rumours could circulate that a couple were married when they knew they were not. Such rumours could make it hard for them to marry

> anyone else. If they went ahead and did so, the rumours would amount to a suspicion that they were living in sin, which the couple might not like, as well as casting doubt on the legitimacy of their children.[70]

The disability imposed by illegitimacy was such that even at the level of royalty, parents worked hard to ensure their children's legitimacy would never come into question. King Henry III's tireless pursuit of documentation concerning his annulment from Joan of Ponthieu, a marriage within forbidden degrees contracted by proxy and never consummated, was a manifestation of this social anxiety to avert doubts about the legitimacy of his children by Eleanor of Provence.[71]

Naturally, because of the heightened anxiety about a child's legitimacy, it was standard practice in petitions for dispensations to remarry despite impediments for parents to express great concern for their children both past and present, requesting (and being awarded) an official statement of their legitimacy. Granted, in terms of inheriting English property, as *Bracton* suggests, the church's declaration acted as a guideline for common law justices only in the High Middle Ages. *Bracton* explains the practice in very lucid terms:

> If between J. and B., man and woman, sentence of divorce has been canonically pronounced, their children should not suffer injury on that account if their parents are known to have been married publicly and without any ecclesiastical objection. Therefore we ordain that their children, born before the divorce or conceived before the final judgment of divorce was pronounced, shall nonetheless be held legitimate and shall succeed to the paternal property by hereditary right and be supported by parental resources.[72]

Soon after *Bracton*, English common law veered away from canon law requirements, adhering to different standards; thus, as Sergeant Pygot declared in 1479, "there are diverse cases where in 'our law' a man is bastard and by the law of Holy Church legitimate."[73] The Statute of Merton (1236) expressly states that a child born before the espousals was a bastard, even if his father later married his mother.[74] An annulment, which declared that a marriage had never been valid, thus bastardized the children in the eyes of the common law, even if the church considered them legitimate. As one justice of Common Pleas bemoaned in 1406 while adjudicating on a matter of inheritance, when a couple divorced, "by their own act they defeated themselves."[75] The one exception was when the couple divorced on grounds of incest, where they both (or at least one of the parties involved) had married in ignorance: *Bracton* makes it clear that in this situation, the offspring are still legitimate.[76] *Bracton*'s exception still applied in the late fifteenth century, when Justice Thomas Bryan pronounced:

> and I say that the law of Holy Church is as has been said, because if I espouse my cousin [relative] within the degrees neither I and nor she knowing [it], and then after we have issue between us, we have notice of this, because of this we are divorced, by the spiritual law the issue is legitimate, but it is otherwise if I am married to a wife, and during this [marriage] I betroth another woman, and have issue [with her], in this case by the law of Holy Church the issue is bastard, and also by our law, because the second espousals are void.[77]

Because most couples protested strenuously that they had been unaware of any kinship, ascertaining whether they actually knew was not easy. Yet, common law justices were willing to impose the full force of the law on those who knowingly entered into an unlawful marriage, even when (or perhaps, especially when) the couple produced an heir who stood to inherit a significant legacy. For example, when the church discovered that Reginald Cobham (of the Barons Cobham of Sterborough, Kent) and his wife, Elizabeth, married knowing full well that they were cousins, it divorced them. To circumvent this obstacle, they purchased a dispensation to remarry. Despite the church's assurance that all children past and present were legitimate, the king's court ruled their son born before the annulment a bastard who could not inherit; their daughter, born after the dispensation, became Reginald's heir.[78]

Justices were cognizant of the differences between canon law and common law in terms of bastardizing a child, and it is noteworthy that common law did not always take the harder line. As Justice Richard Choke explains in a 1479 dispute, sometimes the church was less forgiving. For example, "if a wife elopes [runs away] from her husband and has issue in her adultery, she will lose her dower, and the issue will be legitimate in our law, and again by the spiritual law he is bastard."[79] Granted, a judicial separation did not have the same impact on children. Because the church did not revoke the bonds of matrimony, the children's legitimacy remained intact, and common law justices accepted the church's mandate in this matter. This distinction, though, may not have been widely understood by the English laity. Justices of the Common Bench expressed their frustration that litigants often neglected to explain the nature of their divorce, even though it was material to their case: "if one wants to plead a divorce, he ought to show why the divorce was made, that is by cause of frigidity, or another cause, because some divorce makes the issue bastard, and some does not."[80]

For those children who became bastards by their parents' divorce, the church had a well-established tradition of enforcing payments by the father for illegitimate children. Much like alimony payments, there was a great diversity in the nature of support agreements for bastard children. Many courts enforced weekly payments: in 1371, the dean and chapter of York ordered William of Hexham to pay 2*d*. weekly for the support of his child by Emotta Ripon, with 2*s*. in arrears.[81] Sums of this nature were typical. As R.H. Helmholz has observed, "[t]he Act books do not suggest generosity. The amounts of support vary from one penny per week . . . to six pence. Two pence per week is the sum mentioned most often in the remaining records."[82] Some court orders were more generous. An order from October 1330 to enforce the payment of child support of William del Clay of Markham's bastard children with Beatrice, daughter of John le Spenser de Upton, stipulates yearly payments for a three-year period of 5*s*. sterling, to be paid in equal portions at the feasts of St. Martin and Easter.[83] A late-fifteenth-century order emanating from the archbishop of Canterbury regarding the support of Agnes Rodwell's illegitimate child is particularly charitable. The court ordered John Pynnes, a singleman who impregnated his servant, to pay Agnes 4*d*. per week for her maintenance until the birth of the child and then 8*d*. per week from the birth until her purification. Within three days of her purification, the court required him to pay Agnes 40*s*. and to maintain the child from the time of its birth "as he would were it legitimate."[84] Although such hefty payments must certainly reflect John Pynnes's socioeconomic status, the glaring abuse of his position of authority as Agnes's guardian during her service with him surely explains the punitive nature of the court's award.

The church did not take kindly to fathers who chose not to meet their responsibilities to their children. The bishop of Worcester expected Richard of Timberhanger to pay Constance Brome half a mark yearly for their son in quarterly installments of 20*d*. Ignoring the court's demands had dire consequences: if Richard neglected to make the first payment at the feast of the Purification (that is, roughly three days after the court's session), the court declared that he would find himself excommunicated.[85] As Robert Barker realized in December 1331, this was not an idle threat. When Robert failed to appear in court to respond to Agnes Haukyn's request for child support, the bishop of Rochester excommunicated him. News of his excommunication prompted Robert to appear in court just two days later: the court ordered him to be whipped twice at Fordham church and twice also around the market. The court then ordered him to pay Agnes 1.5*d*. weekly, including the arrears, until the child reached the age of seven. At that time, the child was four years old; thus, the arrears were substantial.[86] The demand to pay arrears for fathers "who had fallen behind in their payments" was a normal part of the process, indicating the church's dedication to enforce fathers into living up to their obligations.[87] The church was determined to find ways to hold men accountable, and thus frequently they included threats in their agreements—and not all penalties were strictly spiritual ones. In 1325, when the bishop of Worcester ordered John Sekestein of Bremesgraue, a chaplain, to pay Agnes, daughter of John Hucheinn, child support of 8*s*. sterling in four separate payments, he added that if the chaplain failed to pay an installment, the whole sum was to be paid immediately.[88]

Of course, not all fathers were obstructionists in meeting their obligations as parents. For example, a case from the bishop of Worcester's register from the year 1323 records an agreement for child support between William le Naym of Seggesberge, chaplain, and Agnes Morice. The register notes that the court decided "with their unanimous consent and goodwill that the son about whom a suit for alimony had been mooted between them should be brought up with the mother": they agreed that William would pay 10*s.* in quarterly installments beginning at Easter for the next two years.[89] In the year 1347, the bishop of Rochester also addressed an amiable case of child support. John Walder and Pauline Galeweye declared that they would gladly marry, but they were too closely related by affinity. Because marriage was impossible, John agreed to pay Pauline one penny a week for the support of their child.[90]

Regrettably, the records typically do not tell us whether a divorce bastardized the children or whether their status was a result of their parents' never marrying in any formal way. However, it is clear that some relationships were long-standing, producing a number of children, and thus were probably considered marriages within their communities. For example, in July 1338, Petronilla super le Grene appeared before the dean and chapter of Lincoln, seeking child support for her four-year-old son and her one-year-old daughter from their father, Robert Northeby. She requested 6*s.* and 8*s.*, respectively, per year, for the next three years.[91] Why did she wait until her oldest child was four before she sought child support? The obvious answer is that before that, she and Robert cohabited, and thus she did not need to seek a formal means of support. Reginald Webbe and Joan Akerman had also been together long enough to produce two children when she appeared in court requesting child support in 1348. Under pain of excommunication, Reginald consented to pay for the support of the elder child and, before midsummer, to find 6*s.* 8*d.* for the support of the younger.[92] The church went to great lengths to enforce the payment of child support for illegitimate children in all of these cases: why should we suppose they were not equally enthusiastic in the defense of legitimate children?

LIFE AFTER DIVORCE

Between high mortality rates and divorce, blended families, uniting the children from a variety of marriages and unions, were the norm in later medieval England.[93] For those children who remained with their mother after a divorce, life with a stepfather, almost immediately after the death of their father, was almost a certainty. The rapidity with which widows remarried most likely reflects the economic difficulties of supporting one's self and one's children in the absence of a husband. Pollock and Maitland's fears that jealousies over property might lead to the abuse and even destruction of the child may have played out in some situations; but the rate of intra-familial homicide was exceedingly low for later medieval England and thus does not suggest that stepfathers were any more exuberant in their correction of stepchildren than they were of their own.[94] Occasional examples of abuse at the hands of a stepfather do appear in the records. For example, an eyre from 1280 notes how Richard le Wynde killed his wife's daughter by whipping her, presumably an overly zealous episode of discipline. The court sentenced Richard to hang.[95] The remarriage of Alice, widow of Walter de Kirkbride, exposed her children to excessive levels of violence. Alice was suing for divorce from her husband of six years, Thomas Lengleys, who was rumored to have caused the death of his wife's unborn child and having broken the back of one of her children by her former marriage.[96] Although Alice's own allegations focus instead on Lengleys's violence towards her, undermining the validity of those rumors, certainly this environment was not a stable one for children. Alice's children, though, were the exception, not the rule. An especially insightful case of desertion from the register of the bishop of Carlisle reveals that social expectations dictated that stepfathers take a more hands-off approach to their wives' children. In a 1331 suit for restitution of conjugal rights between John de Waldene and Beatrice Bridefen, the bishop of Carlisle demanded that Beatrice "chastise her sons and daughter lest they should give her husband cause of offence. If she fails to do so, he may administer gentle chastisement."[97] Although the rebellious behavior of Beatrice's children most certainly drove her husband from the house, it is striking that the bishop very clearly believed their discipline belonged to their mother, even though it was usually a father's responsibility. The bishop was thus drawing an essential distinction between a father's rights and a stepfather's.

On the more positive side, the Year Books recount copious stories of husbands who raised their wives' children as their own. In each of these cases, the reason they appeared before the courts was that someone contested the child's ability to inherit on the grounds of illegitimacy. Yet, justices and pleaders alike adopted an extraordinarily tolerant attitude. A justice of King's Bench in the year 1309 proclaimed that whether a man's son was actually his son was "a very private matter." What mattered most was that he "in his lifetime held him for son and reared him and recognized him as son."[98] A case of bastardy before the Common Bench in 1422 echoed this sentiment, as a pleader declared boldly, "for no one save God knows by whom she is pregnant."[99] In the questions posed to members of the jury, justices of the Common Bench in a case of *mort d'ancestor* in 1285 also focused specifically on a man's behavior towards his wife's son. The jury responded that "Robert was born a good ten years before John married his mother Maud, but we tell you that he was not raised as Roger's son [i.e. her former husband], but once John married he accepted and raised Robert as his son." The justice continued by asking how John treated Robert before the marriage. The jury noted that "John and Maud had fallen out and the Abbot of Reading brought them together, but we cannot deny that he accepted him as his son before the marriage as well as afterward." Despite England's convoluted rules of bastardy, the justices declared the child was legitimate.[100]

Probate evidence also supports the fact that stepfathers frequently treated their stepsons as their own. Jenny Kermode's study of merchant wills from late medieval England provides a number of examples of this nature. One of the more amusing examples is that of John Bedford of Hull. When he died, his will specified that his wife's son from a former marriage would be a co-heir with his own children, providing he did not "molest" his mother.[101] Kermode argues that:

> [d]espite complex family structures, bonds of affection and duty developed between stepchildren, parents, and siblings; between first, second, and even third families; and between present and past spouses. It is worth reflecting that the likelihood of having half-siblings and stepchildren meant that townsfolk had close ties with a far greater number of individuals living nearby than we commonly do today.[102]

Medieval England's unique understanding of family most likely facilitated the acceptance of blended families. *Familia*, as the medieval world defined it, meant "household" rather than strictly the nuclear family as the West defines it today. Especially in urban settings, medieval households often included a broader array of individuals, such as servants and apprentices. Both servants and apprentices shared beds and meals with the rest of the family; their chores also generally included looking after young children. Hence, it is not surprising that close ties often developed between servants, apprentices and their master's family. Their family-like relationship is underscored by bequests in wills; P.J.P. Goldberg notes that "employers regularly remembered their servants and even former servants" in wills.[103] The ease with the medieval *familia* accepted servants and apprentices implies that blood relationships were not central to familial affection; living in a blended family in this environment must have been a very comfortable, normal situation.

EMOTIONAL BAGGAGE?

Tomes claiming to hold the secret of parenting for children scarred by the divorce of their parents line the self-help sections of bookstores today. The emotional baggage typically associated with the children of divorced parents today may also have been a problem in medieval England. In fact, given the subsequent bastardization of many children, many children must have resented their parents for pursuing a path that inevitably transformed their children into legal and social outcasts and severely curtailed their marriage and career choices. An investigation into the unlawful seizure of lands and tenements in Colne, Great Marsden and elsewhere in Essex by John Banastre from his mother, Agnes, uncovered a good deal of resentment harbored by John concerning his parents' divorce. The under-aged son, who in this case was also his father's heir, boldly declared that she had no right to these dower lands, because she had "evilly, perversely, and not womanly disposed towards her husband, but craftily and cunningly" laid the groundwork for a divorce. John recounted how she had taken his sister, Christian, the legitimate child of Agnes and his father, also named John, to be confirmed before John Grene, bishop of the Islands. By acting as her daughter's godmother, she manufactured an impediment of incest by sponsorship to a valid marriage between her husband and herself. Her son John claimed her objective was to engineer a judicial separation, although incest typically barred the marriage altogether.[104] Self-interest (or, at the very least, the interest of the under-aged son's guardian) may explain the son's anger after the death of his father; after all, if his mother had no right to dower, the land would come to him (or to the possession of his guardian until he reached the age of majority). Even if a guardian were primarily responsible for John's lawsuit, the language employed in the records exudes an overriding sense of bitterness and hostility, indicating that John found his mother's self-interested behavior reprehensible.

The legal record clearly articulates John Banastre's explanation for denying his mother her dower lands: how many other sons (or stepsons) also obstructed their mother's claims to dower on similar basis? Dower litigation ultimately pitted sons against their mothers or stepmothers in what might be years of courtroom battles. Because a widow had to plead individual suits for each parcel of land to which she was entitled, the number of suits was often extensive: Eleanor de Ferrers, the widow of the earl of Derby, for example, sued sixty-three different people to retrieve her dower in the thirteenth century.[105] Although the suit itself targeted the occupants of the land, her husband's heir as warrantor was responsible for supporting or rejecting her dower claim. The familial nature of dower suits meant that "[e]motions as well as property were often on trial in dower pleas."[106] Once again, this assumption is tentative, but it seems likely that some bitter examples of dower litigation may well have been motivated out of resentment over an unwanted divorce.

The effect of divorce on the children of separating parents remains the haziest part of this investigation. Canon law upheld a parent's obligation to support his children; nonetheless the records of litigation fail to address the matter altogether. Sufficient evidence does exist, however, to establish that the courts did not neglect the support and custody of children in the process. Young children probably remained in the mother's custody. A father's alimony payments supported not only his wife but also his children. In the case of annulment, the church most likely expected a father to pay child support, as he would to any other bastard child. When fathers did not pay up, the church had a well-established process to intimidate fathers into supporting their children through threats to both their souls and their purses. However, mothers may not have bothered to turn to the courts to enforce fathers to pay child support in this situation. Because most mothers remarried so quickly, stepfathers may have fulfilled this role without questioning their obligation to do so. Although parents did not articulate their concerns for the support and custody of their children in the divorce documentation, they were attuned to the impact divorce had on the legitimacy of their children and worked hard to prevent their children from being denied an inheritance or entrance into religious orders. Yet, because English common law adhered to different standards in terms of defining illegitimacy, those efforts did not always pay off. Like most children's history, these findings are pieced together through often tangential and anecdotal evidence. The picture that emerges, though, is that of a society with many formal and informal processes already in place to make this course of action a relatively easy one.

6 What Happened Next?

Probably the most interesting question to ask about divorce in the medieval context is what happened next. As we have seen, obtaining a divorce in the Middle Ages required great stamina. In court-sanctioned divorces, the expense, the duration of the process, and the vicious attacks on one's character were merely one small part of the equation; supporting one's self and staying safe during the process were even greater concerns. In a self-divorce, relocation to a new environment essentially meant starting one's life over, without the comforts of familiar faces and any sort of financial support network to fall back on. Given the hardships and risks involved in the divorce process to both the couple and those who assisted them, was it worth it? Did women enjoy their newly won independence? How did their communities react? Did the couples ever reconcile? Alternatively, did they simply move on? Questions of this nature are not always easy to answer, but the records do confirm that a declaration by the church that a marriage was invalid was not necessarily the last hurdle in the process of divorce.

PROVING DIVORCE

Obtaining a divorce was one thing; proving it was another altogether. Although the church court drew up documentation concerning the divorce, it seldom reached the hands of the divorced couple. Rather, the church courts archived sentences and produced the necessary evidence on demand when a divorce came into question. A mandate to rescind the excommunication of Alexander de Seton, a Scotsman, reminds us that there was good justification for the church circumspectly holding on to much of the paperwork. In order to obtain a divorce from his wife, Egidia de Hay, Alexander concealed the papal dispensation that had allowed them to marry in the first place in his house and insisted that because of their incestuous relationship, they needed a divorce. He then contracted a second marriage, and Egidia died; his next wife, ostensibly, was the instigator behind his confession, wishing that they be married anew without any past sins to tarnish the validity of their union.[1] As Alexander's deviousness implies, surely, if the paperwork had remained entirely in the hands of individuals rather than in the church archives, destruction through vengeance, intimidation, blackmail, and mere accident would have kept the courts busy continually drafting replacement documents.

Nonetheless, at times, a couple's trust in the church to be a guardian of such important legal documentation was misplaced. A number of cases emphasize that the church was not much better at archiving than it was at enforcing alimony payments. In 1340, when William Botevileyn and his "wife," Margery, were facing a trespass suit for contempt, heavily weighted against them, as it had been perpetuated against one of the justices sitting in judgment on their case and had occurred just moments before in the presence of the entire court, they hoped to quash the bill (and thus go free) on the grounds of a technicality: the bill inaccurately named Margery. She claimed that the two were recently divorced: thus, she was not Margery, wife of William Botevileyn, but Margery of Muyse. In order to validate the accuracy of this detail, the court wrote to the bishop of Rochester to confirm that his court had, indeed, pronounced a divorce between them. The bishop returned that he could not find any such record.[2]

The obvious reason why the court could not find any record of the church annulling their marriage is that William and Margery fabricated the story. The bishop of Rochester's register, though, suggests that Margery may actually have been telling the truth. The two appeared first before the bishop in July 1335, at which time Margery alleged that they could not consummate their marriage due to William's impotence.[3] Fearing a lack of impartiality in her own diocese, Margery appealed directly to the pope. In March of the following year, the pope assigned the archdeacon of Sudbury and the precentor of St. Edmund Bury as his delegates to probe further into the condition of their marriage, as William protested that the allegation of an impediment was false.[4] The register provides no follow-up to this enquiry: in fact, the register does not mention them again except for the writ of *certiorari* from King's Bench in July 1340 requesting confirmation of their divorce, in which the register notes that the bishop of Rochester had returned no such divorce had been pronounced. Given Margery's initial resolve to divorce and her intrepid proclamation in court that she was a newly divorced woman, the church may well have awarded a divorce, but the documentation was simply not where the king's courts expected it to be found.

An investigation by the bishop of Ely into the divorce of Edmund de Duresme and Margaret de Stokes just four years later checks us from jumping to the conclusion that couples purely manufactured stories of divorce. In May 1344, the king commanded the bishop of Ely to search the register of the previous bishop to certify whether a divorce had indeed taken place between Margaret and Edmund (the latter was now deceased). Although the king did not offer an explanation for why he initiated this enquiry, presumably it related somehow to the disposition of Edmund's last will and testament. The bishop replied, "on careful search having been made there is not found in the register that any divorce was celebrated between them nor anything else relating to these persons."[5] In spite of this confident statement, four years later the investigation was ongoing. In November 1348, the bishop of Ely sent a notification to chancery, declaring that, in fact, the archdeacon of Ely had celebrated a divorce between the two during the episcopacy of the former bishop.[6] A notification from December 1348 finally exposed the full truth: the archdeacon, who had previously ruled that a divorce had not taken place between them, had changed his mind when a commissary of the spiritual jurisdiction of the archdeaconry of Ely stumbled across some schedules

> wherein it is written that a divorce was celebrated between the parties, but inasmuch as of such schedules some were not sealed and some were not entire but so decayed that because of their decay they could not in any wise be read through, and others were quite faulty, as was plain and could be plain to any one looking at them, he regarded them as wholly untrustworthy and they should of right be so regarded.[7]

Although Margaret was probably delighted to be vindicated after four years' worth of investigation, the disarray of the church's archives, laid bare by this case, makes clear that the church was a poor repository for the hard-won decisions of those who had fought to end their marriages legitimately with the blessing of the court. If Margaret's divorce had taken place a long time before this, the condition of the archives might be justified, but Margaret and Edmund's divorce dated from the time of John of Hothum as bishop of Ely, who occupied that office from 1316–37.[8] In the worst case, thirty-two years had passed since the divorce, not so long a time given that the church's archives were hundreds of years old.

Even the English church sometimes recognized its own inability to archive documents and share them appropriately with other jurisdictions. For example, in the late fifteenth century, the archbishop of Canterbury summoned Robert Heyde to respond to allegations of bigamy. Appearing in court, Robert swore that he had been legitimately divorced from his first wife by the commissary of the bishop of Lincoln. Rather than write to the diocese of Lincoln for the documentation, the archbishop instead demanded that he reappear in court a month later with letters of testimonial to prove his divorce.[9]

Some individuals did possess personal copies of the documentation provided by the church; but legal records alone were not always sufficient to prove that a divorce had taken place. In an attempt to quash a suit of ravishment at the court of King's Bench in 1421, the plaintiff's "wife" appeared in court with the official record in hand attesting that she had obtained a divorce from the plaintiff. Explaining the "ravishment," as her ex-husband described it, she told the court that the defendant had lain with her, but that the act was consensual. In spite of her rationale, the husband won his case: because a wife did not have power over her body, justices decided she did not have the authority to consent; only the husband did. This decision effectively ignored church certification altogether.[10]

The justices' 1421 decision to dismiss the church's award of a divorce is disconcerting, chiefly because it suggests that the courts continued to see a couple as married even when the church, the publicly recognized authority on matters of marriage, did not. The dichotomy between ecclesiastical and secular perceptions further obscured the sometimes-ambiguous state of marriage. To return to the coerced spousals of Isabella de Scaresbrek and John of York, justices responded in an equally curious manner to John's suit of ravishment.[11] The defendant was Isabella's publicly acknowledged husband, Henry Molineux. When he appeared before justices of assize with evidence of Isabella's court-sanctioned divorce from John on the grounds of coercion (thus, obviously, invalidating a case of the taking of wife and goods), one justice asserted that she was his "wife in possession," if not his "wife in right." Clarifying the matter, the judge argued, "she could be his wife in this county, and perhaps he had another wife in another county, and still both were his wives in possession, although they were not his wives in right."[12] The judge's objective was to uphold a husband's rights (and presumably responsibilities) for wives in possession. The same rationale was put forward also in a case from Common Pleas in 1456.[13] Even though the court did not implement this logic in either suit in the Year Books, we have no way of knowing how persuasive justices found this line of reasoning or whether it was put into operation in other lawsuits. This reading of the case material destabilizes the entire process of divorce: despite the hard work and money a wife spent to get a divorce, the court might very well ignore it and treat her as married anyway.

Only the courts were interested in official proof of divorce. Legal record of the church's decision was therefore only necessary for those who somehow transgressed the law. For the vast majority, the more relevant concern was public proof. Because a husband and wife's livelihoods were so deeply intertwined, some sort of public ritual was necessary to sever that relationship. Native Welsh law, which provided for divorce on very different grounds than those stipulated by the church (much to the dismay of local clergy), dictated a highly public separation:

> [t]he custom was for the wife to remain in the house for nine days after the property division was made and then to leave with her goods traveling immediately in front of her. Only after "the last penny" had gone was she to go herself—her departure, in other words, was itself a dramatic enactment of the satisfaction of her claims and would only have accomplished its purpose in the presence of witnesses.[14]

Robin Chapman Stacey argues that Welsh law compelled this "legal burlesque" for both publicity and education; the law hoped to discourage divorce by transforming it into a public spectacle in which communities gazed on as mortified couples sorted through and divided the belongings of a life together.[15] If the English had followed Welsh traditions, fewer difficulties would have ensued following a divorce, because communities would have been well aware that one had taken place. Although the Anglo-American world eventually came to recognize the benefit of publicity, with nineteenth-century husbands taking out newspaper advertisements to broadcast their newly separated states, the need for public awareness somehow eluded the medieval English.[16]

The custom of buying on credit posed the greatest threat to husbands in the event of a divorce. Under the rules of coverture, the husband was a family's financial manager. A wife was incapable of making purchases, rents, hires or other business decisions without the consent of her husband. Nevertheless, because this legal incapacity lacked practicality, most merchants or workmen were willing to allow wives to acquire relatively inexpensive goods (such as food stuffs, material for clothing and other necessity items) or services without a husband's consent. Such an arrangement was common and vital to the running of medieval households when husbands were frequently away or ill, leaving their wives to run the household and business.[17] If the bill went unpaid, a creditor had legal recourse against the husband, because "by law she had nothing with which to pay."[18] A divorce did not necessarily quash this marital privilege. Buying on credit may well have been a practical method of supporting one's wife during a judicial separation. The doctrine of necessaries, developed at the end of the seventeenth century, adopted precisely this approach for the maintenance of separated wives. It institutionalized a separated wife's right to purchase food and clothing on her husband's credit.[19] This arrangement was not without its difficulties: a separated wife unhappy with a maintenance agreement doubtless believed the best solution to the problem was to go shopping. Who was to prevent her from purchasing goods and simply charging them to her husband's name? At the very least, before a divorce was widely known, a fruitful trip to market might have allowed a newly divorced wife to stock up on necessities, thereby sustaining her for some time before needing to dip into her husband's allowance.

Nicholas Dobson's late-fifteenth-century petition to the chancellor addresses the problem of buying on credit after an informal separation. Nicholas recounts a relatively typical story of a wife's seduction by the local grocer, who "through his inordinate demeaning," convinced Nicholas's wife "to be of no good rule nor conversation, and against God's law, to absent her(self) from her husband." Since her desertion, the wife and grocer had teamed up to harass Nicholas, suing a feigned action of trespass against him before the sheriff's court. More to the point, they had caused others also to sue false writs of trespass against Nicholas for debts his wife had incurred since she had left her husband. Refusing to pay for his wife's newly independent lifestyle, Nicholas was sitting in prison and feared his sojourn might become permanent without the intervention of the chancellor.[20] Nicholas clearly believed his wife's desertion negated his responsibility to support her; but how were those in the marketplace supposed to know that? Concerns for reputation doubly complicated the situation. Surely, Nicholas did not want to announce publicly that his wife had left him for the local grocer? Yet, without this kind of exposure, how were merchants to know that the previous arrangement should no longer continue?

In many respects, paying an estranged wife's shopping expenses was a relatively minor concern. A divorced husband might also have to pay for any loans his ex-wife took out to support herself. A London court condemned John Perveys (unjustly, in his mind) to pay loans worth £20 taken out by his wife, as well as damages of £20 13*s*. 4*d*. and court costs of 26*s*. 3*d*., even though at the time the loan was arranged, John and Elizabeth were divorced, and John was on campaign in Wales with the duke of Buckingham. Of course, as John told it, the story was more intricate than it seemed at first glance: since taking the loan, his wife had married her loan shark, and this second husband was behind the lawsuit, intent on getting his money back.[21] If John's story were legitimate, then Elizabeth's new husband was an exceptionally shrewd man, working around the rules of coverture in order to repay his wife's loan to himself. John's circumstances, though, make us wonder how many other men also were expected to repay their wives' loans, even after their marriages had ended.

Although the financial burdens were probably greater for husbands after a divorce, some wives found themselves in equally uncomfortable situations. When Elizabeth Clyf married John Spenser, he assumed responsibility for the debts she acquired as a singlewoman, as was the custom in English law.[22] Soon after the spousals, anxious to be repaid his debt, Robert Pinson of London sued John for the 26*s*. 8*d*. that Elizabeth owed; when John could not immediately pay up, the sheriff's court threw him in prison. Elizabeth went to Robert and begged that he withdraw the action, declaring that she would act as surety for the money; because she was "covert de baron," Robert denied her request. The court eventually released John when the action was non-suited. Bitter over his imprisonment, John sued at once for a divorce between them. Since that time, the sheriff had arrested Elizabeth as surety in the non-payment of "John's" debt. Once again, as was the case with most bills in chancery, the story was additionally complicated by the fact that she believed Robert and John had teamed up to concoct this plan; but as Elizabeth was now biding her time in a London prison, she had little hope of addressing this problem through normal means.[23] Elizabeth's particular circumstances were unique; however, the underlying problem was endemic. Although divorce might sever a couple's relationship, the ties that bound them ran deep and were not easily uprooted.

The experiences of these couples confirm the intrinsic ambiguity of the marital state that Cordelia Beattie has emphasized in her research. Because the medieval world understood marriage as a process, not an act, there were many opportunities in which "the line between the single and the married might be blurred."[24] We need to recognize "degrees of marriage": cohabiting, separated or divorced couples and women with absent husbands all existed on a "marriage continuum."[25] Divorce was also a process in the medieval world. The same blurring of lines that muddies our understanding of marriage equally problematized the medieval world's recognition of a couple's divorced status.

HOW PERMANENT WAS DIVORCE?

If a canonically valid marriage was not, in fact, permanent, in the Middle Ages, can we expect that a court-sanctioned divorce was? The grim reality is that divorce was no more permanent than a medieval marriage, adding more fuel to the fires of this broader confusion over marital statuses. Certainly, in some cases, the courts expressly stated that a divorce was a temporary solution to the problem and that a couple should not see it as a lasting condition. For example, in judicial separations awarded on any grounds, if a couple exhibited evidence of reconciliation of their own accord, the separation was automatically rescinded without any need for further court appearances.[26] For this reason, a husband determined to prevent a separation sometimes engineered out-of-court negotiations in public settings to prove a wife's change of heart. Simon Munkton and his friends abducted his wife, Agnes Huntington, from a Corpus Christi parade in the hopes of pressuring her to abandon her suit for divorce. When that plan failed, one of his witnesses instead presented a fabricated story of reunion at court, unsupported by other witnesses, in which he saw Simon and Agnes "kiss each other peaceably, voluntarily, and without fear."[27] Simon's witness left no room for speculation by emphasizing the physical nature of their reconciliation; but he did not even have to go to such great lengths to make his point. The oath of separation that Gratian purported the church required all separating couples to swear in court made it clear that separated couples would find it difficult even to live in the same village:

> [h]enceforth you shall, for no reason, unite in marriage or adultery with this woman, your blood relative. You shall not eat with her, drink with her at the same table, or stay with her under one roof. You shall meet her nowhere, except in a church or other public place that is free from scandal, and only out of necessity and in the presence of suitable witnesses.[28]

This oath instantly forces us to consider the process of enacting child visitation rights: clearly, a dedicated father's visit to his wife's home in order to see their children might well have the couple reconciled against their wills. Rather than risk a coerced reunion, a couple did well to avoid each other altogether. Granted, we do need to recognize that some couples may well have wanted to reunite; time spent at a distance may have helped them to overcome their differences. How else do we explain a request by Margaret, wife of John Cronkeshaghe, a mere six months after their divorce *a mensa et thoro* had been awarded to revoke their separation?[29]

Annulments because of impotence or frigidity exemplify divorce as a temporary measure. Canonists grappled with the issue of a marriage dissolved on the grounds of a man's impotence if he then later regained his virility, in part because canonists suspected that a man might fake sexual incapacity in order to obtain a divorce. The church's stance on this issue was well known. In a Year Book discussion of the 1369 suit of ravishment pleaded by Nicholas Cantelowe against a knight referred to as R. Paynel, justices in King's Bench explicitly recognized the impermanence of an annulment in cases of impotence. Learning that Nicholas and his wife had divorced on the grounds of Nicholas's frigidity and impotence, one justice asserted that his rights as husband should still stand. If he "recover[ed] his nature, so that he could perform as a man," then he should have his wife back (and thus, his suit was valid).[30]

An appeal might also revoke a divorce. Not only were the church courts slow and cumbersome in hearing cases of divorce, but because canon law was a constantly evolving field, influenced by the varied and often conflicting views of canon lawyers, there was much room for movement in the church's sentences. Petitions drawing in new court officials paved the way for a fresh interpretation of ecclesiastical laws. Given the regional flavor of medieval canon law, appeals to Rome might also produce an entirely distinct approach to sentencing than what an English judge believed was morally right. Although the records do not always account for the court's decision, it is clear that the church revoked a number of divorces, even though the decision to annul had occurred some time earlier. For example, Maud de Mandeville and Roger de Dauntesseye had been divorced for three years when a royal mandate in 1236 acknowledged their divorce had been revoked by papal authority; the mandate ordered the return of the castle of Kenebauton (*Hunts.*), currently ruled by Maud, to the governance of her husband.[31] The church may have reinstated the divorce sometime after that. Later that same year, Maud died, and her estate passed intact to her heirs from the Bohun family (her first husband's family), implying that Roger did not enjoy his right of curtesy as he would have if the two had had a child together.[32] Sometimes the church rescinded divorces even though the couple had already remarried. An Anglo-Irish case from the mid–fourteenth century recounts how Joan de Tuyt sued for a divorce from Walter Cusak on the grounds of affinity: she discovered that he had cohabited with a woman related to Joan in the third degree before Joan and Walter married. The court awarded a divorce, and Joan remarried. Even though Walter is said not to have appealed, he was presumably responsible for the archbishop of Armagh's abruptly deciding that the divorce was invalid; he ordered Joan and her new husband to divorce and required Joan to return to Walter.[33]

Sometimes the court reversed a decision because it realized the litigants had not been entirely truthful. A commission to the archdeacon of Rochester states this expressly. Although the bishop of Rochester had awarded a divorce to Andrew, son of Roger de Delham, and Joan, daughter of William Hodierne of Halstow, the bishop wanted the archdeacon to investigate their pedigree. If he found that they were related in the fourth and fifth degrees rather than the third and fourth, as they had asserted at their trial, he was to cancel the sentence of divorce.[34] Although this kind of distrust might seem excessive, church officials had good reason to believe that couples might manipulate the laws to their own benefit. Charles Donahue, Jr., has argued that perjury and collusion were defining features that set English marriage litigation apart from the Franco-Belgian equivalent.[35] Fearing the long-term consequences of perjury, far too many Englishmen and -women eventually confessed to their lies. The early-fifteenth-century papal court addressed the deception of Joan Rikil in the divorce of her husband, James Hopwode. The mandate notes that Joan left James to take up with Richard Brune even before suing for divorce. The court record depicts Richard as an unsavory type and the mastermind behind Joan's decision to divorce: "[a]spiring to the great heritage to which she was probably to succeed, [Richard] induced the said James to consent to a sentence of divorce between him and Joan, and suborned a number of witnesses to give, as they afterwards confessed, false depositions, and obtained, by collusion, the promulgation of a sentence of divorce." Since that time, Joan and Richard had contracted marriage and were "living together and committing adultery." The mandate entailed the appearance of Joan and others in court under pain of excommunication; if she admitted to the facts, the bishop was to compel her under ecclesiastical censure, without the possibility of appeal, to abandon Richard and return to James, her husband.[36] Matilda, wife of Thomas le Clerk, also attempted to secure a divorce through false witnesses. Her brother, William in the Lane, testified falsely that her husband, Thomas le Clerk of Camberwell, threatened her in the expectation of obtaining a judicial separation. But Matilda and her brother broke down before the bishop and confessed to their deception in April 1348. The court ordered them to be put to the "discipline of the rod," and Thomas and Matilda were compelled to resume their marriage.[37]

Errors in the process also led to some decisions to revoke a divorce. In 1473, Richard Boteller, an Anglo-Irishman living in the diocese of Cashel, sued for a divorce from Ellen Cantwell. Although the two had been lawfully married and had offspring, and Richard had "kept her for years in his house as his wife," he now alleged that he had contracted marriage with Cathelina Boteller years before and thus was not lawfully married to Ellen. He threw her out of the house and "openly declared that if he had not a sufficient cause to enable him to be separated from her in due time by the judgment of the church, he would not marry her for all the money in the world." In response to his petition, the pope ordered the bishops of Killaloe and Limerick to summon Richard and Ellen to investigate the situation.[38] Richard did not get the reaction he was looking for: the archbishop of Cashel himself mandated Richard to return to his wife and treat her with conjugal affection, under pain of excommunication. Richard refused to obey; the archbishop proceeded with the excommunication, even going so far as to declare that Richard's residence and the places he frequented would fall under interdict. Hoping to work around the archbishop, Richard turned to the bishop of Leighlin, persuading him to pronounce a divorce between the two and to condemn the archbishop for his actions. At this point, Ellen appealed to the pope. Acknowledging that the bishop of Leighlin had no authority or jurisdiction in the matter, the pope repealed his sentence of divorce, declared the marriage to be lawful and ordered Richard to cohabit with his wife. Even so, at the time of the last mandate in July 1476 (three years since the divorce process had first been initiated), Richard had still failed to return to his wife.[39]

Richard Boteller knew well that if you did not get the answer you were looking for from one official, then you went to another. This legal strategy was often successful and lay behind many medieval couples' changes in marital status. William Baron and Marjory Bowis were married and divorced several times over the course of the year 1479. The July mandate responding to William's petition relates how William and Marjory of the diocese of Durham were married before William had reached a marriageable age. Upon turning fourteen, he learned that they were related within the third and fourth degrees and hoped to have their marriage voided. Nonetheless, the diocese upheld the marriage, leading William to appeal to the see. In a subsequent meeting before the abbot of Alnewike and the priors of Tinmouth and Hestildesham, the abbot pronounced a sentence of divorce, declaring the marriage null and William and Marjory free to contract marriage with other persons. Marjory proceeded to appeal to the papal see, and the pope requested the bishop of Carlisle to inspect their marital history further. William then appealed again to the papal see.[40] By August of the same year, William submitted his final appeal after the bishop of Durham (subcommissioned by the bishop of Carlisle) once more determined that William and Marjory were married. The pope's last mandate requested that the bishop of London and the priors of Bowlton in Crawen and Brownhill address the situation in a definitive manner, although there is no record of their final solution. [41]

The English church's stringent application of divorce laws and its eagerness to uphold the sacrament of marriage undoubtedly drove Englishmen and -women into deception in order to achieve their goals of independence. The prevalence of guile and deceitfulness inevitably led to a climate of distrust: their courtroom experiences so jaded England's motley crew of bishops that they assumed the worst from everyone (and regrettably, as much of our case material substantiates, their distrust was well founded). With such dishonesty abounding, ecclesiastical officials had to be prepared to overturn decisions when new evidence was uncovered. A sentence declaring a marriage null and void was thus never as definitive as the church claimed it to be.

LONG-TERM SUPPORT

The church's vacillation in divorce sentences was not the only threat endangering a wife's newfound independence. Even if a woman survived the divorce proceedings, was awarded a judicial separation and worked out an amicable maintenance schedule with her husband, and the two did not reconcile, her rights to sustenance were destined to come under fire upon the death of her husband. Questioning a woman's marital status was a common occurrence in dower litigation by rival claimants hoping to undermine a widow's claim. This tactic was predicated on the proclivity of Englishmen and -women to marry and divorce casually; hopeful heirs were commonly able to lay false claim to estates, discovering that the deceased's wife had no actual proof they had been married. For separated wives, whose marital status was frequently misunderstood, and who could not hope even to bring in witnesses to speak to prolonged cohabitation, the chances of claiming dower were even more tenuous. The fragile nature of the claim happily was not enough to prevent all divorced wives from doing so. The death of Simon le Conestable in the late thirteenth century brought not one but two wives out of the woodwork claiming dower. A reconstruction of Simon's complicated marital history helps to explain the situation. He was first married to Joan, the mother of his heir; although it is not clear how long the two were together, the marriage ended badly. Joan was murdered, and it may well have been his second wife, Katherine, a woman the king pardoned for preparing poison, who assisted in that process. Somewhere in that time, he also married Alice, but their relationship does not appear to have been long-standing. Nevertheless, in court, Alice proved her marriage to Simon and claimed her dower. By then, Simon's heir, Robert, had already granted lands to Katherine, who could not prove her marriage; Katherine got to keep her lands.[42]

Simon's marital history included at least two church-door weddings, one clandestine marriage and one self-divorce. Given the circumstances, it is not surprising that more than one woman believed she was entitled to dower after his death. For many medieval wives, their legitimate marital status meant little until it mattered: in Alice's case, she probably believed she was only separated (even if unofficially) from her husband. He may even have been supporting her through a trust or an informal agreement. Moreover, Katherine probably felt secure in her claim, because she resided with Simon until the time of his death. When it came to the courts, however, whoever produced the best evidence won. Joan, widow of Simon de Percefoil, discovered the importance of corroborating evidence when her nephew contested their marriage. She freely admitted that they had lived separately, although she was quick to assert that she did not desert her husband for a lover: rather, his "harshness" had driven her away. Simon's brother, also his executor, appeared as a witness in her defense. He freely recognized her blamelessness in the marital breakdown and had awarded her dower without complaint.[43] A rival contested the claim of Sibilla, wife of Alan de Whixley, for dower on similar grounds. Her rival was the abbot of Fountains, who remembered distinctly that the church celebrated a divorce between the two before the commissary of the late archbishop of Canterbury. Sibilla passionately denied the divorce; a request to the court at Canterbury to search for evidence of marital dissolution came up empty-handed, and she claimed her dower.[44]

Many separated wives realized too late the need for written evidence of a continuing marital relationship. When evidence did exist, generally the husband's protection, not the wife's, led to its creation. For example, when Henry Wygley separated formally from his wife, Alice, in the years 1487–88, he chose to provide for her future support with a bond for 1,000 marks to be paid by the following Pentecost. The bond states specifically that "Henry shall deliver to her in full satisfaction of all dower and interest that she has in any other part of his estate," providing that "Alice at no time hereafter by assent make any suit or demand in any court, temporal or ecclesiastical, for the said revenues, or procure bodily hurt to him to the breach of the king's peace."[45] The foresight and meticulousness of the bond suggests that Henry had hired a good lawyer. Yet, in drafting the agreement, he was binding not only Alice but himself: if he failed to live up to that obligation, he was going to be in trouble with the law. Henry's bond leads us to consider what happened to wives when the money ran out. Despite the copious attention husbands paid to the creation of reasonable maintenance agreements, an amount that at one time sounded ample eventually may have become inadequate to maintain a wife in her chosen lifestyle. What options did a wife have to renegotiate a maintenance agreement at a later date, particularly when astute lawyers frequently insisted on the insertions of such rigid conditions like those included in Henry Wygley's bond?

A husband's death was the opportune time for a wife to enhance her side of the bargain. For many wives, when a husband's death occurred long after their agreement had been forged, faded memories and ill-informed executors may well have assisted her to increase her portion of the pot. Those cases that appear in the record, of course, represent unsuccessful attempts by wives to renegotiate in their husbands' absence. The separation agreement of Thomas Broune and his wife, Elizabeth, was a typical one for those of their rank; each had a deed of separation drawn up detailing exactly what Elizabeth would receive as a one-time-only payment for her support. According to the petition of William Broune, Thomas's executor, it

> was agreed between the said Thomas and Elizabeth that the same Thomas should deliver to the same Elizabeth and to other persons to her use a certain money and plate and that the same Elizabeth from thenceforth should never vex, trouble, nor sue the said Thomas nor his executors, for any part of his goods, chattels, money or plate, and it was further agreed between the same Thomas and Elizabeth that the same Thomas should be bound to Thomas Fynes, knight, and Godard Oxenbrig, squire, in an obligation in the sum of £200 for the same agreement to be kept on the part of the same Thomas and in like wise the same Elizabeth with other for her should be bound by obligation to that Michael, Prior of the House of St. Mary Overies [London], yet living, and to Richard Morland, deceased, in £200 for the true performance of the said agreement of the said Elizabeth.[46]

Thomas's executor argued further that Elizabeth had received the money and plate as stipulated in the penal bond. His witnesses could attest that she had been given £30 and more as well as "diverse pennies, goblets, salt and spoons to a great value," and that she had been "fully content" with this agreement—that is, until her husband died. Elizabeth's suit in King's Bench against the executor for the sum of £200 she claimed was outstanding on the non-performance of this agreement was the cause of William's petition to the chancellor. Thomas's statement that Elizabeth "should neither vex, trouble, nor sue the said Thomas" in the future was a perceptive inclusion on his behalf in order to prevent any difficulties with double charging—that is, payments for goods that Elizabeth purchased independently and charged to her husband. The intent of this clause was probably to stop Elizabeth from continuing to enjoy these kinds of marital privileges, effectively charging him twice for her support. At the same time, Thomas's decision to opt for a maintenance agreement of this nature highlights the shortsightedness of this kind of arrangement. A settlement of £30 or more and many expensive goods seems fair, but Elizabeth's decision to go to court after Thomas's death makes it plain that the end of the money was in sight. Even if, by law, he was not obligated to support her beyond the agreement, she was still his wife. Should not custom at least dictate a need to support his insolvent wife?

Elizabeth Broune was not the only wife who attempted to improve her lot after the death of her husband. In 1388, Isabella Pledour sued a writ of detinue against her husband's executors for 1,500 marks, as she claimed it, "her portion of the goods and chattels of her late husband according to the custom of the city, whereby a widow took a third part if there were children, and one half if there were no children." When her husband, Richard Lyons, merchant and London alderman, was slain by rebels in 1381,[47] he possessed goods and chattels worth 3,000 marks—cash, but also trading goods from his business, namely "gold and silver in money, silver vessels, linen, woolen and silk cloth, wine in tuns, pepper, ginger and other merchandise." When his executors appeared before the mayor's court, though, they protested that she was not his wife. Rather, in 1363, Richard had sued for a divorce on the grounds of an impediment that no one since remembered, but the bishop of St. Paul had proclaimed the divorce. Isabella refuted these allegations and apparently continued in a long string of lawsuits to retrieve her dower lands. One couple in particular who stood to lose the third part of two messuages of land and sixteen London shops also took her to court. After verifying with the bishop of London, who confirmed that the two had indeed been married lawfully, the court initially sided with Isabella in April 1388; in November 1389, the bishop uncovered further documentation concerning their marriage and sent certification to the justices that the church had, in fact, annulled their union. By June 1391, Isabella was back in court on another writ of detinue against Richard's executors, this time demanding 5,000 marks, purportedly "her widow's portion of her late husband's goods." This time, with the bishop's documentation in hand, the church declared confidently that she was ineligible for dower, because the church had annulled their marriage. It was not prepared for Isabella's response: she swore that she had appealed the divorce to the bishop of London, who instructed his commissary to hear the appeal; the commissary had then voided the divorce and confirmed the marriage. Court proceedings were put off for another day until Isabella could obtain the documentation.

Was Isabella another victim of the church's derisory record keeping? Alternatively, was all of this a lie simply to claim dower lands to which she had no rights? The final decision in this matter no longer exists, but there are several indications that Isabella's story was not altogether frank. At her first appearance in court, she mentioned nothing of the divorce, let alone the appeal to the divorce that ostensibly nullified it. She may have been trying to keep the story simple to avoid confusing court officials, but certainly the complex story of their marital history was a straightforward response to claims that she was not Richard's wife. In addition, why did she originally ask only for 1,500 marks but then three years later attempt to lay claim to 5,000 marks? Surely, there was more to this story than met the eye. Isabella's endeavor to pursue dower after her (ex?) husband's death is a powerful reminder that, even with established maintenance agreements, a wife might well ask for more after the death of her adversary.[48]

At the very least, in a case of separation, a wife in need of additional support could take her case before royal or ecclesiastical officials and hope to find a sympathetic ear. For wives who self-divorced, unless they wanted to be reconciled against their will (which, as we have already seen, was the fate of countless couples who divorced themselves), legal resolution was out of the question. The records illustrate that, for some of these wives, financial independence was not always everything it was cracked up to be.

For example, a court record notes that Margery, wife of John Roseson of Berkswell (*Warks.*), feloniously stole woolen and linen cloth and a copper pan valued at 26*s.* 8*d.* after leaving her husband.[49] Was she driven to thievery because she was incapable of supporting herself? Sandy Bardsley has argued persuasively that women's waged work was "consistently paid at about the same rate as that of other members of the 'second-rate' work-force—boys, old men and disabled men."[50] Moreover, "even the highest wage awarded to women failed to come close to the highest wages of men."[51] The impracticality of supporting oneself independently led some singlewomen into prostitution, so much so that the later medieval period saw the terms "singlewoman" and "prostitute" to be interchangeable.[52] Some runaway wives seem to have fallen into this category. The register of the dean of Salisbury for the year 1412 notes that Katherine, wife of John atte Mulle, had "left her husband and wasted his goods." Even though she swore "to stay and look after him on pain of 100*s.* and six beatings through the market," she failed to do so. The record goes on to note that she was a "common prostitute," cited for adultery with six different men.[53] When Agnes, wife of John atte Pole, left her husband in 1273, she was also reported as having become a prostitute.[54] Were these women actually selling sex? Because of the vagueness in the English use of the term "meretrix," it is hard to draw any sort of firm conclusion. Moreover, an angry husband may have leaked these allegations to the court. Nevertheless, it is important to recognize that these accusations were credible, in large part, because everyone knew how difficult it was for a woman to support herself.

Most women solved the problem of support by remarrying. Because runaway wives technically were still married to their previous husbands, disciplinary actions usually describe their situation as adulterous; however, it is not hard to imagine that many of these long-standing adulterous unions were actually clandestine marriages. For example, Adam le Coke de Wodicote was accused of "long retaining" Juliana, wife of Thomas la Melewarde, in adultery.[55] The records did sometimes state that the wife had actually gone on to another marriage. An *ex officio* act book from the years 1468–74 notes the case of Agnes Erby of Faversham (*Kent*), summoned before the court of Canterbury for not living with her husband and having another husband in Lincoln diocese.[56] Four of the seventeen other runaway wives from the same act book were similarly accused.[57] Many other wives probably lived off the goods that they "stole" from their husbands or lived with their families and friends to stave off poverty and vagrancy. Regardless of the approach, it is clear that most wives after a self-divorce needed to align themselves with men somehow in order to support themselves.

Many medieval English couples self-divorced, because a court-sanctioned divorce was simply not worth all the expense and hard work, especially when there was a good possibility that the church might misplace the documentation or allow it to decay. Moreover, a formal decree that a marriage was invalid was only necessary for court proofs: certainly, a separated wife who hoped to claim dower someday should bolster her case by obtaining legitimate documentation. For most other women, however, a court order was more trouble than it was worth. Self-divorce might even permit a former wife to claim dower when really she had no right to do so otherwise. A man's obligation to support his wife theoretically continued in the absence of a court-sanctioned divorce; thus, it was in a wife's best interest to avoid any action that might revoke his obligation—keeping her options open, so to speak—except in those rare situations where she had her own independent means of support. As most of these examples confirm, being able to prove a divorce in court was not a man's greatest concern. Rather, he needed to be able to publicize his divorce widely in his community in order to sever publicly the relationship that made him responsible for his wife's debts, purchases and even criminal activity. For separated wives hoping to prolong or enhance a husband's support, the rules of coverture, which normally oppressed women, might act as a boon, permitting her to continue to enjoy the benefits of marriage without having to reside with her husband. Granted, not all wives manipulated the system to their own profit. The medieval English very much endorsed the "breadwinner ideal," paying women little for doing the same work as men. Consequently, those women who tried to carry on independently most likely entered into subsequent marriages just to survive.

Conclusions

Because Christianity recognizes marriage as being symbolic of Christ's relationship with the church, it has long proclaimed that matrimony is a sacred, permanent and monogamous union. Among the laity, however, the twenty-first-century Christian world is still waiting for that ideology to sink in. Predisposed by the force of the church's declaration and the overwhelming religiosity of the medieval era, historical thinking has generally supported the perception that divorce (as we understand it today) is a strictly modern invention. Yet, as this study demonstrates, although obtaining divorce was not necessarily easy, it was a regular feature of medieval life. Tracing the marital history of many medieval Englishmen and -women is a challenge, in large part, because individuals frequently participated in a series of long-term monogamous unions. A few examples illustrate this point quite aptly. Lucy Twenge married William le Latimer in 1294 when she was fifteen, and she had a child soon after that, which may or may not have been fathered by William. At twenty-four, she was "abducted" from the family home and soon after moved in with a lover, Nicholas de Meynell, with whom she had an illegitimate child. Around her thirty-second year, the church approved her divorce with William, and she also left Nicholas; by her thirty-third year, she had married Robert de Everingham. During the first year of her new marriage, her former lover, Nicholas, abducted her from her husband, hoping to end their marriage, but apparently nothing came of the incident.[1] When she was thirty-seven, her husband Robert died while fighting the Scots. She remarried when she was thirty-nine, this time to Bartholomew de Fanacourt; the two had no children, but the union seems to have taken: when Lucy died at the age of sixty-seven, she and Bartholomew were still married.[2]

Lucy's complex relationship history makes it clear that the sanctity and permanence of marriage, as the church expounded it, did not deter individuals from following their hearts. Lucy was not an anomaly. A dower dispute in 1365 uncovered a similar marital history for the more ordinary Maud, wife of William de Clopton. Maud appeared in court to claim dower from her previous husband, the recently deceased Robert Pewer. The church denied her plea, however, because it deemed her marriages to Robert and William invalid. Maud had initially been married to Robert of Morton; after he had been abroad for years, she presumed he was dead and exchanged vows with a man referred to only in the record as Walter of T. Then, Robert of Morton returned; the church annulled her union with Walter and ordered her to return to Robert. At some point, though, she abandoned Robert of Morton and married Robert Pewer, and then she married William de Clopton after Robert Pewer passed away. At the time of the dower litigation in 1365, the court discovered that Robert of Morton (the first husband) was, in fact, still alive, and thus none of the subsequent marriages were lawful: her claim to dower in the right of Robert Pewer was denied.[3]

A writ of *mort d'ancestor* sued at the court of Common Pleas in 1338 uncovers another analogous story. Justices were in a quandary as they examined a marital history rivaling that of modern celebrities. Robert and Margery were the first to marry, and their union produced two children, a son and a daughter. Eventually, Robert sued for divorce on the grounds of affinity, and he began a relationship with Sabina but did not marry her. Together, Sabina and Robert also had a child. Some time after this, Robert married Agnes, but he soon realized that it was a mistake: the two did not get on well. He returned to Sabina; Robert and Agnes were divorced (although the record does not reveal the nature or grounds for the divorce). He then married Sabina, and they had another son. Because an annulment bastardized the children of a marriage, and Sabina and Robert had children both before and after they married, the real question, in the justices' minds, was: who exactly was Robert's heir?[4]

Robert's perception of the role played by marriage is distinctly medieval; the medieval laity saw marriage not as a holy union but as a means to climb the social ladder. Robert hesitated to marry Sabina, even though he clearly felt strong affection for her, because she had little to offer him in terms of social and financial advancement. In the end, the needs of his heart overruled those of his purse; regardless, the church's abiding respect for the marital union was absent entirely from his experience. Robert crassly manipulated the church's rules for divorce whenever he felt the need to end a relationship. The marital histories of those living at the end of the Middle Ages were no less intricate, revealing that the church's record of accomplishment in indoctrinating the medieval laity with canonical perceptions of marriage did not improve much over time. Eleanor Grey's 1474 petition to the pope resulted in a mandate to the bishops of Winchester, Bangor and Rathlure, recounting yet another tale of serial monogamy. Eleanor was a widow when she married John Acton of the diocese of London, her husband, Humphrey Grey, having recently passed away.[5] Since her lawful marriage to John, however, she had discovered that he was actually married to Alice Weyght of London. Apparently, John and Alice had married with the blessing of the church and cohabited for several years before self-divorcing, all long before John and Eleanor met. At the time of her petition, Eleanor had deserted her husband, and Alice had died just a short time before. Nevertheless, her petition to the pope requested a formal divorce so that she could be free to remarry.[6] Although Eleanor herself stands out as being anxious to play by the church's rules, confirming that its position had indeed taken root over time, her husband's two lawful marriages and one unlawful divorce illustrate that the church still had quite a ways to go.

The scope of divorce in medieval England was expansive. Medieval Englishmen and -women divorced for a whole host of reasons. Officially, the church granted divorces on the grounds of incest, bigamy, sexual incapacity, coercion, adultery, heresy and domestic violence. Unofficially, spousal incompatibility played a tremendous role. The curial process very much shaped justifications for divorce. Although Richard Thorif sued for a divorce from his wife, Alice, on the grounds of consanguinity, frequent citations for adultery with Isabella de Bloxham from Coleby strongly hint that incest had little to do with his desire to be free of Alice.[7] As the marital histories rehearsed above establish, great tension existed between the practice and ideology of marriage. Although the medieval English primarily saw marriage as an investment in a family's future prosperity, such financially minded concerns only went so far when the couples despised each other. The church's teachings on the permanence of marriage may have fallen well short of the goal, but its highly vocal advocacy of marriage as a union founded on the free consent of bride and groom (to the exclusion of all others) did find a receptive audience. The marriages arranged by parents with great forethought and planning, intending to enhance both the reputations and coffers of the families involved, sometimes dissolved through the individual desires of the couple.

Divorce, in all its forms, was a risky venture. A court-sanctioned divorce involved lengthy, expensive proceedings in which a woman had to expect her good name and reputation to be dragged through the mud. There was also no assurance that the court would grant a divorce. Pre-contract suits, for example, seem to have failed quite often.[8] Even those suits where the situations would seem to warrant divorces had no assurance. The church denied Alice Bonde's request for a divorce, although her marital history demonstrates that she put up with at least ten years of abuse, abandonment and deprivation from her hopelessly adulterous husband. In November 1336, the court of the dean and chapter of Lincoln summoned her husband, William. Despite having sworn an oath on pain of £20 that he would treat his wife well, he had shuffled her off to live with her father. He had apparently arranged for her maintenance, with the hope that "they might abstain from each other perpetually," making sure to keep her marriage portion for himself. When he finally appeared in court, he claimed that "a divorce was coming"; she was merely staying with her father during the proceedings.[9] In November of the following year, he was cited for adultery with two different women (it appears that they were sisters); he paid a fine of 3*s.* 4*d.* in penance.[10] In July 1339, he was cited for adultery again, and then also in November of the same year, with Matilda, wife of William Wykham.[11] By

July 1342, he was back to his affair with one of the sisters and once again cited for adultery.[12] In July 1343, he was cited with a different woman altogether.[13] By July 1346, we discover that the divorce never came through. Alice herself appeared as a plaintiff before the dean and chapter, requesting that William be compelled to live with her, treat her with marital affection and provide her with sustenance. Both appeared in court, and an agreement was forged: William and Alice swore an oath that they would dwell together as husband and wife.[14] By November, William was back in court again, cited for adultery with Margaret Baxter and for not adhering to his wife.[15] When William appeared before the court to discuss his failure to cohabit with Alice, the record notes that although he promised to treat his wife with marital affection and to adhere to her, after that judgment "he beat her beyond measure" and once again denied her food and other supplies.[16] The court cited William once more for adultery in July 1347 before the two disappear for the last time from the court's records.[17]

The documentation provides inadequate detail to gain a better understanding of why Alice's suit for a divorce failed. Presumably, she was suing for a judicial separation on the grounds of cruelty and infidelity; what is most disconcerting is that somehow William's incorrigible behavior did not meet the court's requirements. As Alice's situation reveals, when the court intervened to reconcile couples who did not wish to be reconciled, the outcome might be dreadful. John de Warenne's infamous attempts to divorce his wife and marry his mistress also divulge the church's willingness to stand firm in its morals. John and his mistress, Maud de Nerford, made several attempts to undo his marriage to Joan de Bars. After just five years of marriage to Joan, he abandoned his sixteen-year-old wife, flagrantly living in adultery with his mistress, who, at that time, was also married to someone else. Only after the church passed a sentence of excommunication against him was he willing to return reluctantly to his wife.[18] Five years later, Maud's husband had died, and she was now suing for divorce between John and Joan on the grounds of pre-contract. John simplified the matter by disclosing that they were married within the third and fourth degrees and thus their union was unlawful anyway. During that time, the king ordered John to support his wife, and arrangements were made for what would happen to their lands once the church awarded a divorce.[19] Apparently, Joan's family was hostile enough to the divorce proceedings that John went so far as to request protection from the king during that time.[20] Despite John and Maud's efforts, the church never granted a divorce; Joan was required to stay married to a man referred to by one historian as "a nasty, brutal man with scarcely one redeeming quality."[21] Joan did at least have an opportunity to extract revenge: notwithstanding John's copious attempts to devise his estates to his two illegitimate sons by Maud, Joan thwarted him at every turn, ensuring that they went instead to his nephew Richard, earl of Arundel.[22]

Failed divorces such as these meant that the church behaved as a formidable obstacle, standing in the way of many individual dreams of autonomy.

Thus, before embarking on a suit of divorce, one had to be certain the court might react favorably to one's request. The court process that ensued often was sufficient to deter many couples. Legal battles over maintenance and division of property were every bit as petty and bitter as those appearing in court today. That it was usually women who sought assistance from the courts in property issues after a divorce underscores the oppressive role played by coverture in medieval England. The property implications of coverture, which saw marital property belonging absolutely to the governance of the husband, crippled women in their capacity to achieve independence and forced them to rely instead on the assistance and intervention of both family and the judicial system. Nonetheless, this study reveals that husbands were also constrained by coverture. Ravishment of wife existed as a trespassory category, primarily because men could not sue their wives. The rules of coverture made it impossible for harassed or impoverished husbands to sue the real culprits in their lives. Although self-divorce may have avoided much of the unpleasantness of this process, because a couple had to evade detection by the authorities, the logistics of self-divorce were actually much more difficult, commonly requiring relocation, an option that was simply not available to everyone. On top of all this, one's hard work might have been for naught, as medieval divorces were no more permanent than medieval marriages.

Given the mountain of obstacles, it is striking that anyone divorced in the Middle Ages. For most medieval Englishmen and -women, divorce would not have been a practical option without the impressive networks of support available to them. Although communities expected couples to make a genuine effort to work through their problems to the best of their abilities, when a marriage was beyond repair, families, friends and neighbors all stepped in to help. Legal officials, at all levels and of all jurisdictions, also expended a good deal of resources assisting couples in the process of divorce. The courts mandated financial support and protection for wives (and even sometimes husbands) during the proceedings, and when it came time to divide the marital property, the support of the courts was invaluable. Despite the church's moralizing rhetoric about the sanctity of marriage, it, too, played a key role in the process, from the local clergymen who counseled marriages in distress to bishops who doggedly harassed husbands for failing to live up to their marital duties and support their wives. Not all its efforts were effective; many husbands simply refused to return their wives' property upon divorce, and enforcement of alimony payments was uneven at best. The inefficiency of law enforcement, though, must not overshadow the church's good intentions. The only unknown variable in this entire process is the custody and support of the children of divorced spouses; nonetheless, even if the legal documentation does not elucidate custody arrangements, it does at least demonstrate a high degree of concern for their legitimacy and well-being.

Divorce cases highlight, in particular, how detrimental English patriarchal attitudes were to the welfare of medieval women in the marriage process. Violence often initiated marriage: coerced nuptials, involving especially heiresses and widows, were a normal experience. Age mattered little in these encounters. Margaret, daughter of Robert de Sandford, was only nine years old when, "by force," she married the sheriff of Westmorland's son; whereas Alice Crome was a grown woman, a merchant's widow with good standing in her local community, when John Wylliamson coerced her into marriage.[23] Violence may also have been the glue that kept many marriages together. Countless women in this study tolerated an astonishing level of brutality in their home environments before standing up for themselves. "For a matter of small substance," Thomas St. Nicholas beat his wife "so grievously that it was thought she would die."[24] After a marriage that lasted long enough to produce twelve children, Nicholas Portlond imprisoned his wife "for a long time in iron fetters within a narrow room, without [sufficient] food and other necessities."[25] Many other wives claimed they were fleeing for their lives. Although some wives probably inflated the scale of violence in order to persuade the court to rule against their husbands, many others almost certainly accurately reflected the state of their marriages. To take the two cases already mentioned as examples: in the former, because Thomas St. Nicholas's brother-in-law was imprisoned after intervening in a fight between his sister and her husband, his keen desire to return home, as well as his resentment towards St. Nicholas, probably encouraged him to embellish the violence and thus smear St. Nicholas's character. In the latter, the tale of Nicholas Portlond's wife reached the bishop's ears through public outcry—that is, neighbors determined to see her set free. What motivation did they have to lie?

Although violence clearly kept some marriages together, what is most impressive is that many other wives refused to be victims. Far too much of women's history is a story of women as victims. The experiences of the women in this investigation go far in undermining that perception. This is not a story of women as victims. Divorcing wives actively defied social norms to choose their own fates. Even those wives who demanded the return of delinquent husbands were fighting against victimization, declining to be abandoned, impoverished and ostracized all at the whim of their husbands. Divorce proceedings draw attention to women at their best in terms of gritty resolution and independent action. These wives knew their rights and used England's multiple jurisdictions in shrewd ways to demand support and sometimes independence. Wives who participated in self-divorce, a dicey proposition, endangering not only one's financial stability but also one's soul, exhibited an even greater sense of purpose, placing their own needs over the requirements of ecclesiastical law. This is not a story of women as victims: these wives were active participants, shaping their lives in a world that denied their legal (and often real) existence.

Notes

NOTES TO THE INTRODUCTION

1. *Calendar of Inquisitions Post-Mortem and Other Analogous Documents, v.1: Henry III* (London: His Majesty's Stationery Office, 1904), p. 79.
2. For arguments against seeing medieval divorce as divorce, see R.H. Helmholz, *Marriage Litigation in Medieval England* (New York: Cambridge University Press, 1974), p. 74; Shannon McSheffrey, *Marriage, Sex, and Civic Culture in Late Medieval London* (Philadelphia: University of Pennsylvania Press, 2006), p. 23.
3. Ruth Mazo Karras, *Sexuality in Medieval Europe: Doing unto Others* (New York: Routledge, 2005), p. 68.
4. By the early thirteenth century, incest was defined as entering into marriage with a person related within four degrees (that is, third cousin) by blood (*consanguinity*), by marriage or sexual union (*affinity*) or by sponsorship or spiritual relationship (that is, a godparent).
5. Helmholz, *Marriage Litigation*, pp. 59, 28–31.
6. James A. Brundage, *Law, Sex, and Christian Society in Medieval Europe* (Chicago: University of Chicago Press, 1987), p. 458.
7. 1 Corinthians viii: 8–9.
8. Helmholz, *Marriage Litigation*, pp. 26–27.
9. Canon 51 of the Fourth Lateran Council (1215) stipulates this requirement.
10. For example, see R.H. Helmholz, "Marriage Contracts in Medieval England," in *To Have and To Hold: Marrying and Its Documentation in Western Christendom, 400–1600*, ed. Philip L. Reynolds and John Witte, Jr. (Cambridge: Cambridge University Press, 2007), pp. 260–86.
11. As Helmholz has noted, "[i]t was hard to 'explain away' the receipt of property as being consistent with an intent other than one aimed at marriage," so the exchange of gifts was also key evidence in matrimonial litigation to prove the existence of a marriage. Helmholz, "Marriage Contracts in Medieval England," p. 268; see also Shannon McSheffrey, ed., *Love and Marriage in Late Medieval London* (Kalamazoo, MI: Medieval Institute Publications, 1995), pp. 42–3.
12. Art Cosgrove, "Consent, Consummation and Indissolubility: Some Evidence from Mediaeval Ecclesiastical Courts," *Downside Review* 109 (1991): 98.
13. Philippa C. Maddern, "Moving Households: Geographical Mobility and Serial Monogamy in England, 1350–1500," *Parergon* 24.2 (2007): 69–92. Other scholars who also address the popularity of self-divorce are M.M. Sheehan, "The Formation and Stability of Marriage in Fourteenth-Century England: Evidence of an Ely Register," in *Marriage, Family, and Law in Medieval Europe: Collected Studies*, ed. James K. Farge (Toronto: University

of Toronto Press, 1996), pp. 38–76; Elizabeth M. Makowski, "The Conjugal Debt and Medieval Canon Law," in *Equally in God's Image: Women in the Middle Ages*, ed. Julia Bolton Holloway, Constance S. Wright and Joan Bechtold (New York: Peter Lang, 1990), p. 137.

14. Brundage, *Law, Sex and Christian Society*; Conor McCarthy, *Marriage in Medieval England: Law, Literature and Practice* (Woodbridge: Boydell, 2004); Charles Reid, Jr., *Power over the Body, Equality in the Family: Rights and Domestic Relations in Medieval Canon Law* (Grand Rapids: Wm. B. Eerdmans, 2004).
15. R.H. Helmholz, "Support Orders, Church Courts, and the Rule of *Filius Nullius*: A Reassessment of the Common Law," *Virginia Law Review* 63.383 (1977): 436.
16. David F. Noble, *A World without Women: The Christian Clerical Culture of Western Science* (Oxford: Oxford University Press, 1992).
17. P. Tucker has suggested that chancery bills "were sometimes composed and perhaps even written by the plaintiff himself" (791). See "The Early History of the Court of Chancery: A Comparative Study," *English Historical Review* 115 (2000): 791–811.
18. Helmholz, *Marriage Litigation*, p. 74.
19. Helmholz, *Marriage Litigation*; Frederik Pedersen, *Marriage Disputes in Medieval England* (London: Hambledon, 2000); Charles Donahue, Jr., *Law, Marriage, and Society in the Later Middle Ages* (New York: Cambridge University Press, 2007).
20. Emma Hawkes, "'[S]he Will . . . Protect and Defend Her Rights Boldly by Law and Reason . . . ': Women's Knowledge of Common Law and Equity Courts in Late-Medieval England," in *Medieval Women and the Law*, ed. Noël James Menuge (Woodbridge: Boydell, 2000), pp. 151, 155.
21. Alan Harding, *The Law Courts of Medieval England* (London: Allen and Unwin, 1973), p. 102.
22. Tim Stretton has examined the difficulties associated with coverture and its impact on wives. See *Women Waging Law in Elizabethan England* (Cambridge: Cambridge University Press, 1998), pp. 22–3.
23. A writ designed specifically for the prosecution of husbands for violent trespass against their wives did exist, and thus cases of this nature should have rightfully belonged to the king's courts. Nonetheless, it is clear that wives, whether out of fear or ignorance, did not use the royal courts for this purpose; the records of chancery, then, at the very least demonstrate that wives were not using this court to resolve straightforward issues of domestic violence. For a discussion of domestic violence in the king's courts, see Sara M. Butler, *The Language of Abuse: Marital Violence in Later Medieval England* (Leiden: Brill, 2007).
24. Lawrence Stone, *The Family, Sex and Marriage 1500–1800* (New York: Harper and Row, 1977), p. 117.
25. Judith M. Bennett, *Women in the Medieval English Countryside: Gender and Household in Brigstock before the Plague* (Oxford: Oxford University Press, 1987), p. 103.
26. Ibid.
27. Barbara A. Hanawalt, *The Ties That Bound: Peasant Families in Medieval England* (New York: Oxford University Press, 1986), p. 214; see also Hanawalt, "Violence in the Domestic Milieu of Late Medieval England," in *Violence in Medieval Society*, ed. Richard W. Kaeuper (Woodbridge: Boydell, 2000), pp. 197–214.
28. For a discussion of coverture and a married woman's rights at law, see Janet S. Loengard, "Common Law for Margery: Separate but Not Equal," in

Women in Medieval Western European Culture, ed. Linda E. Mitchell (New York: Garland, 1999), pp. 117–30.
29. Robert C. Palmer, "Contexts of Marriage in Medieval England: Evidence from the King's Court circa 1300," *Speculum* 59.1 (1984): 43.
30. Colin Richmond, "The Pastons Revisited: Marriage and the Family in Fifteenth-Century England," *Bulletin of the Institute of Historical Research* 58.137 (1985): 28.
31. Charles Donahue, Jr., "Female Plaintiffs in Marriage Cases in the Court of York in the Later Middle Ages: What Can We Learn from the Numbers?" in *Wife and Widow in Medieval England*, ed. Sue Sheridan Walker (Ann Arbor: University of Michigan Press, 1993), p. 197.
32. Andrew Finch, "*Repulsa Uxore Sua*: Marital Difficulties and Separation in the Later Middle Ages," *Continuity and Change* 8.1 (1993): 25.
33. Donahue, "Female Plaintiffs," p. 205.
34. This is discussed more in chapter 4.
35. For a discussion of the role of family and friends in marriage, see McSheffrey, *Marriage, Sex, and Civic Culture*. See also Barbara A. Hanawalt, "'Of Good and Ill Repute': The Limits of Community Tolerance," in *"Of Good and Ill Repute": Gender and Social Control in Medieval England* (Oxford: Oxford University Press, 1998), pp. 1–17.
36. *PP: 1342–1419* (1896), p. 528; *CPR* for 1450, p. 330.
37. *CPRRGBI*, v. 11: 1455–1464 (1921), pp. 431–6.
38. *CPRRGBI*, v. 10: 1447–1455 (1915), pp. 641–54.
39. *CPRRGBI*, v. 10: 1447–1455 (1915), pp. 417–29.
40. Dyan Elliott, "Lollardy and the Integrity of Marriage and the Family," in *The Medieval Marriage Scene: Prudence, Passion, Policy*, ed. Sherry Roush and Cristelle L. Baskins (Tempe: Arizona Center for Medieval and Renaissance Studies, 2005), p. 39.
41. As cited in ibid., p. 40.
42. Henry de Bracton, *De Legibus et Consuetudinibus Angliae*, ed. George E. Woodbine, trans. Samuel E. Thorne, 4 vols (Cambridge: Belknap Press at Harvard University Press, 1968), v. 4, p. 335.
43. Tim Stretton, ed. *Marital Litigation in the Court of Requests 1542–1642* (Cambridge: Camden Fifth Series, v. 32, 2008), p. 2.
44. Tim Stretton, "Coverture and Unity of Person in Blackstone's *Commentaries*," in *Blackstone and His* Commentaries*: Biography, Law, History*, ed. Wilfrid Robertson Prest (Oxford: Hart Publishing, 2009), p. 127.
45. Patricia R. Orr, "*Non Potest Appellum Facere*: Criminal Charges Women Could Not—but Did—Bring in Thirteenth-Century English Royal Courts of Justice," in *The Final Argument: The Imprint of Violence on Society in Medieval and Early Modern Europe*, ed. Donald J. Kagay and L.J. Andrew Villalon (Woodbridge: Boydell, 1998), pp. 141–62.
46. Y.B. Pasch. 18 Edw. IV, fo. 4a (1478).
47. Philippa Maddern, "Interpreting Silence: Domestic Violence in the King's Courts in East Anglia, 1422–1442," in *Domestic Violence in Medieval Texts*, ed. Eve Salisbury, Georgiana Donavin and Merrall Llewelyn Price (Gainesville: University Press of Florida, 2002), p. 38.
48. Ibid., p. 42.
49. Frederick Pollock and F.W. Maitland, *The History of English Law before the Time of Edward I*, 2nd ed. (London: Cambridge University Press, 1968, 2 vols.), v. 2, p. 436.
50. Isaac Herbert Jeayes, ed. and trans., *Court Rolls of the Borough of Colchester* (Colchester: W. Gurney, 1921), v. 1, p. 56; this case is also discussed in Butler, *Language of Abuse*, pp. 31–32.

51. Bracton, *De Legibus et Consuetudinibus Angliae*, v. 4, p. 287.
52. C.A.F. Meekings, ed., *Crown Pleas of the Wiltshire Eyre, 1249* (Devizes: Wiltshire Archaeological and Natural History Society, 1961), p. 238, n. 445.
53. Marjorie K. McIntosh, "The Benefits and Drawbacks of *Femme Sole* Status in England, 1300–1630," *Journal of British Studies* 44 (2005): 410–38.
54. Ivo, *Decretum* 8.35, as cited in Brundage, *Law, Sex, and Christian Society*, p. 200.

NOTES TO CHAPTER 1

1. James A. Brundage, *Law, Sex, and Christian Society in Medieval Europe* (Chicago: University of Chicago Press, 1987), p. 94.
2. Ibid., pp. 105, 144.
3. Ibid., p. 295.
4. Ibid.
5. Ibid., p. 480.
6. Charles Donahue, Jr., *Law, Marriage and Society in the Later Middle Ages* (New York: Cambridge University Press, 2007), ch. 10.
7. Thomas Aquinas, *Summa Theologiae*, ed. Timothy McDermott (Grand Rapids: Christian Classics, 1997), II[a] II[ae], q. 154, a. 9.
8. If the individuals came from different parishes, English law stipulated that the banns must be read in both parishes. See Michael M. Sheehan, *Marriage, Family, and Law in Medieval Europe: Collected Studies*, ed. James K. Farge (Toronto: University of Toronto Press, 1996), pp. 148–49.
9. Elizabeth Archibald, *Incest and the Medieval Imagination* (Oxford: Oxford University Press, 2001), ch. 1.
10. *CPRRGBI*, v. 3, pp. 381–88.
11. In July 1482, the pope asked the rector of Everingham to solemnize the marriage of John Suthill and Alice Waslyn, related within the second degree (that is, first cousins). See Eric E. Barker, ed., *The Register of Thomas Rotherham, Archbishop of York, 1480–1500* (Canterbury and York Society, v. 69, 1976), p. 21.
12. The York consistory court offers a number of examples with witness depositions; see YBI CP. G. 971A (1450–1550), CP. F. 202 (1461), CP. F. 257 (1476–77), CP. G. 10 (1504).
13. David D'Avray, *Medieval Marriage: Symbolism and Society* (Oxford: Oxford University Press, 2005), p. 91.
14. R.L. Storey, ed., *The Register of Gilbert Welton, Bishop of Carlisle, 1353–1362* (Canterbury and York Society, v. 88, 1999), p. 24. Affinity seems to have been a relatively popular ground for annulment in the York consistory materials. For example, see YBI CP. E. 33 (1337), CP. E. 140 (1371–72), CP. E. 181.1 (1390), CP. E. 212 (1394–95), CP. F. 187 (1451–52).
15. In 1304, the church heard the plea of Alice, the widow of Walter de Stirchesley, against her husband, William de Chaddeworth, on similar grounds: William had "carnally known the daughter of the said Alice de Stirchesley before he married Alice." See G. Wrottesley and F. Parker, eds., "Plea Rolls for Staffordshire: 32 Edward I," *Staffordshire Historical Collections* 7.1 (1886): 114–26.
16. *CPRRGBI*, v. 6, pp. 188–95.
17. D'Avray, *Medieval Marriage*, p. 95.
18. Ibid. The Lollards of the fourteenth century were appalled by the medieval church's willingness to allow dispensations for incestuous relationships,

which the Lollards categorized as "lechery." See Dyan Elliott, "Lollardy and the Integrity of Marriage and the Family," in *The Medieval Marriage Scene: Prudence, Passion, Policy*, ed. Sherry Roush and Cristelle L. Baskins (Tempe: Arizona Center for Medieval and Renaissance Studies, 2005), p. 39.

19. Georges Duby, *Medieval Marriage: Two Models from Twelfth-Century France*, trans. Elborg Forster (Baltimore: Johns Hopkins University Press, 1978).
20. Frederik Pedersen, "Marriage Contracts and the Church Courts of Fourteenth-Century England," in *To Have and To Hold: Marrying and Its Documentation in Western Christendom, 400–1600*, ed. Philip L. Reynolds and John Witte, Jr. (Cambridge: Cambridge University Press, 2007), p. 314.
21. Conor McCarthy, *Marriage in Medieval England: Law, Literature, and Practice* (Woodbridge: Boydell, 2004), p. 5.
22. Barbara A. Hanawalt, *The Ties That Bound: Peasant Families in Medieval England* (New York: Oxford University Press, 1986), p. 6.
23. Joseph H. Lynch, *The Medieval Church: A Brief History* (New York: Longman, 1992), p. 277.
24. John H. Arnold, *Belief and Unbelief in Medieval Europe* (London: Hodder Arnold, 2005), p. 137.
25. Ibid.
26. Brundage, *Law, Sex, and Christian Society*, p. 141.
27. *CPRRGBI*, v. 7, pp. 208–13.
28. *CPRRGBI*, v. 9, pp. 557–65.
29. *CPRRGBI*, v. 3, pp. 447–61.
30. Michael M. Sheehan, "The Formation and Stability of Marriage in Fourteenth-Century England: Evidence of an Ely Register," in *Marriage, Family, and Law*, pp. 38–76; R.H. Helmholz, *Marriage Litigation in Medieval England* (New York: Cambridge University Press, 1974), ch. 3; Sara McDougall, "Bigamy: A Male Crime in Medieval Europe?" *Gender and History* 22.2 (2010): 430–46.
31. These examples are drawn from R.H. Helmholz, "Marriage Contracts in Medieval England," in *To Have and to Hold*, p. 266.
32. Philippa C. Maddern, "Moving Households: Geographical Mobility and Serial Monogamy in England, 1350–1500," *Parergon* 24.2 (2007): 69–92. Again, the York consistory court offers a number of interesting examples. See YBI CP. E. 87 (1364), CP. E. 155 (1373–74), CP. F. 64 (1412–13), CP. F. 49 (1433), CP. F. 123 (1434–38), CP. F. 248 (1469).
33. Sheehan, "Formation and Stability of Marriage," p. 76.
34. Diana O'Hara, *Courtship and Constraint: Rethinking the Making of Marriage in Tudor England* (Manchester: Manchester University Press, 2000), p. 3. See also Shannon McSheffrey, "'I Will Never Have None Ayenst My Faders Will': Consent and the Making of Marriage in the Late Medieval Diocese of London," in *Women, Marriage and Family in Medieval Christendom*, ed. C.M. Rousseau and J.T. Rosenthal (Kalamazoo, MI: Medieval Institute Publications, 1998), pp. 153–74.
35. Shannon McSheffrey, ed., *Love and Marriage in Late Medieval London* (Kalamazoo, MI: Medieval Institute Publications, 1995), p. 25. Helmholz has noted that, among the many suspensive conditions employed in exchanges of vows, by far the most common was "if my parents, friends, or relatives consent." Helmholz, "Marriage Contracts in Medieval England," p. 266.
36. Noël James Menuge, "Female Wards and Marriage in Romance and Law: A Question of Consent," in *Young Medieval Women*, ed. Katherine J. Lewis, Noël James Menuge and Kim M. Phillips (London: St. Martin's Press, 1999), p. 154.

37. YBI CP. E. 248, m. 23d (1339).
38. YBI CP. E. 248 (1339).
39. Brundage, *Law, Sex, and Christian Society*, p. 374.
40. Sidney Lee and Leslie Stephen, eds., *Dictionary of National Biography* (London: Smith, Elder and Co., 1891), v. 6, pp. 365–66.
41. TNA PRO SC 8/320/E449 (1298). Barbara A. Hanawalt offers a number of interesting examples in "Separation Anxieties in Late Medieval London: Gender in 'The Wright's Chaste Wife,'" in *"Of Good and Ill Repute": Gender and Social Control in Medieval England* (Oxford: Oxford University Press, 1998), pp. 92–94.
42. TNA PRO C 1/15/175 (1443).
43. TNA PRO C 1/15/176 (1443).
44. *CPR* for 1445, p. 339.
45. TNA PRO C 1/44/270 (*c*. 1467–72).
46. TNA PRO C 1/66/317 (1474).
47. D'Avray, *Medieval Marriage*, p. 116.
48. Shannon McSheffrey, *Marriage, Sex, and Civic Culture in Late Medieval England* (Philadelphia: University of Pennsylvania Press, 2006), pp. 5–6.
49. Jeremy Goldberg, *Communal Discord, Child Abduction, and Rape in the Later Middle Ages* (New York: Palgrave Macmillan, 2008), p. 24.
50. Philip Reynolds, "Marrying and Its Documentation in Pre-modern Europe: Consent, Celebration, and Property," in *To Have and To Hold*, p. 3.
51. Helmholz, *Marriage Litigation*, p. 98. The consistory courts also dealt with only a small number of these cases. For example, the York consistory court addressed only six possible cases of this nature during the period under examination: YBI CP. E. 23 (1332–33), CP. E. 76 (1357), CP. F. 119 (1436), CP. G. 101 (1500–1530), CP. G. 19 (1505), CP. G. 24 (1506).
52. *CPRRGBI*, v. 3, pp. 391–413.
53. *CPRRGBI*, v. 3, p. 187.
54. *CPRRGBI*, v. 3, p. 164.
55. *CPRRGBI*, v. 1, pp. 249–59.
56. *CPRRGBI*, v. 3, pp. 349–60.
57. John Pigge was the titular Bishop of Beirut (Syria) but resident in London. *CPRRGBI*, v. 13, p. 458, n. 21.
58. *CPRRGBI*, v. 13, p. 797. In a commission recorded in the *CPR* for October 1481, John Williamson is referred to as "esquire." See *CPR* for 1481, p. 231. An exemplification in June 1486 refers to him specifically as "gentleman." *CPR* for 1486, p. 114.
59. TNA PRO C 1/67/210 (*c*. 1483–85).
60. Sue Sheridan Walker, "Litigation as Personal Quest: Suing for Dower in the Royal Courts, circa 1272–1350," in *Wife and Widow in Medieval England* (Ann Arbor: Michigan University Press, 1993), pp. 81–108.
61. TNA PRO C 1/67/212 (*c*. 1483–85).
62. Presumably Rede, Suffolkshire.
63. TNA PRO C 1/79/71 (1486). Given Alice's sound case, it is not clear why she appeared in chancery. Intimidation, local bias or a need for a hasty resolution certainly are all viable explanations; Alice may also have been appealing to the chancellor after her suit failed in the common law courts. Alice also appears in a later petition in a dispute over the sale of a house in Norwich to William Elsy, servant to the prior of the cathedral church of the Blessed Trinity in Norwich. Interestingly enough, despite the annulment, Elsy refers to Alice here as "Alice Williams naming herself Alice Crome widow." TNA PRO C 1/133/16 (*c*. 1486–93).
64. For a good discussion on this topic, see Y.B. Trin. 7 Edw. IV, fo. 14b (1467).

65. M.A. Farrow, ed., *Consistory Court of Norwich Wills, 1370–1550* (London: British Record Society, 1945), p. 108.
66. The reality intimated by the records also helps to explain the popularity of this trope in literature. See Graham N. Drake, "Not Safe Even in Their Own Castles: Reading Domestic Violence against Children in Four Middle English Romances," in *Domestic Violence in Medieval Texts*, ed. Eve Salisbury, Georgiana Donavin and Merrall Llewelyn Price (Gainesville: University Press of Florida, 2002), pp. 139–63.
67. Helmholz, *Marriage Litigation*, p. 94.
68. YBI CP. F 36 (1411).
69. YBI CP. F. 25 (1477).
70. Georges Duby, "Youth in Aristocratic Society: Northwestern France in the Twelfth Century," in *The Chivalrous Society*, trans. Cynthia Postan (Berkeley: University of California Press, 1981), p. 119.
71. Gwen Seabourne, *Imprisoning Medieval Women: The Non-judicial Confinement and Abduction of Women in England, c. 1170–1509* (Farnham: Ashgate, 2011), p. 99.
72. Caroline Dunn, "The Language of Ravishment in Medieval England," *Speculum* 86 (2011): 92.
73. *CPRRGBI*, v. 4, p. 44.
74. The Year Books refer to Isabella as Alice, but Henry's and John's names are accurately reported. Y.B. Mich. 39 Edw. III, fos. 32a–33a (1365); Y.B. term uncertain, 39 Edw. III, fos. 233b–234a (1365). Chapter 4 addresses this justice's intriguing perspective in greater detail.
75. *CPRRGBI*, v. 2, pp. 108–18.
76. *CPRRGBI*, v. 13, pp. 623–33.
77. Y.B. Hil. 12 Edw. III (1338); as it appears in Alfred J. Horwood and Luke Owen Pike, eds., *Year Books of the Reign of King Edward the Third: Years XI and XII* (Rolls Series no. 31, part B, vol. 1, 1883), pp. 360–63.
78. GLRO MS DL/C/205, fos. 265v–266f; as it appears in McSheffrey, *Love and Marriage*, pp. 81–82.
79. YBI CP. E. 26.
80. Brundage provides a convenient flowchart to encapsulate the church's rules on sex within marriage. See *Law, Sex, and Christian Society*, p. 162.
81. Helmholz, *Marriage Litigation*, pp. 88–89.
82. R.L. Storey, ed., *The Register of Thomas Appleby, Bishop of Carlisle 1363–1395* (Canterbury and York Society, v. 96, 2006), pp. 14–15.
83. Storey, *Register of Gilbert Welton*, p. 22.
84. Edward J. Behrend-Martinez, *Unfit for Marriage: Impotent Spouses on Trial in the Basque Region of Spain 1050–1750* (Reno: University of Nevada Press, 2007), p. 114.
85. Morris S. Arnold, ed. and trans., *Select Cases of Trespass from the King's Courts 1307–1399*, v. 1 (Selden Society, v. 100, 1985), p. 87, no. 8.15 (TNA PRO KB 27/509, m. 26).
86. *CPRRGBI*, v. 13, pp. 487–95.
87. Canterbury X.8.1 *Ex Officio* Act Book (1395–1410), fo. 44d.
88. YBI CP. E. 105 (1370).
89. Sara M. Butler, *The Language of Abuse: Marital Violence in Later Medieval England* (Leiden: Brill, 2007), ch. 4; Philippa Maddern has drawn the same conclusion. See her "Interpreting Silence: Domestic Violence in the King's Courts in East Anglia, 1422–1442," in *Domestic Violence in Medieval Texts*, pp. 42–46.
90. Sharon Wright, "Broken Cups, Men's Wrath, and the Neighbours' Revenge: The Case of Thomas and Alice Dey of Alverthorpe, 1383," *Canadian Journal of History* 43 (2008): 243.

91. This pattern is typically English. Charles Donahue, Jr., has argued that judicial separations were common in Franco-Belgian courts and frequently on the grounds of adultery. See Donahue, *Law, Marriage, and Society*, ch. 10. For medieval Germany, Rudolf Weigand observes that most separations were based on claims of adultery. See R. Weigand, "Zur mittelalterlichen kirchlichen Gerichtsbarkeit. Rechtsvergleichende Untersuchung," *Zeitschrift der Savigny-Stiftung für Rechtsgeschichte* 98 (1981): 247.
92. *CPRRGBI*, v. 13, pp. 510–18.
93. *CPRRGBI*, v. 11, pp. 186–90.
94. *CPRRGBI*, v. 11, pp. 318–24.
95. Elizabeth M. Elvey, ed., *The Courts of the Archdeaconry of Buckingham* (Buckinghamshire Record Society, no. 19, 1975), p. 250.
96. Charles Johnson, ed., *Registrum Hamonis Hethe, Diocesis Roffensis, A.D. 1319–1352*, v. 2 (Canterbury and York Society, v. 49, 1948), p. 973.
97. William Brown, ed., *The Register of John Le Romeyn, Lord Archbishop of York, 1286–1296*, pt. 1 (Surtees Society, v. 123, 1913), pp. 170, 176–77.
98. GLRO MS DL/C/205, fos. 203v–204r; as it appears in McSheffrey, *Love and Marriage in Late Medieval London*, p. 83. The materials for York's consistory court also include a number of interesting depositions. See YBI CP. E. 221 (1395–96), CP. F. 371 (1409–10), CP. F. 235 (1446).
99. Rose Graham, ed. and trans., *Registrum Roberti Winchelsey, Cantuariensis Archiepiscopi, A.D. 1294–1313*, v. 1 (Canterbury and York Society, v. 51, 1952), pp. 45–47.
100. Butler, *Language of Abuse*, pp. 54–59; Elizabeth Foyster, "A Laughing Matter? Marital Discord and Gender Control in Seventeenth-Century England," *Rural History* 4.1 (1993): 5–21; Danièle Alexandre-Bidon and Monique Closson, "L'amour à l'épreuve du temps: Femme battues, maris battus, amants battus à travers les manuscrits enluminés (XIII^{è}–XV^{è} s.)," in *Amour, mariage et transgressions au Moyen Age. Actes du colloque des 24–27 mars 1983*, ed. Danielle Buschinger and André Crépin (Göppingen: Kümmerle, 1984), pp. 493–514.
101. Elvey, *Courts of the Archdeaconry of Buckingham*, p. 144.
102. Ibid., p. 174.
103. Ibid., p. 176.
104. P.E. Hair, ed., *Before the Bawdy Court: Selections from Church Court and Other Records Relating to the Correction of Moral Offences in England, Scotland, and New England, 1300–1800* (New York: Elek Books, 1972), pp. 174–75, no. 435.
105. T.C.B. Timmins, ed. *The Register of John Waltham, Bishop of Salisbury, 1388–1395* (Canterbury and York Society, v. 80, 1994), p. 146.
106. T.C.B. Timmins, ed. *The Register of John Chandler, Dean of Salisbury, 1404–1417* (Wiltshire Record Society, v. 39, 1984), pp. 96–97.
107. A. Hamilton Thompson, ed., *Visitations in the Diocese of Lincoln 1517–1531: Volume 1: Visitations of Rural Deaneries by William Atwater, Bishop of Lincoln, and His Commissaries, 1517–20* (Lincoln Record Society, v. 33, 1940), p. 47.
108. Timmins, *Register of John Waltham*, p. 117, no. 929.
109. E.F. Jacob, ed. *Register of Henry Chichele, Archbishop of Canterbury, 1414–1443*, v. 4 (Canterbury and York Society, v. 47, 1947), pp. 185–86.
110. A.H. Thomas, ed., *Calendar of Early Mayor's Court Rolls of the City of London, A.D. 1298–1307* (Cambridge: Cambridge University Press, 1924), pp. 236–37. These are not the only cases where the wives were in the process of formalizing their separations.

111. For example, see Arnold, *Select Cases of Trespass*, pp. 86–87, no. 8.14 (TNA PRO KB 27/50, m. 36), or pp. 92–93, no. 8.19 (TNA PRO KB 27/518, m. 32d); TNA PRO C 1/343/63 (1500–1515), in which John Obyn of London argues that his wife's assertion of pre-contract with William Sharpe is merely "pretended."
112. Arnold, *Select Cases of Trespass*, pp. 82–83, no. 8.10 (TNA PRO KB 27/434, m. 26d).
113. Storey, *Register of Gilbert Welton*, p. 63. This description was not female-specific. For example, when Christopher de Lancastre left his wife, Joan, he was said to have done so "for frivolous and fictitious reasons" (p. 104).
114. TNA PRO C 1/239/56 (1500–1515).
115. TNA PRO C 1/68/106 (1386–1486); TNA PRO C 1/693/8 (1529–32); R.L. Storey, ed., *The Register of Thomas Langley, Bishop of Durham, 1406–1437*, v. 5 (Surtees Society, v. 177, 1966), pp. 110–11.
116. Shawn Madison Krahmer, "Adam, Eve, and Original Sin in the Works of Bernard of Clairvaux," *Cistercian Studies Quarterly* 37.1 (2002): 5, 9–10.
117. Canterbury, *Sede Vacante Scrapbook* (*SVSB*) I, p. 113.
118. Johnson, *Registrum Hamonis Hethe*, v. 2, p. 973.
119. A.T. Bannister, ed., "Visitation Returns of the Diocese of Hereford in 1397," *English Historical Review* 45 (1930): 100.
120. Timmins, *Register of John Chandler*, p. 4.
121. Warren Ortman, ed., *Court Rolls of the Abbey of Ramsey and of the Honor of Clare* (Yale Historical Publications, v. 9, 1928), p. 252; Timmins, *Register of John Chandler*, pp. 112–13.
122. Ruth Mazo Karras, "Sex and the Singlewomen," in *Singlewomen in the European Past, 1250–1800*, ed. J.M. Bennett and A.M. Froide (Philadelphia: University of Pennsylvania Press, 1999), pp. 130–31.
123. The nature of the divorce is uncertain. The prevalence of accusations of adultery and cruelty would seem to suggest that William was seeking a judicial separation. However, because Isabel's witnesses testify specifically to the solemnization of the marriage, it is possible that he was hoping to deny the marriage altogether but also provide enough evidence for a separation in the event that his first approach failed.
124. GL MS 9065, fo. 95rv, as cited and translated in Shannon McSheffrey, ed., *Consistory: Testimony in the Late Medieval London Consistory Court* (Concordia University, 2008–present), http://digitalhistory.concordia.ca/consistory. Date of access: November 27, 2012.
125. GL MS 9065, fos. 112r and 112rv, ibid.
126. GL MS 9065, fo. 97rv, ibid.
127. GL MS 9065, fo. 97rv, ibid.
128. Physical discipline of an "unruly wife" was necessary to avoid being cuckolded. See Peter Coss, "An Age of Deference," in *A Social History of England 1200–1500*, ed. Rosemary Horrox and W. Mark Ormrod (Cambridge: Cambridge University Press, 2006), p. 50.
129. GL MS 9065, fo. 97v, as cited in McSheffrey, *Consistory*.
130. Brown, *Register of John Le Romeyn*, no. 247, 272–73.
131. Canterbury Y.1.11 *Ex Officio* Act Book, 1468–74, fo. 47.
132. Ibid., fo. 160.
133. Hair, *Before the Bawdy Court*, p. 118, no. 274.
134. For a comparison of numbers, please see Charles Donahue, Jr., "Female Plaintiffs in Marriage Cases in the Court of York in the Later Middle Ages: What Can We Learn from the Numbers?" in *Wife and Widow in Medieval England*, ed. Sue Sheridan Walker (Ann Arbor: University of Michigan Press, 1993), pp. 183–214.

NOTES TO CHAPTER 2

1. L.R. Poos, "The Heavy-Handed Marriage Counselor: Regulating Marriage in Some Later-Medieval English Local Ecclesiastical Court Jurisdictions," *American Journal of Legal History* 29 (1995): 585–607.
2. David D'Avray, "Authentication of Marital Status: A Thirteenth-Century English Royal Annulment Process and Late Medieval Cases from the Papal Penitentiary," *English Historical Review* 120.488 (2005): 990.
3. Wendy R. Childs, "Moving Around," in *A Social History of England 1200–1500,* ed. Rosemary Horrox and W. Mark Ormrod (Cambridge: Cambridge University Press, 2006), pp. 260–75.
4. Barbara A. Hanawalt, "Separation Anxieties in Late Medieval London: Gender in 'The Wright's Chaste Wife,'" in *'Of Good and Ill Repute': Gender and Social Control in Medieval England* (Oxford: Oxford University Press, 1998), p. 88.
5. William Brown, ed., *The Register of John Le Romeyn, Lord Archbishop of York, 1286–1296,* pt. 1 (Surtees Society, v. 123, 1913), p. 191.
6. Despite manifold warnings, the couple persisted in their adultery, until Agnes died in Henry's "unlawful embraces." James Parker, ed., *Register of Bishop Godfrey Giffard, September 23rd, 1268 to August 5th, 1301* (Worcestershire Historical Society, 1902), pp. 95, 98.
7. T. Walter Hall, ed., *A Descriptive Catalogue of Sheffield Manorial Records from the 8th Year of Richard II to the Restoration* (Sheffield, Eng.: Northend, 1920), v. 1, p. 34; TNA PRO C 1/45/46 (1467–70); Rosamond Sillem, ed., *Records of Some Sessions of the Peace in Lincolnshire 1360–1375* (Lincoln Record Society, v. 30, 1936), pp. 20–21.
8. T.C.B. Timmins, ed., *The Register of John Waltham, Bishop of Salisbury, 1388–1395* (Canterbury and York Society, v. 80, 1994), p. 146.
9. Unfortunately, most ecclesiastical records do not mention the occupation of the husband.
10. R.H. Helmholz, *Marriage Litigation in Medieval England* (New York: Cambridge University Press, 1974), p. 161.
11. R.H. Helmholz, *The Oxford History of the Laws of England: Vol. 1, The Canon Law and Ecclesiastical Jurisdiction from 597 to the 1640s* (Oxford: Oxford University Press, 2004), p. 225.
12. Brian L. Woodcock, *Medieval Ecclesiastical Courts in the Diocese of Canterbury* (Oxford: Oxford University Press, 1952), p. 61.
13. YBI CP. E. 248 (1345–46).
14. YBI CP. E. 89 (1365–66).
15. TNA PRO C 1/107/29 (1486).
16. *CCR* for 1497, pp. 363–72.
17. Kathleen Edwards and Dorothy Owens, eds., *The Registers of Roger Martival, Bishop of Salisbury, 1315–1330,* v. 4 (Canterbury and York Society, v. 75, 1968), pp. 10–14.
18. Frederik Pedersen, "Did the Medieval Laity Know the Canon Law Rules on Marriage? Some Evidence from Fourteenth-Century York Cause Papers," *Mediaeval Studies* 56 (1994): 115–16, 150–51.
19. Charles Donahue, Jr., *Law, Marriage, and Society in the Later Middle Ages* (New York: Cambridge University Press, 2007), p. 48.
20. F.R.H. Du Boulay, ed., *Registrum Thome Bourgchier, Cantuariensis Archiepiscopi A.D. 1454–1486* (Canterbury and York Society, v. 54, 1957), pp. 23–24.
21. Helen Birkett, "The Pastoral Application of the Lateran IV Reforms in the Northern Province, 1215–1348," *Northern History* 43.2 (2006): 219.

22. Michael M. Sheehan, "Marriage Theory and Practice," in *Marriage, Family, and Law in Medieval Europe: Collected Studies*, ed. James K. Farge (Toronto: University of Toronto Press, 1996), pp. 118–76.
23. Translated from F.M. Powicke and C.R. Cheney, eds., *Councils and Synods with Other Documents Relating to the English Church* (Oxford: Clarendon Press, 1964), v. 2, p. 87, statute 83.
24. Ibid., v. 2, p. 88, statute 86.
25. John Myrc, *Instructions for a Parish Priest* (London: Trübner and Co., 1868; repr. Elibron Classics, 2005), p. 6.
26. David D'Avray, *Medieval Marriage: Symbolism and Society* (Oxford: Oxford University Press, 2005), p. 204.
27. *CCR* for 1378, pp. 222–23.
28. YBI CP. E. 248, Simon Munkton *c.* Agnes Huntington (1345–46).
29. Cordelia Beattie, "A Room of One's Own? The Legal Evidence for the Residential Arrangements of Women without Husbands in Late-Fourteenth- and Early-Fifteenth-Century York," in *Medieval Women and the Law*, ed. Noël James Menuge, (Woodbridge: Boydell, 2000), p. 46.
30. TNA PRO C1/287/47 (1504–9).
31. It is possible that Thomas's wife had already begun a suit in ecclesiastical court for a judicial separation on the grounds of cruelty, although this author was incapable of finding evidence of such a suit. However, John Baker's initial actions strongly suggest that he did not feel the beating required ecclesiastical intervention; his opinion may have changed with subsequent dealings with his brother-in-law. The bill certainly does not indicate that a suit had been initiated in the church courts, and it seems likely that an appeal to the regular process might well have been mentioned in this case only because it would have strengthened Baker's negative depiction of his brother-in-law.
32. Sue Sheridan Walker, "Punishing Convicted Ravishers: Statutory Strictures and Actual Practice in Thirteenth- and Fourteenth-Century England," *Journal of Medieval History* 13 (1987): 237–50.
33. Ibid., 239.
34. Ibid., 238.
35. Ibid., 246; Henry Ansgar Kelly, "Statutes of Rapes and Alleged Ravishers of Wives: A Context for the Charges against Thomas Malory, Knight," *Viator* 28 (1997): 398–99.
36. The confusion between rape and ravishment is discussed in more detail in chapter 3.
37. TNA PRO C1/83/38 (1487–1504).
38. TNA PRO C1/343/57 (1504–9).
39. TNA PRO C1/492/35 (1515–29).
40. TNA PRO C1/45/46 (1467–70).
41. TNA PRO C1/61/382 (1473–74).
42. Barbara A. Hanawalt, "'Good Governance' in the Medieval and Early Modern Context," *Journal of British Studies* 37 (1998): 248.
43. See Shannon McSheffrey, "Men and Masculinity in Late Medieval London Civic Culture: Governance, Patriarchy and Reputation," in *Conflicted Identities and Multiple Masculinities: Men in the Medieval West,* ed. Jacqueline Murray (New York: Garland, 1999), pp. 243–78.
44. TNA PRO SC 8/89/4402 (*c.* 1428).
45. *CPRRGBI*, v. 3, pp. 244–54.
46. A.T. Bannister, ed., "Visitation Returns of the Diocese of Hereford in 1397," *English Historical Review* 45 (1930): 92, John Comyn, chaplain of Collewalle; Bertha Haven Putnam, ed., *Yorkshire Sessions of the Peace, 1361–1364* (Yorkshire Archaeological Society, v. 100, 1939), p. 26, no. 100,

Thomas de Wartre, chaplain; W.P. Baildon, ed. and trans., *Court Rolls of the Manor of Wakefield, 1297–1309*, v. 2 (Yorkshire Archaeological Record Series, v. 36, 1906), p. 93, Alice, wife of John Hyde of Wakefield, abducted at the parish chaplain's command; William Hudson, ed., *Leet Jurisdiction in the City of Norwich: During the XIIIth and XIVth Centuries* (Selden Society, v. 5, 1891), p. 67, Walter Quell, chaplain; TNA PRO C 1/75/39 (1386–1486); TNA PRO C 1/68/106 (1386–1486); Elisabeth Guernsey Kimball, ed., *Rolls of the Warwickshire and Coventry Sessions of the Peace 1377–1397* (Dugdale Society, v. 16, 1939), p. 160, no. 18, William Fletcher, chaplain; Elisabeth Chapin Furber, ed., *Essex Sessions of the Peace, 1351, 1377–79* (Essex Archaeological Society, v. 3, 1953), p. 98, no. A42, Roger de Harleston, archdeacon of Cambridge; ibid., p. 169, no. B192, William Beverel, chaplain; ibid., p. 171, no. B207, William, rector of the church of Chignall St. James; ibid., p. 203, no. B279, Thomas Isbroud, chaplain; Sillem, *Sessions of the Peace in Lincolnshire*, p. 208, Robert, son of John Haliday of Morton, chaplain; Morris S. Arnold, ed. and trans., *Select Cases of Trespass from the King's Courts 1307–1399*, v. 1 (Selden Society, v. 100, 1985), pp. 78–79, no. 8.5 (TNA KB 27/225, m. 87d), Stephen de Beck, a beneficed clerk; ibid., p. 81, no. 8.8 (TNA KB 27/295, m. 2d), John, parson of Newbold Pacey; ibid., pp. 87–88o, n. 8.15 (TNA KB 27/509, m. 26), Henry, vicar of Swalcliffe.

47. Certainly that happened. The register of the archbishop of Canterbury for the year 1299 includes an interesting series of notifications concerning Simon, son of Gilbert of Walsoken, who was excommunicated for assaulting the rector of Walsoken, whom he caught in bed with his wife. See Rose Graham, *Registrum Roberti Winchelsey,Cantuariensis Archiepiscopi, A.D. 1294–1313*, v. 1 (Canterbury and York Society, v. 51, 1952) pp. 340–42. For a discussion of the continuing problem of sexually active clergy, see Bernhard Schimmelpfennig, "*Ex Fornicatione Nati*: Studies on the Position of Priests' Sons from the Twelfth to the Fourteenth Century," *Studies in Medieval and Renaissance History*, n.s. 2, o.s. 12 (1979): 3–50.
48. Such was the case with Henry, vicar of Swalcliffe.
49. S.F.C. Milsom notes that "[m]any petitions of the fourteenth and fifteenth centuries complain of matters which in principle were remedied by the common law. Special treatment is sought because the petitioner is too poor to sue, or his adversary so powerful that sheriffs will not do their duty or jurors tell the truth." See S.F.C. Milsom, *The Historical Foundations of the Common Law* (London: Butterworths, 1981), p. 83.
50. TNA PRO C1/75/39 (1487–1504).
51. See Edward Powell, "Jury Trial at Gaol Delivery in the Late Middle Ages: The Midland Circuit, 1400–1429," in *Twelve Good Men and True: The Criminal Trial Jury in England, 1200–1800*, ed. J.S. Cockburn and Thomas A. Green (Princeton: Princeton University Press, 1988), pp. 102–3.
52. Kelly, "Statutes of Rape," 408.
53. In her study of consensual abduction, Walker notes the frequency with which the courts identified clergymen as spouse abductors and proposes that these men "may have been acting in their capacity of spiritual advisor." Walker, "Punishing Convicted Ravishers," 245–46.
54. Arnold, *Select Cases of Trespass*, pp. 78–79, no. 8.5 (TNA KB 27/225, m. 87d).
55. Sequestration to prevent the plaintiff from experiencing undue force was a common procedure in the canonical courts. For example, in the period 1463–1505, Canterbury act books record at least nine cases of sequestration. See Canterbury Y.1.6, fo. 21; Y.1.15, fos. 160 and 201; Y.1.16, fo. 253; Y.1.17, fo. 13; Y.1.19, in which the folios are unnumbered but the cases are

those of Ralph Huddingfeld of Smorden and his wife, Amica Humfrey, and Lodan de Betrysden and his wife, Elisabeth Barker; and finally, Y.2.2, fos. 37 and 110.

56. "Force and arms" was a legal requirement that was often fictitiously manipulated in order to have a case brought before the king's court. Milsom, *Historical Foundations,* pp. 283–313.
57. TNA PRO C1/295/4 (1504–9), *Certiorari.*
58. Judicial separations were very infrequent. For example, for the ecclesiastical province of York from the fourteenth to the early sixteenth centuries, there are only six identifiable cases of applications for separation on the grounds of cruelty.
59. R.N. Swanson, "Angels Incarnate: Clergy and Masculinity from Gregorian Reform to Reformation," in *Masculinity in Medieval Europe,* ed. D.M. Hadley (New York: Longman, 1999), p. 170.
60. TNA PRO JUST 1/483, m. 57 (1271–72).
61. *CPRRGBI*, v. 12, pp. 398–401.
62. Ibid., pp. 404–8.
63. *CCR* for 1384, p. 588.
64. *CPR* for 1355, p. 220.
65. Ibid., p. 304. The legal trail of the divorce seems to end here; however, Sir John Avenel died in 1359, so the marriage ended in one way or another not long after Margery initiated divorce proceedings. W.R. Powell, *A History of the County of Essex* (Victoria County History, v. 5, 1966), pp. 97–114.
66. TNA PRO SC 8/295/14727 (*c.* 1377–79).
67. TNA PRO SC 8/146/7264 (*c.* 1377).
68. *CCR* for 1377, pp. 553–57.
69. GL, MS 9065, fo. 38rv, as cited in Shannon McSheffrey, ed. *Consistory: Testimony in the Late Medieval London Consistory Court* (Concordia University, 2008-present). http://digitalhistory.concordia.ca/consistory. Date of access: November 27, 2012.
70. They were certainly married by September 1375, when the king sent an order to his escheator not to meddle further with a manor that was to come into the hands of Margaret, daughter of John de Nerford, "whom John Brewes has taken to wife." *CCR* for 1375, p. 158.
71. *CPR* for 1378, p. 260.
72. Ibid., p. 299. The relationship with Robert Howard is noted in Douglas Richardson and Kimball G. Everingham, *Magna Carta Ancestry: A Study in Colonial and Medieval Families* (Baltimore: Genealogical Pub. Co., 2005), p. 816.
73. *CPR* for 1378, p. 301.
74. Ibid., p. 307.
75. TNA PRO SC 8/18/889 (1378).
76. *CCR* for 1378, pp. 222–23.
77. *CPR* for 1379, p. 374.
78. *CPR* for 1380, p. 530.
79. Colin Richmond and Margaret Aston, *Lollardy and the Gentry in the Later Middle Ages* (Stroud: Sutton, 1997), p. 16; Mary Carpenter Erler, "The Library of a London Vowess, Margery de Nerford," *Women Reading, and Piety in Late Medieval England* (Cambridge: Cambridge University Press, 2002), p. 48.
80. Erler, "Library of a London Vowess," pp. 48–67. Her will is in GL MS 9171/2, fos. 384r–v.
81. Gwen Seabourne, *Imprisoning Medieval Women: The Non-judicial Confinement and Abduction of Women in England, c. 1170–1509* (Farnham: Ashgate, 2011), p. 131.

82. *CPMRCL*, v. 2, pp. 114–23.
83. Ibid., pp. 163–81.
84. Elizabeth's standing as an heiress is recorded in *CCR* for 1380.
85. *CCR* for 1385, pp. 541–42.

NOTES TO CHAPTER 3

1. Judith M. Bennett and A.M. Froide, "A Singular Past," in *Singlewomen in the European Past* (Philadelphia: University of Pennsylvania Press, 1999), p. 13. Emphasis in original.
2. Cordelia Beattie, *Medieval Single Women: The Politics of Social Classification in Late Medieval England* (Oxford: Oxford University Press, 2007), p. 121.
3. Natalie Zemon Davis, *The Return of Martin Guerre* (Cambridge: Harvard University Press, 1983), p. 33.
4. Cordelia Beattie, "A Room of One's Own? The Legal Evidence for the Residential Arrangements of Women without Husbands in Late-Fourteenth- and Early-Fifteenth-Century York," in *Medieval Women and the Law*, ed. Noël James Menuge (Woodbridge: Boydell, 2000), p. 52.
5. Amy Erickson has made the same argument for lone women in the early modern era. See Amy Louise Erickson, *Women and Property in Early Modern England* (London: Routledge, 1993), p. 202.
6. Matthew 19:6.
7. See James A. Brundage, "Domestic Violence in Classical Canon Law," in *Violence in Medieval Society*, ed. Richard W. Kaeuper (Woodbridge: Boydell, 2000), pp. 183–95.
8. TNA PRO C 1/19/152 (1452–54).
9. Ruth Mazo Karras, *Sexuality in Medieval Europe: Doing unto Others* (New York: Routledge, 2005), pp. 50–52. P.J.P. Goldberg includes a fascinating case in his *Women in England, c. 1275–1525* (Manchester: Manchester University Press, 1995), p. 256, in which charges of rape brought by a pregnant woman named Joan were dismissed because, as the court ruled, "it was said that this was a wonder because a child could not be engendered without the will of both."
10. Y.B. Mich. 5 Edw. IV, fos. 58a–61b (1465).
11. Shannon McSheffrey, "Men and Masculinity in Late Medieval London Civic Culture: Governance, Patriarchy and Reputation," in *Conflicted Identities and Multiple Masculinities: Men in the Medieval West*, ed. Jacqueline Murray (New York: Garland, 1999), pp. 243–78.
12. Karen Jones, *Gender and Petty Crime in Late Medieval England: The Local Courts in Kent, 1460–1560* (Woodbridge: Boydell, 2006), p. 131.
13. Y.B. Hil. Hen VII, fos. 6a–7b (1486).
14. For an excellent discussion of this facet of divorce, see Philippa C. Maddern, "Moving Households: Geographical Mobility and Serial Monogamy in England, 1350–1500," *Parergon* 24.2 (2007): 69–92. Granted, it is critical to note that relocation for a woman was much more difficult than it was for a man. Barbara A. Hanawalt has argued that space was highly gendered in medieval England: "[w]hen women did move out of their space, they had to do so with proper escort or risk humiliation or even rape." See Barbara A. Hanawalt, "At the Margins of Women's Space," in *"Of Good and Ill Repute": Gender and Social Control in Medieval England* (Oxford: Oxford University Press, 1998), p. 84. A woman attempting to relocate independently to an area without family and friends would have faced countless obstacles.

15. R.M. Haines, ed., *Calendar of the Register of Adam de Orleton, Bishop of Worcester 1327–1333* (London: Historical Manuscripts Commission, no. 27, 1979), p. 141.
16. For example, see Agnes Curtyes de Est Deping, in Margaret Bowker, ed., *An Episcopal Court Book for the Diocese of Lincoln 1514–1520* (Lincoln Record Society, v. 61, 1967), p. 88. For an excellent discussion of excommunication, see Elisabeth Vodola, *Excommunication in the Middle Ages* (Berkeley and Los Angeles: University of California Press, 1986).
17. Charles Johnson, ed., *Registrum Hamonis Hethe, Diocesis Roffensis, A.D. 1319–1352*, v. 1 (Canterbury and York Society, v. 48, 1915), pp. 148–50.
18. L.R. Poos, ed., *Lower Ecclesiastical Jurisdiction in Late-Medieval England: The Courts of the Dean and Chapter of Lincoln, 1336–1349, and the Deanery of Wisbech, 1458–1484* (Records of Social and Economic History, New Series v. 32, 2001), p. 6.
19. Poos, *Lower Ecclesiastical Jurisdiction*, p. 368.
20. T.C.B. Timmins, ed., *The Register of John Chandler, Dean of Salisbury, 1404–1417* (Wiltshire Record Society, v. 39, 1984), pp. 96–97.
21. P.E. Hair, ed., *Before the Bawdy Court: Selections from Church Court and Other Records Relating to the Correction of Moral Offences in England, Scotland, and New England, 1300–1800* (New York: Elek Books, 1972), no. 36.
22. T.C.B. Timmins, ed., *The Register of John Waltham, Bishop of Salisbury, 1388–1395* (Canterbury and York Society, v. 80, 1994), pp. 150, 151.
23. Joseph Henry Parry, ed., *Registrum Johannis Gilbert, Episcopi Herefordensis A.D. 1375–1389* (Canterbury and York Society, v. 18, 1915), pp. 82–83.
24. Rowland Alwyn Wilson, ed. and trans., *The Register of Walter Reynolds, Bishop of Worcester, 1308–1313* (Dugdale Society, v. 9, 1928), pp. 28–29.
25. C.T. Flower and M.C.B. Dawes, eds., *Registrum Simonis de Gandavo, Diocesis Saresbiriensis A.D. 1297–1315*, v. 1 (Canterbury and York Society, v. 40, 1934), pp. 414–15.
26. Flower and Dawes, *Registrum Simonis de Gandavo*, v. 1, pp. 419–20.
27. Susan M. Keeling and C.P. Lewis, "The Rape and Honour of Lewes," in *History of the County of Sussex* (Victoria County History, v. 7, 1940), pp. 1–7.
28. Johnson, *Registrum Hamonis Hethe*, v. 1, pp. 197, 227–28.
29. E.F. Jacob, ed., *The Register of Henry Chichele, Archbishop of Canterbury, 1414–1443*, v. 4 (Canterbury and York Society, v. 47, 1947), pp. 185–86.
30. R.L. Storey, ed., *The Register of Thomas Langley, Bishop of Durham, 1406–1437*, v. 2 (Surtees Society, v. 166, 1951), p. 134.
31. TNA PRO SC 8/275/13736 (1305).
32. Joyce M. Horn, ed., *The Register of Robert Hallum, Bishop of Salisbury, 1407–17* (Canterbury and York Society, v. 72, 1982), p. 140.
33. At least one wife in this sampling returned of her own initiative. A tourn from the year 1307 at Wakefield describes the case of Alice, wife of John Kyde of Wakefield, who participated in a consensual abduction by Nicholas, the parish chaplain of Wakefield. Although the record notes that "afterwards Alice returned to her husband," the very long list of items taken with her and their value would suggest that John Kyde was hoping to receive compensation for the items she did not bring home. William Paley Baildon, ed., *Court Rolls of the Manor of Wakefield, 1297–1309*, v. 2 (Yorkshire Archaeological Society Record Series, v. 36, 1906), p. 93.
34. Timmins, *Register of John Chandler*, pp. 112–13, no. 315.
35. Poos, *Lower Ecclesiastical Jurisdiction*, p. 219.
36. C. Eveleigh Woodruff, ed., "Some Early Visitation Rolls Preserved at Canterbury," *Archaeologia Cantiana* 32 (1917): 154.

37. This issue is discussed at greater length in Sara M. Butler, *The Language of Abuse: Marital Violence in Later Medieval England* (Leiden: Brill, 2007).
38. R.L. Storey, ed., *The Register of Gilbert Welton, Bishop of Carlisle, 1353–1362* (Canterbury and York Society, v. 88, 1999), p. 63.
39. Bowker, *Episcopal Court Book for the Diocese of Lincoln*, p. 88.
40. J.W. Willis Bund, ed., *Episcopal Registers, Diocese of Worcester. Register of Bishop Godfrey Giffard, September 23rd, 1268 to August 15th, 1301* (Worcestershire Historical Society, 1902), p. 76.
41. J. Raine, ed., *Depositions and Other Ecclesiastical Proceedings from the Courts of Durham Extending from 1311 to the Reign of Elizabeth* (Surtees Society, v. 21, 1854), p. 37.
42. A.T. Bannister, ed., "Visitation Returns of the Diocese of Hereford in 1397," *English Historical Review* 45 (1930): 92.
43. A. Hamilton Thompson, ed., *Visitations in the Diocese of Lincoln 1517–1531: Volume 1: Visitations of Rural Deaneries by William Atwater, Bishop of Lincoln, and His Commissaries, 1517–20* (Lincoln Record Society, v. 33, 1940), p. 139.
44. Hair, *Before the Bawdy Court*, pp. 116–17, no. 268.
45. Storey, *Register of Gilbert Welton*, p. 63; Timmins, *Register of John Chandler*, p. 116.
46. E.M. Elvey, ed., *The Courts of the Archdeaconry of Buckingham 1483–1523* (Buckinghamshire Record Society, no. 19, 1975), p. 250.
47. J.B. Post, "Ravishment of Women and the Statutes of Westminster," in *Legal Records and the Historian*, ed. J.H. Baker (London: Royal Historical Society, 1978), p. 158.
48. Y.B. Mich. 20 Hen. VII, fos. 2a–2b (1504). The same case is also addressed in Y.B. Hil. 21 Hen. VII, fos. 13a–13b (1506).
49. Morris S. Arnold, ed. and trans., *Select Cases of Trespass from the King's Courts 1307–1399*, v. 1 (Selden Society, v. 100, 1985), pp. 89–90, no. 817 (TNA KB 27/514, m. 19).
50. Please see chapter 2 for a good discussion of the assistance of family.
51. Arnold, *Select Cases of Trespass*, v. 1, p. 80, no. 8.6 (TNA PRO KB 27/225, m. 1).
52. Ibid., pp. 80–81, no. 8.7 (TNA PRO KB 27/232, m. 64d).
53. *CPR* for 1359, p. 191.
54. Maureen Mulholland, "Trial in Manorial Courts in Late Medieval England," in *Judicial Tribunals in England and Europe, 1200–1700: The Trial in History*, ed. Maureen Mulholland and Brian Pullan, v. I (Manchester: Manchester University Press, 2003), p. 88.
55. The necessity that the case involve substantial goods was not spelled out in statute law until 1487; 3 Henry VII, c. 2, in A. Luders, T.E. Tomlins, J. France, W.E. Taunton and J. Raithby, eds. *Statutes of the Realm* (London: Record Commission, 1810–27), v. 2, p. 512. For a discussion of the 1487 act, see E.W. Ives, "'Agaynst Taking Awaye of Women': The Inception and Operation of the Abduction Act of 1487," in *Wealth and Power in Tudor England: Essays Presented to S.T. Bindoff*, ed. E.W. Ives, R.J. Knecht and J.J. Scarisbrick (London: Athlone Press, 1978), pp. 21–45.
56. Essex Record Office D/DPr66; as cited in Alan Macfarlane, ed., *Earls Colne, Essex: Records of an English Village, 1375–1854* (University of Cambridge, 2002), http://linux02.lib.cam.ac.uk/earlscolne/ecrolls2/54201104.htm.
57. J.P. Walker, ed. and trans., *Court Rolls of the Manor of Wakefield, 1322–1331*, v. 5 (Yorkshire Archaeological Society Record Series, v. 109, 1945), p. *viii*. Other examples of cases of ravishment in manorial courts are William Brok of Hertisheved, who ravished the wife of Godard in July 1277, see

Baildon, *Manor of Wakefield*, v. 1, p. 173; John Bokke, who carried off the wife of Henry Hauke, see Baildon, *Manor of Wakefield*, v. 1, p. 34; Richard de Berton, who carried off the wife of William Steadfast in 1299–1300, see William Hudson, ed., *Leet Jurisdiction in the City of Norwich: During the XIIIth and XIVth Centuries* (Selden Society, v. 5, 1891), p. 52; Walter Quell, chaplain, who carried off the wife of Robert de Costessey three times with goods and chattels, see Hudson, *Leet Jurisdiction in the City of Norwich*, p. 67.

58. Baildon, *Manor of Wakefield*, v. 1, p. 234. The resolution to this case does not seem to have survived, although both John and Cicely turn up in later records. Cicely appears at another tourn in November 1296 for brewing weak ale (p. 244), and John of Sibbe appears as a pledge in a brush-wood case in 1297 (p. 271).
59. Gervase Le Gros, ed., *Rolls of the Assizes Held in the Channel Islands in the 2nd Year of the Reign of King Edward II, 1309* (Société Jersiase, no. 18, 1903), p. 190.
60. Arnold, *Select Cases of Trespass*, v. 1, pp. 73–74, no. 8.1 (TNA KB 27/191, m. 7). Walker does note it was possible to be pardoned for ravishment; however, a pardon only forgave what was due to the crown, not to the plaintiff. See Sue Sheridan Walker, "Punishing Convicted Ravishers: Statutory Strictures and Actual Practice in Thirteenth- and Fourteenth-Century England," *Journal of Medieval History* 13 (1987): 245.
61. Emma Hawkes, "'She Was Ravished against Her Will, What So Ever She Say': Female Consent in Rape and Ravishment in Late-Medieval England," *Limina* 1 (1995): 47.
62. For a discussion of the dangers of such confusing terminology, see Christopher Cannon, "*Raptus* in the Chaumpaigne Release and a Newly Discovered Document Concerning the Life of Geoffrey Chaucer," *Speculum* 68 (1993): 74–94.
63. Hawkes, "She Was Ravished against Her Will," p. 48.
64. Elizabeth Chapin Furber, ed., *Essex Sessions of the Peace 1351, 1377–79* (Essex Archaeological Society, v. 3, 1953), p. 98, no. A42.
65. Elisabeth Guernsey Kimball, ed., *Rolls of the Warwickshire and Coventry Sessions of the Peace 1377–1397* (Dugdale Society, v. 16, 1939), p. 151, no. 133.
66. Furber, *Essex Sessions of the Peace*, p. 169, no. B192.
67. Bertha Haven Putnam, ed., *Yorkshire Sessions of the Peace, 1361–64* (Yorkshire Archaeological Society, v. 100, 1939), p. 34, no. 8. I first examined this phenomenon of the language used in cases of ravishment in a 2006 article published in the *Journal of Social History* (40.2), entitled "Runaway Wives: Husband Desertion in Medieval England," pp. 337–59, from which this portion of the chapter is drawn. Since then, Caroline Dunn has done a more exhaustive statistical study of the language used by the courts for her doctoral dissertation, published in part in "The Language of Ravishment in Medieval England," *Speculum* 86 (2011): 79–116. The main distinction in her findings is that she sees changes over time in the clarity of terminology used by juries.
68. T.D. Hardy, ed., *Registrum Palatinum Dunelmense*, pt. 3 (Rolls Series, v. 62, 1878), p. 281.
69. See also the records of the Deanery of Wisbech from the year 1464, which note the case of Roger Palfrayman, who detained the wife of John Botery. He was warned to remove her and return her to her husband, under pain of judgment. He is not described as her lover, as the church was usually very careful to do. Was he another well-meaning neighbor or brother trying to

help a runaway wife? Poos, *Lower Ecclesiastical Jurisdiction*, p. 479. See Storey, *Register of Thomas Langley*, v. 3, p. 65, no. 695.

70. Frederik Pedersen, *Marriage Disputes in Medieval England* (London: Hambledon Press, 2000), p. *vii*.
71. TNA PRO C1/82/87 (1487–1503).
72. TNA PRO JUST 2/67, m. 6.
73. TNA PRO JUST 1/998A, m. 26d (1268).
74. TNA PRO JUST 1/998A, m. 40d (1268).
75. Timmins, *Register of John Waltham*, p. 23.
76. Warren Ortman, ed., *Court Rolls of the Abbey of Ramsey and of the Honor of Clare* (Yale Historical Publications, v. 9, 1928), p. 246.
77. TNA PRO C 1/693/8 (1529–32).
78. TNA PRO C1/71/139 (1487–1503).
79. William Brown, ed., *Cartularium Prioratus de Gyseburne, Ebor. Dioceseos, Ordinis S. Augustini* (Selden Society, v. 86, 1889), p. 124*n*.
80. *CCR* for 1304, p. 126.
81. Y.B. 32 Edw. I (1304); as it appears in Alfred J. Horwood, ed., *Year Books of the Reign of Edward the First: Years XXXII and XXXIII (1304–1305)* (Rolls Series n. 31, pt. A, v. 4, 1864), pp. 316–21.
82. TNA PRO SC 8/324/E641 (1305).
83. TNA PRO SC 8/324/E640 (1305).
84. Nicholas de Meynell also came from a rather scurrilous family background. In 1290, his father claimed his wife had tried to poison him and was also an adulteress; two years later, his mother left his father because of his cruel behavior. See William Brown, ed. *The Register of John Le Romeyn, Lord Archbishop of York, 1286–1296*, v. 1 (Surtees Society, v. 123, 1913), pp. 170–71, 176–77.
85. William Page, *A History of the County of York: North Riding* (Victoria County History, v. 2, 1923), pp. 309–19.
86. TNA PRO SC 8/35/1705 (1305).
87. William Brown and A. Hamilton Thompson, eds., *The Register of William Greenfield, Lord Archbishop of York, 1306–1315*, pt. 3 (Surtees Society, v. 151, 1936), pp. 13–14.
88. Ibid., pt. 3, pp. 15–16, 19–20.
89. Brown and Thompson, *Register of William Greenfield*, pt. 1 (Surtees Society, v. 145, 1931), p. 126.
90. Brown and Thompson, *Register of William Greenfield*, pt. 3, pp. 49–50.
91. John Wilfred Wardell, *A History of Yarm, an Ancient North Riding Town* (Yarm: Sunderland, 1957), p. 18.
92. Brown and Thompson, *Register of William Greenfield*, pt. 3, pp. 72–73.
93. *CCR* for 1312, pp. 540–41.
94. Douglas Richardson and Kimball G. Everingham, *Magna Carta Ancestry: A Study in Colonial and Medieval Families* (Baltimore: Genealogical Pub. Co., 2005), p. 517.
95. Ibid.
96. Jacob, *Register of Henry Chichele*, v. 4, pp. 185–86.
97. Storey, *Register of Thomas Langley*, v. 3, pp. 40–41.
98. TNA PRO C 1/6/195 (1424–26).
99. Richardson and Everingham, *Magna Carta Ancestry*, p. 517.
100. TNA PRO C 1/6/318 (1424–6); C 1/6/319 (1424–26); C 1/6/320 (1424–26); C 1/6/321 (1424–26).
101. October 1407. C. Given-Wilson, ed., *The Parliament Rolls of Medieval England, 1275–1504 (PROME)* (Leicester: Scholarly Digital Editions, 2005).

102. Dean and Chapter of Durham (DCD) Cart. IV, f. 278v–279r. It is not clear when Margery died, but she seems to have had a relatively active life in her elderly years. She petitioned the chancellor once more, this time against Sir Henry Pierrepont and her son Ralph as well as others, claiming that they were meddling with lands bequeathed to her by her husband Nicholas. Unfortunately, the petition has been dated incorrectly to 1475–80 or 1483–85, dates that are simply not possible, as Margery would have been well over a hundred years old. See TNA PRO C 1/67/229.
103. William Page and W.J. Hardy, eds., *Manuscripts of Rye and Hereford Corporations* (London: Eyre and Spottiswoode, 1892), pp. 421–94.
104. *CPR* for 1385, p. 86.
105. TNA PRO SC 8/146/7276 (*c.* 1391).
106. TNA PRO SC 8/103/5109 (*c.* 1390).

NOTES TO CHAPTER 4

1. See Maria L. Cioni, *Women and Law in Elizabethan England with Particular Reference to the Court of Chancery* (New York: Garland, 1985), p. 172.
2. For a synopsis of the laws of coverture, see Emma Hawkes, "'[S]he Will . . . Protect and Defend Her Rights Boldly by Law and Reason . . . ': Women's Knowledge of Common Law and Equity Courts in Late-Medieval England," in *Medieval Women and the Law*, ed. Noël James Menuge (Woodbridge: Boydell, 2000), pp. 146–47.
3. M. Bateson, ed., *Borough Customs* (Selden Society v. 18, 1904), pp. 224–25; as cited in Cordelia Beattie, "'Living as a Single Person': Marital Status, Performance and the Law in Late Medieval England," *Women's History Review* 17.3 (2008): 336. Emphasis included in Beattie.
4. G.D.G. Hall, trans. and ed., *The Treatise on the Laws and Customs of the Realm of England Commonly Called Glanvill* (Oxford: Oxford University Press, 1965), p. 68.
5. Ibid. Adultery as a bar to a wife's claim to dower might have also been common outside England. Canon law also stipulated that an adulterous wife lose her dower. See James A. Brundage, *Law, Sex, and Christian Society in Medieval Europe* (Chicago: University of Chicago Press, 1987), p. 408. As well, Venetian statutes excluded adulterous wives from claiming dower. Moreover, as we see also in the Statute of Westminster II (1285), the Venetians stipulated that a wife's rights were re-activated only if her husband received her back into his home and forgave her. See Linda Guzzetti, "Separations and Separated Couples in Fourteenth-Century Venice," in *Marriage in Italy, 1300–1650*, ed. Trevor Dean and K.J.P. Lowe (Cambridge: Cambridge University Press, 1998), pp. 254–55.
6. Henry de Bracton, *De Legibus et Consuetudinibus Angliae*, ed. George E. Woodbine, trans. Samuel E. Thorne, 4 vols (Cambridge: Belknap Press at Harvard University Press, 1968), v. 2, pp. 266–67.
7. Francis M. Nichols, ed., *Britton: The French Text Carefully Revised with an English Translation, Introduction and Notes* (Oxford: Clarendon Press, 1865), v. 2, pp. 264–65.
8. Joseph Biancalana, "Widows at Common Law: The Development of Common Law Dower," *Irish Jurist*, n.s. 23 (1988): 257, 259, 288–92; Paul Brand, "'Deserving' and 'Undeserving' Wives: Earning and Forfeiting Dower in Medieval England," *Journal of Legal History* 22.1 (2001): 1–11.
9. Biancalana, "Widows at Common Law," 257.

10. Brand, "'Deserving' and 'Undeserving' Wives," 8, 1.
11. Westminster II, c. 34, in A. Luders, T.E. Tomlins, J. France, W.E. Taunton, J. Raithby, eds, *Statutes of the Realm* (London: Record Commission, 1810–27), v. 1, p. 87.
12. 6 Richard II, st. 1, c. 6, in *Statutes of the Realm*, v. 2, p. 27.
13. Sue Sheridan Walker, "Litigation as Personal Quest: Suing for Dower in the Royal Courts, circa 1272–1350," in *Wife and Widow in Medieval England* (Ann Arbor: Michigan University Press, 1993), pp. 88–89.
14. Y.B. Trin. 43 Edw. III, fos. 19b–20a (1369).
15. Y.B. Trin. 10 Edw. III, fos. 35a–36b (1336).
16. Y.B. Trin. 18 Edw. II, fos. 617–619 (1325).
17. For a good discussion of the legal treatises on this matter, see Frederick Pollock and F.W. Maitland, *The History of English Law before the Time of Edward I*, v. 2 (London: Cambridge University Press, 1895, repr. 1968), pp. 393–95.
18. James A. Brundage, "Domestic Violence in Classical Canon Law," in *Violence in Medieval Society*, ed. Richard W. Kaeuper (Woodbridge: Boydell, 2000), p. 189.
19. L.R. Poos, ed., *Lower Ecclesiastical Jurisdiction in Late-Medieval England: The Courts of the Dean and Chapter of Lincoln, 1336–1349, and the Deanery of Wisbech, 1458–1484* (Records of Social and Economic History, New Series v. 32, 2001), p. 276.
20. For example, see the case of Sir Geoffrey de Upsall and his wife. Rosalind M.T. Hill, ed., *Register of William Melton, Archbishop of York, 1317–1340*, v. 2 (Canterbury and York Society, v. 71, 1977), p. 85.
21. Dom S.F. Hockey, ed., *The Register of William Edington, Bishop of Winchester, 1346–1366*, pt. 2 (Hampshire Record Series, v. 8, 1987), p. 63.
22. Unfortunately, the failure of the record to note the amount and frequency of payment is a common feature of alimony disputes. For other cases of this nature, see YBI CP. E. 14, Margery de Toft *c.* William Maynebag (1324); or YBI CP. E. 132, Lord William Claxton *c.* Lady Elizabeth, dowager of Lord Randalph Ebyr (1420–22).
23. See Mavis E. Mate, *Daughters, Wives and Widows after the Black Death: Women in Sussex, 1350–1535* (Woodbridge: Boydell, 1998), pp. 100–113.
24. *CPR* for 1316, p. 434.
25. *CCR* for 1320, p. 236.
26. Canterbury U.4.1, fos. 70r–70v; Canterbury Y.1.4, fo. 79r.
27. Kent County Record Office, Rochester DRb Pa I, fos. 129r, 140r; transcribed in R.H. Helmholz, *Marriage Litigation in Medieval England* (New York: Cambridge University Press, 1974), pp. 219–20.
28. Kathleen Edwards and Dorothy M. Owen, eds., *The Registers of Roger Martival, Bishop of Salisbury 1315–1330*, v. 4 (Canterbury and York Society v. 68, 1975), pp. 10–14.
29. Canterbury Y.1.3, fos. 112 and 116.
30. Ernest Harold Pearce, ed., *The Register of Thomas de Cobham, Bishop of Worcester, 1317–1327* (Worcestershire Historical Society, 1930), p. 18.
31. Poos, *Lower Ecclesiastical Jurisdiction* , pp. 162, 193.
32. YBI Cons. AB/1, fos. 177r–177v.
33. William Brown and A. Hamilton Thompson, eds, *The Register of William Greenfield, Lord Archbishop of York, 1306–1315*, v. 1 (Surtees Society, v. 145, 1931), p. 163. It is possible that Henry de Leck and his wife arranged to live chastely not because of marital discord but rather because they had religious aspirations, much like Margery Kempe and her husband, John (although in the case of Margery and John Kempe, it seems clear that it was

entirely Margery's decision to pursue a celibate lifestyle). Irrespective of the motivations for the separation, the court's determination to force Henry to support his wife despite their arrangement is meaningful.

34. L[incolnshire] A[rchives] O[ffice] D[ean]&C[hapter] A/2/24 fo. 33v, as cited in L.R. Poos, "The Heavy-Handed Marriage Counsellor: Regulating Marriage in Some Later-Medieval English Local Ecclesiastical-Court Jurisdictions," *American Journal of Legal History* 39 (1995): 302.
35. The record does not make it clear what kind of divorce is referred to in this instance: an annulment or a judicial separation. Charles Johnson, ed., *Registrum Hamonis Hethe, Diocesis Roffensis, A.D. 1319–1352*, v. 1 (Canterbury and York Society, v. 48, 1915), p. 213.
36. Charles Trice Martin, ed., *Registrum Epistolarum Fratris Johannis Peckham, Archiepiscopi Cantuariensis*, v. 2 (Rolls Series, v. 77, pt. 2, 1882), p. 505.
37. J.W. Willis Bund, ed. and trans., *Register of Bishop Godfrey Giffard, September 23rd, 1268 to August 15th, 1301* (Worcestershire Historical Society, 1902), p. 394.
38. Janet S. Loengard, "Common Law for Margery: Separate but not Equal," in *Women in Medieval Western European Culture*, ed. Linda E. Mitchell (New York: Garland, 1999), p. 121.
39. R.L. Storey, ed., *The Register of John Kirkby, Bishop of Carlisle, 1332–1352, and the Register of John Ross, Bishop of Carlisle, 1325–32* (Canterbury and York Society, v. 79, 1993), p. 135.
40. TNA PRO SC 8/46/2291 (*c.* 1383).
41. TNA PRO C 1/6/318 (1424–25).
42. S.F.C. Milsom, *Historical Foundations of the Common Law* (London: Butterworths, 1981), p. 168.
43. *PP*, p. 471.
44. Husbands might also sue for a divorce; however, it was very rare to find a male plaintiff.
45. R.L. Storey, ed., *The Register of Gilbert Welton, Bishop of Carlisle, 1353–1362* (Canterbury and York Society, v. 88, 1999), pp. 28, 37–38.
46. Edwards and Owen, *Registers of Roger Martival*, v. 4, pp. 52–54.
47. Ibid., p. 51.
48. Ibid., pp. 74, 89.
49. Ibid., p. 75.
50. Unfortunately, the records give no reason for the seizure of Plokenet's property. Ibid, p. 89.
51. Ibid., p. 91.
52. A.T. Bannister, ed., *Registrum Ade de Orleton, Episcopi Herefordensis, A.D. MCCCXVII–MCCCXXVII* (Canterbury and York Society, v. 5, 1908), p. 260.
53. *CCR* for 1323–1327, p. 409 (Oct. 17, 1325).
54. On August 10, 1325, a license was awarded to Alan to grant the manor of Logwardyn (*co. Here*) to Master Thomas de Chaundos for life. See *CPR* for 1324–1327, p. 159 (Aug. 10, 1325).
55. *CCR* for 1323–1327, p. 409 (Oct. 17, 1325); p. 510 (Oct. 10, 1325); pp. 86–87 (Mar. 17, 1327); p. 505 (Sept. 20, 1329).
56. Or "Lengleis," as his name appears in the *CPR* for 1340–1343, p. 38.
57. Storey, *Register of John Kirkby*, p. 113.
58. Ibid., p. 135.
59. *CPR* for 1338–40, p. 332.
60. Storey, *Register of John Kirkby*, pp. 135–37.
61. LAO D&C A/2/24 fo. 33v. Transcribed in Poos, *Lower Ecclesiastical Jurisdiction*, p. 302.

62. London, *Acta correct.*, v. 11, fo. 237r (July 1511–July 1516). As discussed by Richard M. Wunderli, *London Church Courts and Society on the Eve of the Reformation* (Cambridge: Medieval Academy of America, 1981), p. 121.
63. Y.B. Pasch. 8 Edw. II, fos. 41 (1315); as it appears in William Craddock Bolland, ed., *Year Books of Edward II*, v. 17: 8 Edward II (1314–1315) (Selden Society, v. 41, 1925), pp. 108–11.
64. TNA PRO C1/365/37 (1504–9).
65. Isaac Herbert Jeayes, ed., *Court Rolls of the Borough of Colchester*, v. 1 (Colchester: W. Gurney, 1921), p. 16.
66. TNA PRO C1/266/23 (*c.* 1500–1509).
67. R.H. Helmholz notes that the growth of trusts for women by the fifteenth century was substantial enough to explain, in part, why married women no longer felt inclined to make wills of their own. See Helmholz, "Married Women's Wills in Later Medieval England," in *Wife and Widow in Medieval England*, ed. Sue Sheridan Walker (Ann Arbor: University of Michigan Press, 1993), pp. 165–82.
68. Poos, *Lower Ecclesiastical Jurisdiction*, p. 7.
69. TNA PRO C 1/60/177 (1486–93 or 1504–15).
70. Y.B. Mich. 47, Edw. III, fo. 18a (1373).
71. Johnson, *Registrum Hamonis Hethe*, v. 1, pp. 228–29.
72. Amy Louise Erickson, "Coverture and Capitalism," *History Workshop Journal* 59 (2005): 7–8.
73. *CPR* for 1250, p. 76.
74. H.C. Maxwell Lyte, ed., *A Descriptive Catalogue of Ancient Deeds* (History of Parliament Trust, v. 5, 1906), pp. 349–66.
75. Y.B. Trin. 5 Edw. 4, fo. 3b (1465).
76. *Decretals of Gregory IX*, bk 4, t. xvii, c. 2; as it appears in John T. Noonan, Jr., trans., and Augustine Thompson, ed. and suppl., "Marriage Canons from the Decretum of Gratian and the Decretals, Sext, Clementines and Extravagantes," (Catholic University of America, 1993), http://faculty.cua.edu/Pennington/Canon%20Law/marriagelaw.htm. Date of access: November 27, 2012.
77. Rose Graham, ed. and trans., *Registrum Roberti Winchelsey, Cantuariensis Archiepiscopi, A.D. 1294–1313*, v. 1 (Canterbury and York Society v. 51, 1952), pp. 163–66.
78. *CPRRGBI*, v. 8, pp. 321–34.
79. *CPR* for 1254, p. 298.
80. A.H. Thomas, ed., *Calendar of Early Mayor's Court Rolls of the City of London, A.D. 1298–1307* (Cambridge: Cambridge University Press, 1924), pp. 228–52.
81. Y.B. Trin. 20 Edw III (1346); as it appears in Luke Owen Pike, ed., *Year Books of the Reign of King Edward the Third: Year XX (Second Part)* (Rolls Series no. 31, part B, v. 15, 1911), pp. 72–81. See also Y.B. Mich. 14 Edw. I (1286); as it appears in Paul A. Brand, *The Earliest English Law Reports*, v. 2 (Selden Society, v. 112, 1996), pp. 253–54.
82. For a good discussion on this topic, see Y.B. Trin. 7 Edw. IV, fo. 14b (1467).
83. TNA PRO C 1/28/511 (1460–65).
84. TNA PRO C 1/40/94 (1467–72).
85. TNA PRO C 1/33/113 (1465–71).
86. *Bracton*, v. 2, p. 179.
87. Janet S. Loengard, "'Which May Be Said to Be Her Own': Widows and Goods in Late-Medieval England," in *Medieval Domesticity: Home, Housing and*

Household in Medieval England, ed. Maryanne Kowaleski and P.J.P. Goldberg (Cambridge: Cambridge University Press, 2008), p. 165.

88. Ibid.
89. Ibid., p. 169.
90. Ibid., p. 171.
91. Natasha Korda, *Shakespeare's Domestic Economies: Gender and Property in Early Modern England* (Philadelphia: University of Pennsylvania Press, 2002), p. 152.
92. TNA PRO C 1/3/49 (1386). The other wife was Baroness Eleanor Maltravers. For a period during 1384, the church required Eleanor and Reginald to divorce on the grounds of consanguinity. It is always possible that Reginald and Margaret met and married during that time. A dispensation from the archbishop of Canterbury, though, permitted Eleanor and Reginald to remarry shortly after their divorce. Frederick Lewis Weis, Walter Lee Shepherd, and David Faris, *Ancestral Roots of Certain American Colonists Who Came to America before 1700* (Lancaster: Genealogical Publishing Company, 1964), lines 9–33, 21–32, 59–135, 212–34.
93. TNA PRO REQ 2/4/189, m. 3 (*c.*1492–1547).
94. TNA PRO C 1/66/286 (1475–80 or 1483–85); Roger Virgue has suggested that the date of the petition was most likely 1474. See Roger Virgue, "Sir John Risley (1443–1512), Courtier and Councillor," *Norfolk Archaeology* 38 (1982): 140–48.
95. Daniel Lysons, *The Environs of London*, v. 4 (1796), pp. 148–182, repr. University of London and History of Parliament Trust: British History Online, 2011, http://www.british-history.ac.uk/source.aspx?pubid=330. Date of access: November 27, 2012. See also Colin Richmond, *John Hopton: A Fifteenth-Century Suffolk Gentleman* (Cambridge: Cambridge University Press, 1981), p. 215, no. 230.
96. *CCR* for 1285, p. 357.
97. George Thomas Clark and Francisque Michel, *The Land of Morgan: Being a Contribution Towards the History of the Lordship of Glamorgan* (Whiting: University of California Press, 1862), p. 139.
98. TNA PRO C 1/17/1 (*c.* 1407–56).
99. TNA PRO C 1/153/74 (1486–93 or 1504–15).
100. TNA PRO C 1/29/511 (*c.* 1460–65).
101. Y.B. 2 Edw. II (1309). This cases appears in print in F.W. Maitland, ed., *Year Books of Edward II*, v. 2 (Selden Society, v. 194, 1904), p. 19; Elsie Shanks and S.F.C. Milsom, eds., *Novae Narrationes* (Selden Society, v. 115, 1963), p. 80.
102. Y.B. Pasch. 19 Edw. III (1345), as it appears in Luke Owen Pike, *Year Books of the Reign of King Edward the Third: Year XIX* (Rolls Series no. 31, part B, v. 13, 1906), pp. 14–17; also Y.B. term uncertain, 19 Edw. III, fo. 60b (1345).

NOTES TO CHAPTER 5

1. Charles Reid, Jr., "The Rights of Children in Medieval Canon Law," in *The Vocation of the Child*, ed. Patrick McKinley Brennan (Grand Rapids: Wm. B. Eerdmans, 2008), p. 265.
2. James A. Brundage, *Law, Sex, and Christian Society in Medieval Europe* (Chicago: University of Chicago Press, 1987), p. 245.
3. Gratian, *Decretum*, as cited in Jessica Goldberg, "The Legal Persona of the Child in Gratian's *Decretum*," *Bulletin of Medieval Canon Law* 24, n.s.

(2000): 19–20. Although it is hard to imagine how not providing for one's child might be considered by some to be an act of asceticism, Barbara Newman's work on female saints suggests that it may actually have been a popular misconception. Medieval mothers sometimes considered their children to be an extension of themselves; the process of self-denial, then, not only meant denying one's self proper sustenance but also one's child. See Barbara Newman, *From Virile Woman to WomanChrist: Studies in Medieval Religion and Literature* (Philadelphia: University of Pennsylvania Press, 1995), ch. 3.

4. *Decretals of Gregory IX*, Bk. 4, t. xvii, c. 2, as it appears in John T. Noonan, Jr., trans., and Augustine Thompson, ed. and suppl., "Marriage Canons from the Decretum of Gratian and the Decretals, Sext, Clementines and Extravagantes" (Washington, D.C.: Catholic University of America, 1993), http://faculty.cua.edu/Pennington/Canon%20Law/marriagelaw.htm. Date of access: November 27, 2012.
5. R.H. Helmholz, "Support Orders, Church Courts, and the Rule of *Filius Nullius*: A Reassessment of the Common Law," *Virginia Law Review* 63.383 (1977): 435.
6. Ibid., 436.
7. *The Decretals of Gregory IX*, Bk. 2, t. 33, c. 2, "*De Conversione Infidelium*." Many thanks to Dr. Mark Gossiaux of the Philosophy Department at Loyola University New Orleans for his valuable assistance in this translation.
8. *Codex Iuris Canonici*, ca. 1132. Linda Guzzetti has mistakenly argued that this ruling existed also in the fourteenth century. Although the *Codex* is basically a reorganization and clarification of medieval canon law, it is a twentieth-century creation; nowhere in medieval canon law is this statement made clearly. See Linda Guzzetti, "Separations and Separated Couples in Fourteenth-Century Venice," in *Marriage in Italy, 1300–1650*, ed. Trevor Dean and K.J.P. Lowe (Cambridge: Cambridge University Press, 1998), p. 269. Guzzetti does note that Venetian separations did not address the issue of child custody or support either.
9. York M 2(1) c, fo. 15.
10. Philippe Ariès, *Centuries of Childhood: A Social History of Family Life*, trans. Robert Baldick (New York: Alfred Knopf, 1962); Lloyd de Mause, "The Evolution of Childhood," in *The History of Childhood* (New York: Psychohistory Press, 1974), pp. 1–74; Edward Shorter, *The Making of the Modern Family* (New York: Basic Books, 1975); Lawrence Stone, *The Family, Sex, and Marriage in England, 1500–1800* (New York: Harper and Row, 1977). For arguments against this perception, see Anthony Burton, "Looking Forward from Ariès? Pictorial and Material Evidence for the History of Childhood and Family Life," *Continuity and Change* 4.2 (1989): 203–29; Danièle Alexandre-Bidon and Didier Lett, *Children in the Middle Ages: Fifth to Fifteenth Centuries*, trans. Jody Gladding (Notre Dame, IN: University of Notre Dame Press, 1999); Barbara A. Hanawalt, "Medievalists and the Study of Childhood," *Speculum* 77 (2002): 440–60; Jean E. Jost, "Loving Parents in Middle English Literature," in *Childhood in the Middle Ages and the Renaissance: The Results of a Paradigm Shift in the History of Mentality*, ed. Albrecht Classen (Berlin: Walter de Gruyter, 2005), pp. 307–28.
11. H.E. Salter, ed., *Records of Mediaeval Oxford: Coroners' Inquests, the Walls of Oxford, etc.* (Oxford: Oxford Chronicle Company, Ltd, 1912), pp. 7–8.
12. TNA PRO JUST 2/119C, m. 4 (1411–21).
13. TNA PRO JUST 2/24, mm. 6d and 7 (1375–84).

14. Shulamith Shahar, *Childhood in the Middle Ages* (London: Routledge, 1990), p. 152.
15. J.V. Bullard and H. Chalmer Bell, eds., *Lyndwood's Provinciale: The Text of the Canons Therein Contained, Reprinted from the Translation Made in 1534* (London: Faith Press, 1929), p. 133.
16. TNA PRO C 1/142/18 (1486–92 or 1504–15).
17. TNA PRO C 1/46/162 (1433–43 or 1467–72).
18. Henry Maxwell Lyte, ed., *The Registers of Oliver King Bishop of Bath and Wells 1496–1503, and Hadrian de Castello Bishop of Bath and Wells 1503–1518* (Somerset Record Society, v. 54, 1939), p. 82.
19. W. Brown, ed., *The Register of John Le Romeyn, Lord Archbishop of York, 1286–1296*, pt. 1 (Surtees Society, v. 123, 1913), p. 267.
20. Sara M. Butler, "A Case of Indifference? Child Murder in Later Medieval England," *Journal of Women's History* 19.4 (2007): 64–66. See also R.H. Helmholz, "And Were There Children's Rights in Early Modern England? The Canon Law and 'Intra-family Violence' in England, 1400–1640," *International Journal of Children's Rights* 1 (1992): 23–32.
21. Barbara A. Hanawalt, "Narratives of a Nurturing Culture: Parents and Neighbors in Medieval England," *Essays in Medieval Studies* 12 (1995), http://www.illinoismedieval.org/ems/EMSpdf/V12/V12Hanawalt.pdf . Date of access: November 27, 2012.
22. TNA PRO JUST 1/635, m. 45 (1329–30).
23. TNA PRO JUST 1/1078, m. 9 (1279–81).
24. TNA PRO JUST 1/184, m. 16d (1281–82).
25. TNA PRO JUST 2/18, m. 10 (1340–66).
26. TNA PRO JUST 2/18, m. 12d (1340–66).
27. TNA PRO JUST 2/18, m. 45 (1340–66).
28. Margaret Archer, ed., *The Register of Bishop Philip Repingdon 1405–1419*, v. 3 (Lincoln Record Society, v. 74, 1982), p. 431.
29. Eleanora C. Gordon, "Accidents among Medieval Children as Seen from the Miracles of Six English Saints and Martyrs," *Medical History* 35 (1991): 160.
30. Ibid.
31. Ibid., 163.
32. R.H. Helmholz, "Roman Law of Guardianship in England, 1300–1600," *Tulane Law Review* 52 (1978): 255.
33. Lisi Oliver, ed., *The Beginnings of English Law* (Toronto: University of Toronto Press, 2002), pp. 79, 112, 129. Although it has been argued that the Anglo-Saxon laws permitted divorce and even allowed a mother custody in those situations, Lisi Oliver's definitive study has demonstrated that this interpretation rests on a misunderstanding of how the clauses fit together. In reality, the laws are discussing what happens to a child after the death of his or her father. See Oliver, pp. 113–14.
34. Ibid., p. 112.
35. Sue Sheridan Walker, "The Feudal Family and the Common Law Courts: The Pleas Protecting Rights of Wardship and Marriage, c. 1225–1375," *Journal of Medieval History* 14 (1988): 15.
36. Ibid.
37. Frederick Pollock and F.W. Maitland, *The History of English Law before the Time of Edward I*, 2nd ed., v. 1 (London: Cambridge University Press, 1968), p. 307.
38. Ibid.
39. As cited in ibid., p. 306.
40. Walker, "Feudal Family and the Common Law Courts," 17.

41. *CPR* for 1238, p. 229.
42. *CPR* for 1338, p. 160. Other examples of mothers as guardians: Agnes, wife of John de Lokton, *CPR* for 1390, p. 273; Mabel, late wife of Roger Torpell, *CPR* for 1242, p. 301; Alice, late wife of Richard de Cramlyngton, *CPR* for 1323, p. 322; wife of William, earl of Ulster, *CPR* for 1339, p. 305.
43. Walker, "Feudal Family and the Common Law Courts," 14.
44. G.D.G. Hall, trans. and ed., *The Treatise on the Laws and Customs of the Realm of England Commonly Called Glanvill* (Oxford: Oxford University Press, 1965), pp. *vii*, 9; Henry de Bracton, *De Legibus et Consuetudinibus Angliae,* ed. George E. Woodbine, trans. Samuel E. Thorne, 4 vols. (Cambridge: Belknap Press at Harvard University Press, 1968), v. 2, pp. 250–55.
45. Elaine Clark, "City Orphans and Custody Laws in Medieval England," *American Journal of Legal History* 34 (1990): 176. Jenny Kermode has made a similar observation in her investigation of the evidence of merchant wills. See Jenny Kermode, "Sentiment and Survival: Family and Friends in Late Medieval English Towns," *Journal of Family History* 24.1 (1999): 8.
46. R.R. Sharpe, ed., *Calendar of Letter Book E: 1314–1337* (London: J.E. Francis, 1903), pp. 262–271.
47. Ibid., p. 47.
48. Barbara A. Hanawalt, *Growing Up in Medieval London: The Experience of Childhood in History* (Oxford: Oxford University Press, 1993), p. 95.
49. Sharpe, *Calendar of Letter Book E: 1314–1337* (1903), p. 57.
50. Sharpe, *Calendar of Letter Book H: 1375–1399* (1907), p. 45.
51. Sharpe, *Calendar of Letter Book I: 1400–1422* (1909), pp. 167–175.
52. Sharpe, *Calendar of Letter Book K: Henry VI* (1911), pp. 121, 118.
53. Sharpe, *Calendar of Letter Book D: 1309–1314* (1902), pp. 223–24.
54. Sharpe, *Calendar of Letter Book E: 1314–1337* (1903), pp. 47–48.
55. *Gunnlaugs saga ormstungu*, ed. Sigurður Nordal and Guðni Jónnson (Reykjavik: Hið Íslenzka Fornritafélag, 1938), ch. 3. For more examples, see John Boswell, *The Kindness of Strangers: The Abandonment of Children in Western Europe from Late Antiquity to the Renaissance* (New York: Pantheon Books, 1988), ch. 10.
56. "The Boy whose Mother's Prayers Freed him from Captivity," in Stephen Parkinson, *et al.*, ed. and trans., "The Oxford Cantigas de Santa Maria Database" (Oxford, 2007), http://csm.mml.ox.ac.uk/index.php?p=poemdata_view&rec=62 . Date of access: November 27, 2012.
57. *Calendar of Inquisitions Post-Mortem and Other Analogous Documents*, v. 10, p. 132, no. 142. This case is cited in Philippa Maddern, "Between Households: Children in Blended and Transitional Households in Late-Medieval England," *Journal of the History of Childhood and Youth* 3.1 (2010): 75. Many thanks to Philippa Maddern for bringing this instructive case to my attention.
58. Mavis E. Mate, "Work and Leisure," in *A Social History of England 1200–1500*, ed. Rosemary Horrox and W. Mark Ormrod (Cambridge: Cambridge University Press, 2006), p. 276.
59. TNA PRO REQ 2/4/189 (1492–1547).
60. William Brown and A. Hamilton Thompson, eds., *The Register of William Greenfield, Lord Archbishop of York, 1306–1315*, pt. 3 (Surtees Society, v. 151, 1936), pp. 152–53.
61. A.T. Bannister, ed., "Visitation Returns of the Diocese of Hereford in 1397," *English Historical Review* 45 (1930): 451.
62. Rose Graham, ed. and trans., *Registrum Robert Winchelsey,Cantuariensis Archiepiscopi, A.D. 1294–1313*, v. 2 (Canterbury and York Society, v. 52, 1956), pp. 193–94.

63. TNA PRO JUST 1/1107, m. 91 (1305–7).
64. A. Hamilton Thompson, ed., *Visitations in the Diocese of Lincoln, 1517–1531: Volume I: Visitations of Rural Deaneries by William Atwater, Bishop of Lincoln, and His Commissaries, 1517–20* (Lincoln Record Society, v. 33, 1940), p. 60.
65. Pollock and Maitland, v. 1, p. 307.
66. Graham, *Registrum Roberti Winchelsey*, v. 2, pp. 744–45.
67. David Allen, "A Fourteenth-Century Divorce in Stoke-by-Nayland," *Proceedings of the Suffolk Institute of Archaeology and History* 38.1 (1993): 1.
68. Y.B. Pasch. 9 Edw. IV, fos. 1a–1b (1469).
69. Y.B. Mich. 12 Hen. VII, fo. 14a (1496).
70. David D'Avray, "Authentication of Marital Status: A Thirteenth-Century English Royal Annulment Process and Late Medieval Cases from the Papal Penitentiary," *English Historical Review* 120.488 (2005): 990.
71. D'Avray, "Authentication of Marital Status," 987–1013.
72. *Bracton*, v. 3, pp. 372–73.
73. Y.B. Hil. 18 Edw. IV, fos. 29a–30b (1479).
74. *Statute of Merton* (1236), 20 Hen. III, ch. 9, in A. Luders, T.E. Tomlins, J. France, W.E. Taunton, J. Raithby, eds, *Statutes of the Realm* (London: Record Commission, 1810–27), v. 1, p. 4.
75. Y.B. Trin. 7 Hen. IV, fos. 16b–17a (1406).
76. *Bracton*, v. 3, pp. 363–64.
77. Y.B. Hil. 18 Edw. IV, fos. 29a–30b (1479). For an example of bastardization following a divorce on the grounds of pre-contract, see John P. Collas and William S. Holdsworth, eds., *Year Books of Edward II*, v. 22: Edward II (1317–1318) (Selden Society, v. 61, 1942), pp. 262–63.
78. Y.B. Hil. 5 Hen. V, fos. 2a–3a (1418).
79. Y.B. Hil. 18 Edw. IV, fos. 29a–30b (1479). Granted, not all justices and pleaders saw this as self-evident. In a bastardy case before justices of assize in the year 1364, justices waffled regarding whether Alice Oliver's child was legitimate. Technically the child was born while she was married to her husband; however, by then they had been separated (without church sanction) for seven years, and the child was fathered by her lover, William of Kerr. After great discussion, the child was deemed illegitimate. See Y.B. term uncertain, 38 Edw. III, fos. 224b–225a (1364).
80. Y.B. Trin. 11 Hen. VII, fos. 26b–27a (1496).
81. York Consistory Court Act Book M 2(1) c, fo. 24 (1372–75).
82. Helmholz, "Support Orders" 443.
83. Reginald Brocklesby, ed., *The Register of William Melton, Archbishop of York 1317–1340*, v. 4 (Canterbury and York Society, v. 85, 1997), p. 145.
84. Christopher Harper-Bill, ed., *The Register of John Morton, Archbishop of Canterbury, 1486–1500*, v. 3 (Canterbury and York Society, v. 89, 2000), p. 153.
85. Ernest Harold Pearce, ed., *The Register of Thomas de Cobham, Bishop of Worcester 1317–1327* (Worcestershire Historical Society, 1930), p. 147.
86. Charles Johnson, ed., *Registrum Hamonis Hethe, Diocesis Roffensis, A.D. 1319–1352* (Canterbury and York Society, v. 48, 1946–8), pp. 454–55.
87. Helmholz, "Support Orders," p. 445.
88. Pearce, *Register of Thomas de Cobham*, p. 186.
89. Ibid., p. 149.
90. Johnson, *Registrum Hamonis Hethe,* v. 2, p. 951.
91. L.R. Poos, ed., *Lower Ecclesiastical Jurisdiction in Late-Medieval England: The Courts of the Dean and Chapter of Lincoln, 1336–1349, and the Deanery of Wisbech, 1458–1484* (Records of Social and Economic History, New Series v. 32, Oxford University Press, 2001), p. 64.

92. Johnson, *Registrum Hamonis Hethe*, v. 2, p. 1004
93. Maddern, "Between Households," 65–86; Kermode, "Sentiment and Survival," 6–9.
94. Butler, *Language of Abuse*, pp. 95–96.
95. TNA PRO JUST 1/784, m. 28d (1280).
96. R.L. Storey, ed., *The Register of John Kirkby I, Bishop of Carlisle* (Canterbury and York Society, v. 79, 1992), p. 113.
97. Johnson, *Registrum Hamonis Hethe*, v. 1, p. 455.
98. Y.B. term uncertain, 2 Edw. II (1309); as it appears in F.W. Maitland, ed., *Year Books of Edward II, v. 1: 1 & 2 Edward II (1307–1309)* (Selden Society, v. 17, 1903), pp. 184–87.
99. Y.B. Mich. 1 Hen VI (1422); as it appears in C.H. Williams, ed., *Year Books of Henry VI: 1 Henry VI* (Selden Society, v. 50, 1933), pp. 24–30.
100. Y.B. Hil. 13 Edw. I (1285); as it appears in Paul A. Brand, *The Earliest English Law Reports*, v. 2 (Selden Society, v. 185, 1996), p. 112. .
101. Kermode, "Sentiment and Survival," 8.
102. Ibid., pp. 12–13.
103. P.J.P. Goldberg, "Marriage, Migration, and Servanthood: The York Cause Paper Evidence," in *Woman Is a Worthy Wight* (Stroud: Sutton, 1992), p. 2.
104. William Farrer, ed., *The Court Rolls of the Honor of Clitheroe in the County of Lancaster,* v. 1 (Manchester: Emmott & Co., 1897), pp. 224–26.
105. Paula Dobrowolski, "Women and Their Dower in the Long Thirteenth Century 1265–1329," in *Thirteenth Century England VI: Proceedings of the Durham Conference 1995*, ed. Michael Prestwich, R.H. Britnell and Robin Frame (Woodbridge: Boydell, 1997), p. 159.
106. Sue Sheridan Walker, "Litigation as Personal Quest: Suing for Dower in the Royal Courts, circa 1272–1350," in *Wife and Widow in Medieval England* (Ann Arbor: Michigan University Press, 1993), p. 95.

NOTES TO CHAPTER 6

1. *CPRRGBI*, v. 9, pp. 68–74.
2. Y.B. 14 Edw. III (1340), as it appears in Luke Owen Pike, ed., *Year Books of the Reign of King Edward the Third: Year XIV* (Rolls Series no. 31, part B, v. 4, 1888), pp. 322–31.
3. Charles Johnson, ed., *Registrum Hamonis Hethe, Diocesis Roffensis, A.D. 1319–1352*, v. 1 (Canterbury and York Society, v. 49, 1948), p. 30.
4. Johnson, *Registrum Hamonis Hethe*, v. 1, p. 329.
5. *CPR* for 1344, p. 253.
6. *CPR* for 1348, p. 205.
7. *CPR* for 1348, p. 218.
8. Sidney Lee, *Dictionary of National Biography: Index and Epitome* (Cambridge: Harvard University Press, 1903), p. 646.
9. Christopher Harper-Bill, ed., *The Register of John Morton, Archbishop of Canterbury 1486–1500*, v. 3 (Canterbury and York Society, v. 89, 2000), p. 154.
10. Y.B. Mich. 9 Hen. V (1421), as it appears in Ralph V. Rogers, ed., *Year Books of the Reign of King Henry the Fifth* (Wurzburg: Privately Printed, 1948), pp. 30–31.
11. This case is discussed at length in chapter 2.
12. The Year Books refer to Isabella as Alice, but Henry and John's name are accurately reported. Y.B. Mich. 39 Edw. III, fos. 32a–33a (1365); Y.B. term uncertain, 39 Edw. III, fos. 233b–234a (1365).

13. Y.B. 35 Hen. VI, fos. 9a–10a (1456).
14. Robin Chapman Stacey, "Divorce, Medieval Welsh Style," *Speculum* 77 (2002): 1119.
15. Ibid., 1120.
16. Sarah Leavitt, "'She Hath Left My Bed and Board': Runaway Wives in Rhode Island, 1790–1810," *Rhode Island History* 58.3 (2000): 91–104.
17. J.H. Baker notes that by 1300, a wife could bind her husband "to a sale of goods which came to his use or profit." Cited in Janet S. Loengard, "Common Law for Margery: Separate but Not Equal," in *Women in Medieval Western European Culture*, ed. Linda E. Mitchell (New York: Garland, 1999), p. 123 (for a discussion of women's market rights, see pp. 123–25). For a much lengthier discussion of this subject, see William C. Jordan, *Women and Credit in Pre-industrial and Developing Societies* (Philadelphia: University of Pennsylvania Press, 1992). The literary evidence from the time suggests that creditors permitted wives a good deal of flexibility in this respect. For example, in Chaucer's "The Shipman's Tale," the wife of a merchant tells Daun John that she needs 100 franks to pay off her dress bill, owing the following week. The implication is that she must pay it off before her husband finds out the bill even exists.
18. Loengard, p. 124.
19. The earliest cases indicating the existence of the doctrine of necessaries are drawn from 1698. See "The Unnecessary Doctrine of Necessaries," *Michigan Law Review* 82.7 (1984): 1767*n*.
20. TNA PRO C 1/61/382 (1473–74 or 1485).
21. TNA PRO C 1/218/22 (1493–1500).
22. This exact situation is discussed in Y.B. Mich. 9 Hen. IV, fos. 5b–6a (1407).
23. TNA PRO C1/59/42 (1475–80 or 1483–85).
24. Cordelia Beattie, "Living as a Single Person: Marital Status, Performance and the Law in Medieval England," *Women's History Review* 17.3 (2007): 329.
25. Ibid., 328.
26. R.H. Helmholz, *Marriage Litigation in Medieval England* (New York: Cambridge University Press, 1974), p. 100.
27. YBI CP. E. 248/26c.
28. Gratian, *The Decretum*, q. vi, c. 9, as it appears in John T. Noonan, Jr., trans., and Augustine Thompson, ed. and suppl., "Marriage Canons from the *Decretum* of Gratian and the Decretals, Sext, Clementines and Extravagantes" (Catholic University of America, 1993), http://faculty/cua.edu/Pennington/Canon%20Law/marriagelaw.htm. Date of access: November 27, 2012.
29. A.M. Cooke, ed., *Act Book of the Ecclesiastical Court of Whalley, 1510-1538* (Princeton: Chetham Society, 1901), pp. 105–6.
30. Y.B. 43 Edw. III, fo. 23a (1369).
31. *CPR* for 1236, p. 154.
32. Ralph V. Turner, "The Mandeville Inheritance, 1189–1236," *Haskins Society Journal* 1 (1989): 157.
33. *CPRRGBI*, v. 4, pp. 36–47.
34. Johnson, *Registrum Hamonis Hethe*, v. 2, pp. 743–44.
35. Charles Donahue, J., *Law, Marriage, and Society in the Later Middle Ages* (New York: Cambridge University Press, 2007), p. 558.
36. *CPRRGBI*, v. 8, pp. 544–50.
37. Dom S.F. Hockey, ed., *The Register of William Edington, Bishop of Winchester 1346–1366*, pt. 2 (Hampshire Record Series, v. 8, 1987), p. 20.

38. *CPRRGBI*, v. 13, pp. 17–22.
39. Ibid., pp. 524–31.
40. Ibid., pp. 659–63.
41. Ibid.
42. Sue Sheridan Walker, "Litigation as Personal Quest: Suing for Dower in the Royal Courts, circa 1272–1350," in *Wife and Widow in Medieval England* (Ann Arbor: Michigan University Press, 1993), pp. 93–95.
43. Ibid., p. 88.
44. Ibid., p. 95.
45. *CCR* for 1487–88, p. 85.
46. TNA PRO C1/289/33 (1504–9).
47. Sylvia Thrupp, *The Merchant Class of Medieval London, 1300–1500* (Chicago: University of Chicago Press, 1948), p. 354.
48. For a similar discussion, see Geoffrey and Joan Fresel *v.* Herbert de Bexville (1268), in Paul Brand, ed., *Earliest English Law Reports* (Selden Society, v.3, 1995), pp. 1–2.
49. Elisabeth Guernsey Kimball, ed., *Rolls of the Warwickshire and Coventry Sessions of the Peace 1377–1397* (Dugdale Society, v. 16, 1939), p. 123, no. 20.
50. Sandy Bardsley, "Women's Work Reconsidered: Gender and Wage Differentiation in Late Medieval England," *Past and Present* 165.1 (1999): 22–23.
51. Ibid., 29.
52. Ruth Mazo Karras, "Sex and the Singlewoman," in *Singlewomen in the European Past, 1250–1800*, ed. Judith M. Bennett and Amy Froide (Philadelphia: University of Pennsylvania Press, 1999), pp. 127–45.
53. T.C.B. Timmins, ed., *The Register of John Chandler, Dean of Salisbury 1404–17* (Wiltshire Record Society, v. 39, 1984), pp. 112–13.
54. Warren Ortman, ed., *Court Rolls of the Abbey of Ramsey and of the Honor of Clare* (Yale Historical Publications, v. 9, 1928), p. 246.
55. Ernest Harold Pearce, ed., *The Register of Thomas de Cobham, Bishop of Worcester, 1317–1327* (Worcestershire Historical Society, 1930), p. 192.
56. Canterbury Y.1.11, fo. 120.
57. Agnes Edward of St. Mary's Parish in Northgate, Canterbury Y.1.11, fo. 55; Mariora Pokelyn, Canterbury Y.1.11, fo. 156d; Elena Dryykdestor of St. Agatha, Canterbury Y.1.11, fo. 183d; Joanna Boyce de Thornton, Canterbury Y.1.11, fo. 337.

NOTES TO THE CONCLUSIONS

1. William Brown and A. Hamilton Thompson, eds., *The Register of William Greenfield, Lord Archbishop of York, 1306–1315*, v. 3 (Surtees Society, v. 151, 1931–40), pp. 207–8; *CPR* for 1307–13, pp. 548–50.
2. J. Raine, ed., *Testamenta Eboracensia*, pt. 1 (Surtees Society, v. 4, 1836), pp. 32–33. Chapter 3 discusses Lucy's relationship with William le Latimer at great length.
3. Y.B. Trin. 39 Edw. III, fos. 15b–16a (1365).
4. Y.B. Pasch. 12 Edw. III (1338), as it appears in Alfred J. Horwood and Luke Owen Pike, eds., *Year Books of the Reign of King Edward the Third: Years XI and XII* (Rolls Series no. 31, part B, v. 1, London, 1883), pp. 480–87.
5. *CCR* for 1475 (1953), pp. 369–77.
6. *CPRRGI*, v. 13, pp. 396–99.
7. L.R. Poos, ed., *Lower Ecclesiastical Jurisdiction in Late-Medieval England: The Courts of the Dean and Chapter of Lincoln, 1336–1349, and the*

Deanery of Wisbech, 1458–1484 (Records of Social and Economic History, New Series v. 32, 2001), pp. 13, 29, 68, 148, 162, 165, 192–93, 256.

8. For example, see Beatrice la Albaster *c.* Thomas de Ormesby (1323), in Reginald Brocklesby, ed., *The Register of William Melton, Archbishop of York 1317–1340*, v. 4 (Canterbury and York Society, v. 85, 1997), pp. 71–72.
9. Poos, *Lower Ecclesiastical Jurisdiction*, p. 7.
10. Ibid., p. 35.
11. Ibid., pp. 90, 92, 99.
12. Ibid., p. 145.
13. Ibid., p. 160.
14. Ibid., pp. 197–98.
15. Ibid., pp. 206, 208, 259.
16. Ibid., p. 209.
17. Ibid., p. 214.
18. Rowland Alwyn Wilson, ed. and trans., *The Register of Walter Reynolds, Bishop of Worcester, 1308–1313* (Dugdale Society, v. 9, 1928), pp. 28–29.
19. *CPR* for 1316, p. 434.
20. Ibid., p. 401.
21. Alison Weir, *Queen Isabella: Treachery, Adultery and Murder in Medieval England* (New York: Balantine Books, 2005), p. 41.
22. Susan M. Keeling and C.P. Lewis, "The Rape and Honour of Lewes," in *History of the County of Sussex* (Victoria County History, v. 7, 1940), pp. 1–7.
23. TNA PRO SC 8/23/1108 (*c.*1406); TNA PRO C 1/67/210 (*c.* 1483–85).
24. TNA PRO C1/287/47 (1504–9).
25. T.C.B. Timmins, ed., *The Register of John Waltham, Bishop of Salisbury, 1388–1395* (Canterbury and York Society, v. 80, 1994), p. 23.

Works Cited

MANUSCRIPT SOURCES

Borthwick Institute of Historical Research, York

CP. E.: Cause papers, fourteenth century
CP. F.: Cause papers, fifteenth century
CP. G.: Cause papers, sixteenth century

Canterbury Cathedral Archives, Canterbury

Sede Vacante Scrapbooks, I, II and III: Cause Papers, mainly thirteenth century
Y.1.1: Act book, 1372–75
U.4.1: Act book, 1393–95
X.8.1: Ex officio Act book, 1395–1410
Y.1.2: Act book, 1398–99
X.10.1: Deposition Book, 1410–21
Y.1.3: Act book, 1416–23
Y.1.4: Act book, 1419–25
X.1.1: Ex officio Act book, 1449–57
Y.1.5: Act book, 1454–57
Y.1.7: Act book, 1459–63
X.8.3: Act book, 1462–68
Y.1.6: Act book, 1463–68
Y.1.8: Act book, 1468–74
Y.1.11: Ex officio Act book, 1468–74
Y.1.12: Act book, 1474–79
Y.1.13: Act book, 1479–85
Y.1.14: Act book, 1485–88
Y.1.15: Act book, 1488–92
Y.1.16: Act book, 1492–96
Y.1.17: Act book, 1496–99
Y.1.18: Act book, 1499–1500
Y.1.19 Ex officio Act book, 1364
Y.2.1 Act book, 1503–5
Y.2.2 Act book, 1500–1502

York Minster Library, York

M 2(1) c: Consistory Court Act Book, 1372–75

The National Archives, Public Record Office, Kew, Surrey

C 1, Early Chancery Proceedings
CP, Court of Common Pleas
JUST 1, Eyre Rolls, Assize Rolls, etc.
JUST 2, Coroners' Rolls
JUST 3, Gaol Delivery Rolls
REQ 2, Court of Requests
SC 2, Court Rolls, Manorial
SC 8, Special Collections, Ancient Petitions

PRINTED PRIMARY SOURCES

Aquinas, Saint Thomas. *Summa theologiae*. Ed. Timothy McDermott. Grand Rapids: Christian Classics, 1997.

Archer, Margaret, ed. *The Register of Bishop Philip Repingdon 1405–1419*, v. 3. Lincoln Record Society, v. 74, 1982.

Arnold, Morris S., ed. and trans. *Select Cases of Trespass from the King's Courts 1307–1399*, v. 1. Selden Society, v. 100, 1985.

Baildon, W.P., ed. and trans. *Court Rolls of the Manor of Wakefield, 1297–1309*, v. 2. Yorkshire Archaeological Society Record Series, v. 36, 1906.

Baildon, W.P., ed. *Court Rolls of the Manor of Wakefield, 1274–1297*, v. 1. Yorkshire Archaeological Society Record Series, v. 29, 1901.

Bannister, A.T., ed. "Visitation Returns of the Diocese of Hereford in 1397." *English Historical Review* 45 (1930): 279–89.

Bannister, A.T., ed. *Registrum Ade de Orleton, Episcopi Herefordensis, A.D. MCCCXVII–MCCCXXVII*. Canterbury and York Society, v. 5, 1908.

Barker, Eric E., ed. *The Register of Thomas Rotherham, Archbishop of York, 1480–1500*. Canterbury and York Society, v. 69, 1976.

Bateson, M., ed. *Borough Customs*. Selden Society v. 18, 1904.

Bliss, W.H., ed. *Calendar of Entries in the Papal Registers Relating to Great Britain and Ireland. Petitions to the Pope* [1342–1419]. London: Her Majesty's Stationery Office, 1896.

Bolland, William Craddock, ed. *Year Books of Edward II*, v. 17: 8 Edward II (1314–1315). Selden Society, v. 41, 1925.

Bowker, Margaret, ed. *An Episcopal Court Book for the Diocese of Lincoln 1514–1520*. Lincoln Record Society, v. 61, 1967.

Bracton, Henry de. *De Legibus et Consuetudinibus Angliae*. Ed. George E. Woodbine. Trans. Samuel E. Thorne, 4 vols. Cambridge: Belknap Press at Harvard University Press, 1968.

Brand, Paul, ed. *Earliest English Law Reports*. Selden Society, v. 123, 1995.

Brocklesby, Reginald, ed. *The Register of William Melton, Archbishop of York 1317–1340*, v. 4. Canterbury and York Society, v. 85, 1997.

Brown, William, ed. *The Register of John Le Romeyn, Lord Archbishop of York, 1286–1296*, 2 vols. Surtees Society, v. 123, 128, 1913–7.

Brown, William, ed. *Cartularium Prioratus de Gyseburne, Ebor. Dioceseos, Ordinis S. Augustini*. Selden Society, v. 86, 1889.

Brown, William, and A. Hamilton Thompson, eds. *The Register of William Greenfield, Lord Archbishop of York, 1306–1315*, 5 vols. Surtees Society, v. 145, 149, 151–3, 1931–40.

Bullard, J.V., and H. Chalmer Bell, eds. *Lyndwood's Provinciale: The Text of the Canons Therein Contained, Reprinted from the Translation Made in 1534*. London: Faith Press, 1929.

Bund, J.W. Willis, ed. *Register of Bishop Godfrey Giffard, September 23rd, 1268 to August 15th, 1301*. Worcestershire Historical Society, 1902.
Calendar of Close Rolls, 1272–1485, 45 vols. London, 1911–63.
Calendar of Entries in the Papal Registers Relating to Great Britain and Ireland. Papal Letters [1198–1513], 19 vols. London: His Majesty's Stationery Office, 1893–1998.
Calendar of Inquisitions Post-Mortem and Other Analogous Documents, v. 1: Henry III. London: His Majesty's Stationery Office, 1904.
Calendar of Patent Rolls, 1216–1509, 55 vols. London, 1891–1916.
Collas, John P., and William S. Holdsworth, eds. *Year Books of Edward II*, v. 22: Edward II (1317–1318). Selden Society, v. 61, 1942.
Cooke, A.M. ed. *Act Book of the Ecclesiastical Court of Whalley, 1510–1538*. Princeton: Chetham Society, 1901.
Du Boulay, F.R.H., ed. *Registrum Thome Bourgchier, Cantuariensis Archiepiscopi A.D. 1454–1486*. Canterbury and York Society, v. 54, 1957.
Edwards, Kathleen, and Dorothy M. Owens, eds. *The Registers of Roger Martival, Bishop of Salisbury, 1315–1330*, v. 4. Canterbury and York Society, v. 68, 1975.
Elvey, Elizabeth M., ed. *The Courts of the Archdeaconry of Buckingham*. Buckinghamshire Record Society, no. 19, 1975.
Farrer, William, ed. *The Court Rolls of the Honor of Clitheroe in the County of Lancaster,* v. 1. Manchester: Emmott & Co., 1897.
Farrow, M.A., ed. *Consistory Court of Norwich Wills, 1370–1550*. London: British Record Society, 1945.
Flower, C.T., and M.C.B. Dawes, eds. *Registrum Simonis de Gandavo, Diocesis Saresbiriensis A.D. 1297–1315*, v. 1. Canterbury and York Society, v. 40, 1934.
Furber, Elisabeth Chapin, ed. *Essex Sessions of the Peace, 1351, 1377–79*. Essex Archaeological Society, v. 3, 1953.
Gasparii, Pietro, ed. *Codex Iuris Canonici Pii X Pontificis Maximi Iussu Digestus, Benedicti Papae X Auctoritate Promulgatus*. New York: P.J. Kennedy and Sons, 1918.
Given-Wilson, C., ed. *The Parliament Rolls of Medieval England, 1275–1504 (PROME)*. Leicester: Scholarly Digital Editions, 2005.
Goldberg, P.J.P., ed. *Women in England, c. 1275–1525*. Manchester: Manchester University Press, 1995.
Graham, Rose, ed. and trans. *Registrum Roberti Winchelsey, Cantuariensis Archiepiscopi, A.D. 1294–1313*, 2 vols. Canterbury and York Society, vols. 51 and 52, 1952–6.
Haines, R.M., ed. *Calendar of the Register of Adam de Orleton, Bishop of Worcester 1327–1333*. London: Historical Manuscripts Commission, no. 27, 1979.
Hair, P.E., ed. *Before the Bawdy Court: Selections from Church Court and Other Records Relating to the Correction of Moral Offences in England, Scotland, and New England, 1300–1800*. New York: Elek Books, 1972.
Hall, G.D.G., trans. and ed. *The Treatise on the Laws and Customs of the Realm of England Commonly Called Glanvill*. Oxford: Oxford University Press, 1965.
Hall, T. Walter, ed. *A Descriptive Catalogue of Sheffield Manorial Records from the 8th Year of Richard II to the Restoration*, v. 1. Sheffield, England: Northend, 1920.
Hardy, T.D., ed. *Registrum Palatinum Dunelmense*, pt. 3. Rolls Series, v. 62, 1873–8.
Harper-Bill, Christopher, ed. *The Register of John Morton, Archbishop of Canterbury 1486–1500*, v. 3. Canterbury and York Society, v. 89, 2000.
Harper-Bill, Christopher, ed. *The Register of John Morton, Archbishop of Canterbury 1486–1500*, 2 parts. Canterbury and York Society, v. 75, 1987.

Hill, Rosalind M.T., ed. *Register of William Melton, Archbishop of York, 1317–1340*. 3 vols. Canterbury and York Society, vols. 70, 71, 76, 1977–88.
Hockey, Dom S.F., ed. *The Register of William Edington, Bishop of Winchester 1346–1366*, pt. 2. Hampshire Record Series, v. 8, 1987.
Horn, Joyce M., ed. *The Register of Robert Hallum, Bishop of Salisbury, 1407–17*. Canterbury and York Society, v. 72, 1982.
Horwood, Alfred J., and Luke Owen Pike, eds. *Year Books of the Reign of King Edward the Third: Years XI and XII*. Rolls Series n. 31, part B, v. 1, London, 1883.
Horwood, Alfred J., ed. *Year Books of the Reign of Edward the First: Years XXXII and XXXIII (1304–1305)*. Rolls Series n. 31, pt A, v. 4, London, 1864.
Hudson, William, ed. *Leet Jurisdiction in the City of Norwich: During the XIIIth and XIVth Centuries*. Selden Society, v. 5, 1891.
Jacob, E.F., ed. *Register of Henry Chichele, Archbishop of Canterbury, 1414–1443*, 4 vols. Canterbury and York Society, vols. 42, 45, 46, 47, 1938–47.
Jeayes, Isaac Herbert, ed. and trans. *Court Rolls of the Borough of Colchester*, 3 vols. Colchester: W. Gurney, 1921–41.
Johnson, Charles, ed. *Registrum Hamonis Hethe, Diocesis Roffensis, A.D. 1319–1352*, 2 vols. Canterbury and York Society, vols. 48 and 49, 1946–48.
Kimball, Elisabeth Guernsey, ed. *Rolls of the Warwickshire and Coventry Sessions of the Peace 1377–1397*. Dugdale Society, v. 16, 1939.
Le Gros, Gervase, ed. *Rolls of the Assizes Held in the Channel Islands in the 2nd Year of the Reign of King Edward II, 1309*. Société Jersiase, no. 18, 1903.
Luders, A., T.E. Tomlins, J. France, W.E. Taunton and J. Raithby, eds. *Statutes of the Realm*. London: Record Commission, 1810–27.
Lysons, Daniel. *The Environs of London*, v. 4, 1796. Repr. University of London and History of Parliament Trust: British History Online, 2011. http://www.british-history.ac.uk/source.aspx?pubid=330. Date of Access: November 27, 2012.
Lyte, H.C. Maxwell, ed. *The Registers of Oliver King Bishop of Bath and Wells 1496–1503, and Hadrian de Castello Bishop of Bath and Wells 1503–1518*. Somerset Record Society, v. 54, 1939.
Lyte, H.C. Maxwell, ed. *A Descriptive Catalogue of Ancient Deeds*. History of Parliament Trust, v. 5, 1906.
Macfarlane, Alan, ed. *Records of an English Village Earls Colne, 1400–1750*. Cambridge: Chadwyck-Healey, 1980–81. http://linux02.lib.cam.ac.uk/earlscolne/
Maitland, F.W., ed. *Year Books of Edward II*, v. 2. Selden Society, v. 19, London, 1904.
Maitland, F.W., ed. *Year Books of Edward II, v. 1: 1 & 2 Edward II (1307–1309)*. Selden Society, v. 17, 1903.
Martin, Charles Trice, ed. *Registrum Epistolarum Fratris Johannis Peckham Archiepiscopi Cantuariensis*, v. 2. Rolls Series, v. 77, pt. 2, 1882.
McSheffrey, Shannon, ed. *Consistory: Testimony in the Late Medieval London Consistory Court*. Concordia University, 2008–present. http://digitalhistory.concordia.ca/consistory. Date of Access: November 27, 2012.
McSheffrey, Shannon, ed. *Love and Marriage in Late Medieval London*. Kalamazoo, MI: Medieval Institute Publications, 1995.
Meekings, C.A.F., ed. *Crown Pleas of the Wiltshire Eyre, 1249*. Devizes: Wiltshire Archaeological and Natural History Society, 1961.
Myrc, John. *Instructions for a Parish Priest*. London: Trübner and Co., 1868. Repr. Elibron Classics, 2005.
Nichols, Francis M. ed. *Britton: The French Text Carefully Revised with an English Translation, Introduction and Notes*. Oxford: Clarendon Press, 1865.
Noonan, John T., Jr., trans., and Augustine Thompson, ed. and suppl. "Marriage Canons from the Decretum of Gratian and the Decretals, Sext, Clementines and

Extravagantes." Catholic University of America, 1993. http://faculty.cua.edu/Pennington/Canon%20Law/marriagelaw.htm. Date of Access: November 27, 2012.

Nordal, Sigurður, and Guðni Jónnson, eds. *Gunnlaugs saga ormstungu*. Reykjavik: Hid Íslenzka Fornritafélag, 1938.

Oliver, Lisi, ed. *The Beginnings of English Law*. Toronto: University of Toronto Press, 2002.

Ortman, Warren, ed. *Court Rolls of the Abbey of Ramsey and of the Honor of Clare*. Yale Historical Publications, v. 9, 1928.

Page, William, and W.J. Hardy, eds. *Manuscripts of Rye and Hereford Corporations*. London: Eyre and Spottiswoode, 1892.

Parker, James, ed. *Register of Bishop Godfrey Giffard, September 23rd, 1268 to August 5th, 1301*. Worcestershire Historical Society, 1902.

Parkinson, Stephen, *et al.*, ed. and trans. "The Oxford Cantigas de Santa Maria Database." Oxford, 2007. http://csm.mml.ox.ac.uk/index.php?p=poemdata_view&rec=62 . Date accessed: November 27, 2012.

Parry, Joseph Henry, ed. *Registrum Johannis Gilbert, Episcopi Herefordensis A.D. 1375–1389*. Canterbury and York Society, v. 18, 1915.

Pearce, Ernest Harold, ed. *The Register of Thomas de Cobham, Bishop of Worcester, 1317–1327*. Worcestershire Historical Society, 1930.

Pike, Luke Owen, ed. *Year Books of the Reign of King Edward the Third: Year XX (Second Part)*. Rolls Series no. 31, part B, vol. 15, 1911.

Pike, Luke Owen, ed. *Year Books of the Reign of King Edward the Third: Year XIX*. Rolls Series no. 31, part B, vol. 13, 1906.

Pike, Luke Owen, ed. *Year Books of the Reign of King Edward the Third: Year XIV*. Rolls Series no. 31, part B, vol. 4, 1888.

Poos, L.R., ed. *Lower Ecclesiastical Jurisdiction in Late-Medieval England: The Courts of the Dean and Chapter of Lincoln, 1336–1349, and the Deanery of Wisbech, 1458–1484*. Records of Social and Economic History, New Series v. 32, 2001.

Powicke, F.M., and C.R. Cheney, eds. *Councils and Synods with Other Documents Relating to the English Church*, 2 vols. Oxford: Clarendon Press, 1964.

Putnam, Bertha Haven, ed. *Yorkshire Sessions of the Peace, 1361–1364*. Yorkshire Archaeological Society, v. 100, 1939.

Raine, J., ed. *Depositions and Other Ecclesiastical Proceedings from the Courts of Durham Extending from 1311 to the Reign of Elizabeth*. Surtees Society, v. 21, 1854.

Raine, J. ed. *Testamenta Eboracensia*, pt. 1. Surtees Society, v. 4, 1836.

Rogers, Ralph V., ed. *Year Books of the Reign of King Henry the Fifth*. Wurzburg: Privately Printed, 1948.

Salter, H.E. ed. *Records of Mediaeval Oxford: Coroners' Inquests, the Walls of Oxford, etc.* Oxford: Oxford Chronicle Company, Ltd., 1912.

Shanks, Elsie, and S.F.C. Milsom, eds. *Novae Narrationes*. Selden Society, v. 115, 1963.

Sharpe, R.R., ed. *Calendar of Letter Books of the City of London, A–L (1275–1497)*, 11 vols. London: J.E. Francis, 1889–1912.

Sillem, Rosamond, ed. *Records of Some Sessions of the Peace in Lincolnshire 1360–1375*. Lincoln Record Society, v. 30, 1936.

Storey, R.L., ed. *The Register of Thomas Appleby, Bishop of Carlisle, 1363–1395*. Canterbury and York Society, v. 96, 2006.

Storey, R.L., ed. *The Register of Gilbert Welton, Bishop of Carlisle, 1353–1362*. Canterbury and York Society, v. 88, 1999.

Storey, R.L. ed. *The Register of John Kirkby, Bishop of Carlisle, 1332–1352, and the Register of John Ross, Bishop of Carlisle, 1325–32*. Canterbury and York Society, v. 79, 1993.

Storey, R.L. ed. *The Register of John Kirkby I, Bishop of Carlisle*. Canterbury and York Society, v. 79, 1992.

Storey, R.L., ed. *The Register of Thomas Langley, Bishop of Durham, 1406–1437*, 6 vols. Surtees Society, vols. 164, 166, 169, 170, 177, 182, 1951–67.

Stretton, Tim, ed. *Marital Litigation in the Court of Requests 1542–1642*. Camden Fifth Series, v. 32, 2008.

Thomas, A.H., ed. *Calendar of Early Mayor's Court Rolls of the City of London, A.D. 1298–1307*. Cambridge: Cambridge University Press, 1924.

Thompson, A. Hamilton, ed. *Visitations in the Diocese of Lincoln 1517–1531: Volume 1: Visitations of Rural Deaneries by William Atwater, Bishop of Lincoln, and His Commissaries, 1517–20*. Lincoln Record Society, v. 33, 1940.

Timmins, T.C.B., ed. *The Register of John Waltham, Bishop of Salisbury, 1388–1395*. Canterbury and York Society, v. 80, 1994.

Timmins, T.C.B., ed. *The Register of John Chandler, Dean of Salisbury, 1404–1417*. Wiltshire Record Society, v. 39, 1984.

Walker, J.P., ed. and trans. *Court Rolls of the Manor of Wakefield, 1322–1331*, v. 5. Yorkshire Archaeological Society Record Series, v. 109, 1945.

Williams, C.H., ed. *Year Books of Henry VI: 1 Henry VI*. Selden Society, v. 50, 1933.

Wilson, Rowland Alwyn, ed. and trans. *The Register of Walter Reynolds, Bishop of Worcester, 1308–1313*. Dugdale Society, v. 9, 1928.

Woodruff, C. Eveleigh, ed. "Some Early Visitation Rolls Preserved at Canterbury." *Archaeologia Cantiana* 32 (1917): 143–80.

Wrottesley, G., and F. Parker, eds. "Plea Rolls for Staffordshire: 32 Edward I." *Staffordshire Historical Collections* 7.1 (1886): 114–26.

Year Books. 11 vols. London: George Sawbridge, William Rawlins, Samuel Roycroft, 1679–80.

SECONDARY SOURCES

Alexandre-Bidon, Danièle, and Didier Lett. *Children in the Middle Ages: Fifth to Fifteenth Centuries*. Trans. Jody Gladding. Notre Dame, IN: University of Notre Dame Press, 1999.

Alexandre-Bidon, Danièle, and Monique Closson. "L'amour à l'épreuve du temps: Femme battues, maris battus, amants battus à travers les manuscrits enluminés (XIIIè- XVè s.)." In *Amour, mariage et transgressions au Moyen Age. Actes du colloque des 24–27 mars 1983*, edited by Danielle Buschinger and André Crépin, 493–514. Göppingen: Kümmerle, 1984.

Allen, David. "A Fourteenth-Century Divorce in Stoke-by-Nayland." *Proceedings of the Suffolk Institute of Archaeology and History* 38.1 (1993): 1–7.

Archibald, Elizabeth. *Incest and the Medieval Imagination*. Oxford: Oxford University Press, 2001.

Ariès, Philippe. *Centuries of Childhood: A Social History of Family Life*. Trans. Robert Baldick. New York: Alfred Knopf, 1962.

Arnold, John H. *Belief and Unbelief in Medieval Europe*. London: Hodder Arnold, 2005.

Bardsley, Sandy. "Women's Work Reconsidered: Gender and Wage Differentiation in Late Medieval England." *Past and Present* 165.1 (1999): 3–29.

Beattie, Cordelia. "Living as a Single Person: Marital Status, Performance and the Law in Medieval England." *Women's History Review* 17.3 (2007): 327–40.

Beattie, Cordelia. *Medieval Single Women: The Politics of Social Classification in Late Medieval England*. Oxford: Oxford University Press, 2007.

Beattie, Cordelia. "A Room of One's Own? The Legal Evidence for the Residential Arrangements of Women without Husbands in Late-Fourteenth- and Early-Fifteenth-Century York." In *Medieval Women and the Law*, edited by Noël James Menuge, 41–56. Woodbridge: Boydell, 2000.

Behrend-Martinez, Edward J. *Unfit for Marriage: Impotent Spouses on Trial in the Basque Region of Spain 1050–1750*. Reno: University of Nevada Press, 2007.

Bennett, Judith M., and Amy M. Froide, eds. "A Singular Past." In *Singlewomen in the European Past*, 1–37. Philadelphia: University of Pennsylvania Press, 1999.

Bennett, Judith M. *Women in the Medieval English Countryside: Gender and Household in Brigstock before the Plague*. Oxford: Oxford University Press, 1987.

Biancalana, Joseph. "Widows at Common Law: The Development of Common Law Dower." *Irish Jurist*, n.s. 23 (1988): 255–329.

Birkett, Helen. "The Pastoral Application of the Lateran IV Reforms in the Northern Province, 1215–1348." *Northern History* 43.2 (2006): 199–219.

Boswell, John. *The Kindness of Strangers: The Abandonment of Children in Western Europe from Late Antiquity to the Renaissance*. New York: Pantheon Books, 1988.

Brand, Paul. "'Deserving' and 'Undeserving' Wives: Earning and Forfeiting Dower in Medieval England." *Journal of Legal History* 22.1 (2001): 1–11.

Brundage, James A. "Domestic Violence in Classical Canon Law." In *Violence in Medieval Society*, edited by Richard W. Kaeuper, 183–95. Woodbridge: Boydell, 2000.

Brundage, James. A. *Law, Sex, and Christian Society in Medieval Europe*. Chicago: University of Chicago Press, 1987.

Burton, Anthony. "Looking Forward from Ariès? Pictorial and Material Evidence for the History of Childhood and Family Life." *Continuity and Change* 4.2 (1989): 203–29.

Butler, Sara M. "A Case of Indifference? Child Murder in Later Medieval England." *Journal of Women's History* 19.4 (2007): 59–82.

Butler, Sara M. *The Language of Abuse: Marital Violence in Later Medieval England*. Leiden: Brill, 2007.

Butler, Sara M. "Runaway Wives: Husband Desertion in Medieval England." *Journal of Social History* 40.2 (2006): 337–59.

Butler, Sara M. "'I Will Never Consent to Be Wedded with You!': Coerced Marriage in the Courts of Medieval England." *Canadian Journal of History* 39.2 (2004): 247–70.

Cannon, Christopher. "*Raptus* in the Chaumpaigne Release and a Newly Discovered Document Concerning the Life of Geoffrey Chaucer." *Speculum* 68 (1993): 74–94.

Childs, Wendy. "Moving Around." In *A Social History of England 1200–1500*, edited by Rosemary Horrox and W. Mark Ormrod, 260–75. Cambridge: Cambridge University Press, 2006.

Cioni, Maria L. *Women and Law in Elizabethan England with Particular Reference to the Court of Chancery*. New York: Garland, 1985.

Clark, Elaine. "City Orphans and Custody Laws in Medieval England." *American Journal of Legal History* 34 (1990): 168–87.

Clark, George Thomas, and Francisque Michel, *The Land of Morgan: Being a Contribution Towards the History of the Lordship of Glamorgan*. Whiting: University of California Press, 1862.

Cosgrove, Art. "Consent, Consummation and Indissolubility: Some Evidence from Mediaeval Ecclesiastical Courts." *Downside Review* 109 (1991): 94–104.

Coss, Peter. "An Age of Deference." In *A Social History of England*, edited by Rosemary Horrox and W. Mark Ormrod, 31–73. Cambridge: Cambridge University Press, 2006.

Davis, Natalie Zemon. *The Return of Martin Guerre.* Cambridge: Harvard University Press, 1983.

D'Avray, David. *Medieval Marriage: Symbolism and Society.* Oxford: Oxford University Press, 2005.

D'Avray, David. "Authentication of Marital Status: A Thirteenth-Century English Royal Annulment Process and Late Medieval Cases from the Papal Penitentiary." *English Historical Review* 120.488 (2005): 987–1013.

De Mause, Lloyd, ed. "The Evolution of Childhood." In *The History of Childhood*, 1–74. New York: Psychohistory Press, 1974.

Dobrowolski, Paula. "Women and Their Dower in the Long Thirteenth Century 1265–1329." In *Thirteenth Century England VI: Proceedings of the Durham Conference 1995*, edited by Michael Prestwich, R.H. Britnell and Robin Frame, 157–64. Woodbridge, Suffolk: Boydell, 1997.

Donahue, Charles, Jr. *Law, Marriage, and Society in the Later Middle Ages.* New York: Cambridge University Press, 2007.

Donahue, Charles, Jr. "Female Plaintiffs in Marriage Cases in the Court of York in the Later Middle Ages: What Can We Learn from the Numbers?" In *Wife and Widow in Medieval England*, edited by Sue Sheridan Walker, 183–213. Ann Arbor: University of Michigan Press, 1993.

Drake, Graham N. "Not Safe Even in Their Own Castles: Reading Domestic Violence against Children in Four Middle English Romances." In *Domestic Violence in Medieval Texts*, edited by Eve Salisbury, Georgiana Donavin and Merrall Llewelyn Price, 139–63. Gainesville: University Press of Florida, 2002.

Duby, Georges. *The Chivalrous Society.* Trans. Cynthia Postan. Berkeley: University of California Press, 1981.

Duby, Georges. *Medieval Marriage: Two Models from Twelfth-Century France.* Trans. Elborg Forster. Baltimore: Johns Hopkins University Press, 1978.

Dunn, Caroline. "The Language of Ravishment in Medieval England." *Speculum* 86 (2011): 79–116.

Elliott, Dyan. "Lollardy and the Integrity of Marriage and the Family." In *The Medieval Marriage Scene: Prudence, Passion, Policy*, edited by Sherry Roush and Cristelle L. Baskins, 37–54. Tempe: Arizona Center for Medieval and Renaissance Studies, 2005.

Erickson, Amy Louise. "Coverture and Capitalism." *History Workshop Journal* 59 (2005): 1–16.

Erickson, Amy Louise. *Women and Property in Early Modern England.* London: Routledge, 1993.

Erler, Mary Carpenter. *Women, Reading, and Piety in Late Medieval England.* Cambridge: Cambridge University Press, 2002.

Finch, Andrew. "Sexual Morality and Canon Law: The Evidence of the Rochester Consistory Court." *Journal of Medieval History* 20 (1994): 261–75.

Finch, Andrew. "*Repulsa Uxore Sua:* Marital Difficulties and Separation in the Later Middle Ages." *Continuity and Change* 8.1 (1993): 11–38.

Foyster, Elizabeth. "A Laughing Matter? Marital Discord and Gender Control in Seventeenth-Century England." *Rural History* 4.1 (1993): 5–21.

Galloway, Andrew. "Marriage Sermons, Polemical Sermons, and *The Wife of Bath's Prologue*: A Generic Excursus." *Studies in the Age of Chaucer* 14 (1992): 3–30

Goldberg, Jeremy. *Communal Discord, Child Abduction, and Rape in the Later Middle Ages.* New York: Palgrave Macmillan, 2008.

Goldberg, Jessica. "The Legal Persona of the Child in Gratian's *Decretum*." *Bulletin of Medieval Canon Law* 24, n.s. (2000): 10–53.
Goldberg, P.J.P. *Medieval England: A Social History, 1250–1550*. London: Hodder Arnold, 2004.
Goldberg, P.J.P. *Women, Work, and Life Cycle in a Medieval Economy: Women in York and Yorkshire c.1300–1520*. Oxford: Oxford University Press, 1992.
Goldberg, P.J.P., ed. "Marriage, Migration, and Servanthood: The York Cause Paper Evidence." In *Woman Is a Worthy Wight*, 1–15. Stroud: Sutton, 1992.
Gordon, Eleanora C. "Accidents among Medieval Children as Seen from the Miracles of Six English Saints and Martyrs." *Medical History* 35 (1991): 145–163.
Guzzetti, Linda. "Separations and Separated Couples in Fourteenth-Century Venice." In *Marriage in Italy, 1300–1650*, edited by Trevor Dean and K.J.P. Lowe, 249–74. Cambridge: Cambridge University Press, 1998.
Hanawalt, Barbara A. "Medievalists and the Study of Childhood." *Speculum* 77 (2002): 440–60.
Hanawalt, Barbara A. "Violence in the Domestic Milieu of Late Medieval England." In *Violence in Medieval Society*, edited by Richard W. Kaeuper, 197–214. Woodbridge: Boydell, 2000.
Hanawalt, Barbara A. "'Good Governance' in the Medieval and Early Modern Context." *Journal of British Studies* 37 (1998): 246–57.
Hanawalt, Barbara A. *"Of Good and Ill Repute": Gender and Social Control in Medieval England*. Oxford: Oxford University Press, 1998.
Hanawalt, Barbara A. "Narratives of a Nurturing Culture: Parents and Neighbors in Medieval England." *Essays in Medieval Studies* 12 (1995). http://www.illinoismedieval.org/ems/EMSpdf/V12/V12Hanawalt.pdf. Date of Access: November 27, 2012.
Hanawalt, Barbara A. *Growing Up in Medieval London: The Experience of Childhood in History*. Oxford: Oxford University Press, 1993.
Hanawalt, Barbara A. *The Ties That Bound: Peasant Families in Medieval England*. New York: Oxford University Press, 1986.
Harding, Alan. *The Law Courts of Medieval England*. London: Allen and Unwin, 1973.
Hawkes, Emma. "'[S]he Will . . . Protect and Defend Her Rights Boldly by Law and Reason . . . ': Women's Knowledge of Common Law and Equity Courts in Late-Medieval England." In *Medieval Women and the Law*, edited by Noël James Menuge, 145–61. Woodbridge: Boydell, 2000.
Hawkes, Emma. "'She Was Ravished against Her Will, What So Ever She Say': Female Consent in Rape and Ravishment in Late-Medieval England." *Limina* 1 (1995): 47–53.
Helmholz, R.H. "Marriage Contracts in Medieval England." In *To Have and To Hold: Marrying and Its Documentation in Western Christendom, 400–1600*, edited by Philip L. Reynolds and John Witte, Jr., 260–86. Cambridge: Cambridge University Press, 2007.
Helmholz, R.H. *The Oxford History of the Laws of England: Vol. 1, The Canon Law and Ecclesiastical Jurisdiction from 597 to the 1640s*. Oxford: Oxford University Press, 2004.
Helmholz, R.H. "Married Women's Wills in Later Medieval England." In *Wife and Widow in Medieval England*, edited by Sue Sheridan Walker, 165–82. Ann Arbor: University of Michigan Press, 1993.
Helmholz, R.H. "And Were There Children's Rights in Early Modern England? The Canon Law and 'Intra-family Violence' in England, 1400–1640." *International Journal of Children's Rights* 1 (1992): 23–32.
Helmholz, R.H. "Roman Law of Guardianship in England, 1300–1600." *Tulane Law Review* 52 (1978): 223–57.

Helmholz, R.H. "Support Orders, Church Courts, and the Rule of *Filius Nullius*: A Reassessment of the Common Law." *Virginia Law Review* 63.383 (1977): 431–48.

Helmholz, R.H. *Marriage Litigation in Medieval England*. New York: Cambridge University Press, 1974.

Ives, E.W. "'Agaynst Taking Awaye of Women': The Inception and Operation of the Abduction Act of 1487." In *Wealth and Power in Tudor England: Essays Presented to S.T. Bindoff*, edited by E.W. Ives, R.J. Knecht and J.J. Scarisbrick, 21–45. London: Athlone Press, 1978.

Jones, Karen. *Gender and Petty Crime in Late Medieval England: The Local Courts in Kent, 1460–1560*. Woodbridge: Boydell, 2006.

Jordan, William C. *Women and Credit in Pre-industrial and Developing Societies*. Philadelphia: University of Pennsylvania Press, 1992.

Jost, Jean E. "Loving Parents in Middle English Literature." In *Childhood in the Middle Ages and the Renaissance: The Results of a Paradigm Shift in the History of Mentality*, edited by Albrecht Classen, 307–28. Berlin: Walter de Gruyter, 2005.

Karras, Ruth Mazo. *Sexuality in Medieval Europe: Doing unto Others*. New York: Routledge, 2005.

Karras, Ruth Mazo. "Sex and the Singlewomen." In *Singlewomen in the European Past, 1250–1800*, edited by Judith M. Bennett and Amy M. Froide, 127–45. Philadelphia: University of Pennsylvania Press, 1999.

Keeling, Susan M., and C.P. Lewis."The Rape and Honour of Lewes." In *History of the County of Sussex*, 1–7. Victoria History of the Counties of England, v. 7, 1940.

Kelly, Henry Ansgar. "Statutes of Rapes and Alleged Ravishers of Wives: A Context for the Charges against Thomas Malory, Knight." *Viator* 28 (1997): 361–419.

Kermode, Jenny. "Sentiment and Survival: Family and Friends in Late Medieval English Towns." *Journal of Family History* 24.1 (1999): 5–18.

Korda, Natasha. *Shakespeare's Domestic Economies: Gender and Property in Early Modern England*. Philadelphia: University of Pennsylvania Press, 2002.

Krahmer, Shawn Madison. "Adam, Eve, and Original Sin in the Works of Bernard of Clairvaux." *Cistercian Studies Quarterly* 37.1 (2002): 3–12.

Leavitt, Sarah. "'She Hath Left My Bed and Board': Runaway Wives in Rhode Island, 1790–1810." *Rhode Island History* 58.3 (2000): 91–104.

Lee, Sidney. *Dictionary of National Biography: Index and Epitome*. Cambridge: Harvard University Press, 1903.

Lee, Sidney, and Leslie Stephen, eds. *Dictionary of National Biography*. 63 vols. London: Smith, Elder, and Co., 1885–1900.

Loengard, Janet S. "'Which May Be Said to Be Her Own': Widows and Goods in Late-Medieval England." In *Medieval Domesticity: Home, Housing and Household in Medieval England*, edited by Maryanne Kowaleski and P.J.P. Goldberg, 162–76. Cambridge: Cambridge University Press, 2008.

Loengard, Janet S. "Common Law for Margery: Separate but Not Equal." In *Women in Medieval Western European Culture*, edited by Linda E. Mitchell, 117–30. New York: Garland, 1999.

Lynch, Joseph H. *The Medieval Church: A Brief History*. New York: Longman, 1992.

Maddern, Philippa C. "Between Households: Children in Blended and Transitional Households in Late-Medieval England." *Journal of the History of Childhood and Youth* 3.1 (2010): 65–86.

Maddern, Philippa C. "Moving Households: Geographical Mobility and Serial Monogamy in England, 1350–1500." *Parergon* 24.2 (2007): 69–92.

Maddern, Philippa C. "Interpreting Silence: Domestic Violence in the King's Courts in East Anglia, 1422–1442." In *Domestic Violence in Medieval Texts*, edited by Eve Salisbury, Georgiana Donavin and Merrell Llewelyn Price, 42–46. Gainesville: University Press of Florida, 2002.

Makowski, Elizabeth M. "The Conjugal Debt and Medieval Canon Law." In *Equally in God's Image: Women in the Middle Ages*, edited by Julia Bolton Holloway, Constance S. Wright and Joan Bechtold, 129–43. New York: Peter Lang, 1990.

Mate, Mavis E. "Work and Leisure." In *A Social History of England 1200–1500*, edited by Rosemary Horrox and W. Mark Ormrod, 276–92. Cambridge: Cambridge University Press, 2006.

Mate, Mavis E. *Daughters, Wives and Widows after the Black Death: Women in Sussex, 1350–1535*. Woodbridge: Boydell, 1998.

McCarthy, Conor. *Marriage in Medieval England: Law, Literature and Practice*. Woodbridge: Boydell, 2004.

McDougall, Sara. "Bigamy: A Male Crime in Medieval Europe?" *Gender and History* 22.2 (2010): 430–46.

McIntosh, Marjorie K. "The Benefits and Drawbacks of *Femme Sole* Status in England, 1300–1630." *Journal of British Studies* 44 (2005): 410–38.

McSheffrey, Shannon. *Marriage, Sex, and Civic Culture in Late Medieval London*. Philadelphia: University of Pennsylvania Press, 2006.

McSheffrey, Shannon. "Men and Masculinity in Late Medieval London Civic Culture: Governance, Patriarchy and Reputation." In *Conflicted Identities and Multiple Masculinities: Men in the Medieval West*, edited by Jacqueline Murray, 243–78. New York: Garland, 1999.

McSheffrey, Shannon. "'I Will Never Have None Ayenst My Faders Will': Consent and the Making of Marriage in the Late Medieval Diocese of London." In *Women, Marriage and Family in Medieval Christendom*, edited by C.M. Rousseau and J.T. Rosenthal, 153–74. Kalamazoo, MI: Medieval Institute Publications, 1998.

Menuge, Noël James. "Female Wards and Marriage in Romance and Law: A Question of Consent." In *Young Medieval Women*, edited by Katherine J. Lewis, Noël James Menuge and Kim M. Phillips, 153–71. London: St. Martin's Press, 1999.

Milsom, S.F.C. *The Historical Foundations of the Common Law*. London: Butterworths, 1981.

Mulholland, Maureen. "Trial in Manorial Courts in Late Medieval England." In *Judicial Tribunals in England and Europe, 1200–1700: The Trial in History, Volume I*, edited by Maureen Mulholland and Brian Pullan, 81–101. Manchester: Manchester University Press, 2003.

Newman, Barbara. *From Virile Woman to WomanChrist: Studies in Medieval Religion and Literature*. Philadelphia: University of Pennsylvania Press, 1995.

Noble, David F. *A World without Women: The Christian Clerical Culture of Western Science*. Oxford: Oxford University Press, 1992.

O'Hara, Diana. *Courtship and Constraint: Rethinking the Making of Marriage in Tudor England*. Manchester: Manchester University Press, 2000.

Orr, Patricia R. "*Non Potest Appellum Facere*: Criminal Charges Women Could Not—but Did—Bring in Thirteenth-Century English Royal Courts of Justice." In *The Final Argument: The Imprint of Violence on Society in Medieval and Early Modern Europe*, edited by Donald J. Kagay and L.J. Andrew Villalon, 141–62. Woodbridge: Boydell, 1998.

Page, William. *A History of the County of York: North Riding*. Victoria County History, v. 2, 1923.

Palmer, Robert C. "Contexts of Marriage in Medieval England: Evidence from the King's Court circa 1300." *Speculum* 59.1 (1984): 42–67.

Pedersen, Frederik. "Marriage Contracts and the Church Courts of Fourteenth-Century England." In *To Have and To Hold: Marrying and Its Documentation in Western Christendom, 400–1600*, edited by Philip L. Reynolds and John Witte, Jr., 287–331. Cambridge: Cambridge University Press, 2007.

Pedersen, Frederik. *Marriage Disputes in Medieval England*. London: Hambledon, 2000.

Pedersen, Frederik. "Did the Medieval Laity Know the Canon Law Rules on Marriage? Some Evidence from Fourteenth-Century York Cause Papers." *Mediaeval Studies* 56 (1994): 111–53.

Pollock, Frederick, and F.W. Maitland. *The History of English Law before the Time of Edward I*, 2nd ed. London: Cambridge University Press, 1968. 2 vols.

Poos, L.R. "The Heavy-Handed Marriage Counselor: Regulating Marriage in Some Later-Medieval English Local Ecclesiastical Court Jurisdictions." *American Journal of Legal History* 29 (1995): 585–607.

Post, J.B. "Ravishment of Women and the Statutes of Westminster." In *Legal Records and the Historian*, edited by J.H. Baker, 150–64. London: Royal Historical Society, 1978.

Powell, Edward. "Jury Trial at Gaol Delivery in the Late Middle Ages: The Midland Circuit, 1400–1429." In *Twelve Good Men and True: The Criminal Trial Jury in England, 1200–1800*, edited by J.S. Cockburn and Thomas A. Green, 78–116. Princeton: Princeton University Press, 1988.

Powell, W.R. *A History of the County of Essex*. Victoria County History, v. 5, 1966.

Reid, Charles, Jr. "The Rights of Children in Medieval Canon Law." In *The Vocation of the Child*, edited by Patrick McKinley Brennan, 243–65. Grand Rapids: Wm. B. Eerdmans, 2008.

Reid, Charles, Jr. *Power over the Body, Equality in the Family: Rights and Domestic Relations in Medieval Canon Law*. Grand Rapids: Wm. B. Eerdmans, 2004.

Reynolds, Philip. "Marrying and Its Documentation in Pre-modern Europe: Consent, Celebration, and Property." In *To Have and To Hold: Marrying and Its Documentation in Western Christendom, 400–1600*, edited by Philip L. Reynolds and John Witte, Jr., 1–42. Cambridge: Cambridge University Press, 2007.

Richardson, Douglas, and Kimball G. Everingham, *Magna Carta Ancestry: A Study in Colonial and Medieval Families*. Baltimore: Genealogical Pub. Co., 2005.

Richmond, Colin. "The Pastons Revisited: Marriage and the Family in Fifteenth-Century England." *Bulletin of the Institute of Historical Research* 58.137 (1985): 25–36.

Richmond, Colin. *John Hopton: A Fifteenth-Century Suffolk Gentleman*. Cambridge: Cambridge University Press, 1981.

Richmond, Colin, and Margaret Aston. *Lollardy and the Gentry in the Later Middle Ages*. Stroud: Sutton, 1997.

Schimmelpfennig, Bernhard. "*Ex fornicatione Nati*: Studies on the Position of Priests' Sons from the Twelfth to the Fourteenth Century." *Studies in Medieval and Renaissance History*, n.s. 2, o.s. 12 (1979): 3–50.

Seabourne, Gwen. *Imprisoning Medieval Women: The Non-judicial Confinement and Abduction of Women in England, c. 1170–1509*. Farnham: Ashgate, 2011.

Shahar, Shulamith. *Childhood in the Middle Ages*. London: Routledge, 1990.

Sheehan, M.M. *Marriage, Family, and Law in Medieval Europe: Collected Studies*. Ed. James K. Farge. Toronto: University of Toronto Press, 1996.

Shorter, Edward. *The Making of the Modern Family*. New York: Basic Books, 1975.

Stacey, Robin Chapman. "Divorce, Medieval Welsh Style," *Speculum* 77 (2002): 1107–27.

Stone, Lawrence. *The Family, Sex and Marriage 1500–1800*. New York: Harper and Row, 1977.

Stretton, Tim. "Coverture and Unity of Person in Blackstone's *Commentaries*." In *Blackstone and His* Commentaries*: Biography, Law, History*, edited by Wilfrid Robertson Prest, 111–28. Oxford: Hart Publishing, 2009.

Stretton, Tim. *Women Waging Law in Elizabethan England*. Cambridge: Cambridge University Press, 1998.

Swanson, R.N. "Angels Incarnate: Clergy and Masculinity from Gregorian Reform to Reformation." In *Masculinity in Medieval Europe*, edited by D.M. Hadley, 160–77. New York: Longman, 1999.

Thrupp, Sylvia. *The Merchant Class of Medieval London, 1300–1500*. Chicago: University of Chicago Press, 1948.

Tucker, P. "The Early History of the Court of Chancery: A Comparative Study." *English Historical Review* 115 (2000): 791–811.

Turner, Ralph V. "The Mandeville Inheritance, 1189–1236." *Haskins Society Journal* 1 (1989): 147–72.

Virgue, Roger. "Sir John Risley (1443–1512), Courtier and Councillor." *Norfolk Archaeology* 38 (1982): 140–48.

Vodola, Elisabeth. *Excommunication in the Middle Ages*. Berkeley and Los Angeles: University of California Press, 1986.

Walker, Sue Sheridan. "Litigation as Personal Quest: Suing for Dower in the Royal Courts, circa 1272–1350." In *Wife and Widow in Medieval England*, 81–108. Ann Arbor: Michigan University Press, 1993.

Walker, Sue Sheridan. "The Feudal Family and the Common Law Courts: The Pleas Protecting Rights of Wardship and Marriage, c. 1225–1375." *Journal of Medieval History* 14 (1988): 13–31.

Walker, Sue Sheridan. "Punishing Convicted Ravishers: Statutory Strictures and Actual Practice in Thirteenth- and Fourteenth-Century England." *Journal of Medieval History* 13 (1987): 237–50.

Wardell, John Wilfred. *A History of Yarm, an Ancient North Riding Town*. Yarm: Sunderland, 1957.

Weigand, R. "Zur mittelalterlichen kirchlichen Gerichtsbarkeit. Rechtsvergleichende Untersuchung." *Zeitschrift der Savigny-Stiftung für Rechtsgeschichte* 98 (1981): 213–47.

Weir, Alison. *Queen Isabella: Treachery, Adultery and Murder in Medieval England*. New York: Balantine Books, 2005.

Weis, Frederick Lewis, Walter Lee Shepherd and David Faris. *Ancestral Roots of Certain American Colonists Who Came to America before 1700*. Lancaster: Genealogical Publishing Company, 1964.

Woodcock, Brian L. *Medieval Ecclesiastical Courts in the Diocese of Canterbury*. Oxford: Oxford University Press, 1952.

Wright, Sharon. "Broken Cups, Men's Wrath, and the Neighbours' Revenge: The Case of Thomas and Alice Dey of Alverthorpe, 1383." *Canadian Journal of History* 43 (2008): 241–51.

Wunderli, Richard M. *London Church Courts and Society on the Eve of the Reformation*. Cambridge: Medieval Academy of America, 1981.

Index

An environmentally friendly book printed and bound in England by www.printondemand-worldwide.com

PEFC Certified
This product is from sustainably managed forests and controlled sources
www.pefc.org
PEFC
PEFC/16-33-415

FSC
www.fsc.org
MIX
Paper from responsible sources
FSC® C004959

This book is made entirely of sustainable materials; FSC paper for the cover and PEFC paper for the text pages.

#0104 - 160514 - C0 - 229/152/11 [13] - CB